A HISTORY OF STEPFAMILIES

IN EARLY AMERICA

A HISTORY OF

Stepfamilies
in Early America

Lisa Wilson

The University of North Carolina Press *Chapel Hill*

This book was published with the assistance of the
Anniversary Endowment Fund of the University of North Carolina Press.

© 2014 THE UNIVERSITY OF NORTH CAROLINA PRESS

All rights reserved. Designed by Sally Scruggs. Set in Miller by codeMantra. Manufactured in the United States of America. The paper in this book meets the guidelines for permanence and durability of the Committee on Production Guidelines for Book Longevity of the Council on Library Resources. The University of North Carolina Press has been a member of the Green Press Initiative since 2003.

Library of Congress Cataloging-in-Publication Data
Wilson, Lisa, 1957–
A history of stepfamilies in early America / Lisa Wilson.
pages cm.
Includes bibliographical references and index.
ISBN 978-1-4696-1842-5 (pbk : alk. paper) — ISBN 978-1-4696-1843-2 (ebook)
1. Stepfamilies—United States—History. 2. Families—United States—History
3. United States—History—Colonial period, ca. 1600–1775. I. Title.
HQ535.W55 2014
306.874'70973—dc23
2014017086

18 17 16 15 14 5 4 3 2 1

*To the memory of my mother, Constance Hall Wilson,
and my grandmother, Constance Patton Hall*

CONTENTS

ILLUSTRATIONS

PREFACE

About Cinderella . . . Charles Perrault, in his *Tales of Mother Goose*, published the story in 1697 as an adult tale designed to entertain members of the French royal court.[1] By the early nineteenth century, other fairy tales specifically written for children included evil stepmothers. But at first, the Grimm Brothers, at least, had the formula wrong.[2] For example, in their initial version, Snow White explains to the dwarfs that "her mother"—not her stepmother—"had tried to kill her." A few years later, the Grimms realized their error and revised the story so that "as soon as the child was born, the queen [Snow White's mother] died," and the king "took himself another wife." In this version, Snow White's stepmother hires the huntsman to kill her stepdaughter.[3]

Likewise, in the Grimms' first version of Hansel and Gretel, their mother urges their father to abandon them in the woods to save on food, while in the new and improved version, their stepmother becomes the culprit.[4] Stories about evil mothers were no longer conventional by the time of the fourth edition in 1840.[5] Mothers were by definition loving, so the culture gave stepmothers the baggage of cruelty that mothers had left behind.

ACKNOWLEDGMENTS

I am a stepchild. In fact, I have been a part of a stepfamily of one sort or another practically all of my life. My deep personal experience with stepfamilies helped bring me to this topic. This book comes as well from my experience as a historian of the family and gender in early America. My earlier work on widows in Pennsylvania and men in colonial New England helped me see the prevalence of these families in the past. In addition, through my research, I have come to realize that scholars of literature, sociology, and anthropology are the experts on stepfamilies, with very few historians tackling the topic. One of the reasons for this gap in the historical literature, I am convinced, is the difficulty of the task. These families were literally everywhere in the past, yet they are often difficult to untangle with the information available in surviving documents. I hope that others will take on the subject and answer the many questions that I have left unanswered.

I could not have completed this book without two years of grant-supported leave from my teaching obligations at Connecticut College. First, I received a Massachusetts Historical Society (MHS)/National Endowment for the Humanities long-term fellowship for the 2006–7 academic year. I spent a wonderful year researching in the MHS's extraordinary collections. My (fellow) fellow, Ruth Wallis Herndon, became a great colleague and friend as we worked side by side throughout those months, and she kindly read a draft of this manuscript. I also benefited from the incredible MHS staff, particularly Conrad Wright and Peter Drummey. Finally, I attended the multiple seminars and brown-bag events at the society, meeting many researchers and fellows as they came to work on the collections or to give presentations. In the 2010–11 academic year, an American Antiquarian Society (AAS)/National Endowment for the Humanities long-term fellowship provided me with another wonderful opportunity to work on this project. I particularly thank Laura Wasowicz, curator of children's literature at the AAS, for suggestions that helped me find the stepchildren at the society. I spent the year living in the Goddard Daniels House, which was home to an extraordinary community of scholars. We long-termers created a writing group, reading each other's work and sharing meals and more than a little wine. This scholarly paradise was and is cultivated by Paul Erickson, director of academic programs, who has earned my deep gratitude for providing the peace, solitude, and fun that makes the AAS a unique place to conduct research. I also thank Elizabeth Maddock Dillon, Sean Harvey, Daniel Rood, and Kyle Volk for their time and attention to my work. Kyle and I have continued reading each other's work and cheering each other on, and I cannot thank him enough for sharing his extraordinary intellect and friendship.

I have presented my work at various venues, including the annual meeting of the Society for Historians of the Early American Republic in July 2012, the AAS Seminar in October 2010 and April 2011, the annual meeting of the American Historical Association in January 2002 and January 2010, the MHS Brown Bag Series in April 2007, the Boston Area Early American History Seminar in October 2006, the Heroism, Nationalism, and Human Rights Conference at the University of Connecticut in February 2006, and the Association for the Study of Connecticut History spring meeting in April 2002. I am very thankful for all the comments I received at these sessions.

Others who have read all or part of this book include Allegra di Bonaventura, Steven Bullock, Marc Forster, Katherine Hermes, Shan Holt, and Mike Zuckerman. I particularly thank Shan Holt for her ongoing friendship, intellectual and otherwise. I am grateful as always for Mike Zuckerman and his ongoing support of my work and belief in me. In addition, I thank my editor, Chuck Grench, for the calm encouragement that sustained me through multiple revisions.

Finally, I thank a great stepfather and husband, Dave Kanen, and my son, Alex Waciega, for their constant love and support.

A HISTORY OF STEPFAMILIES
IN EARLY AMERICA

INTRODUCTION

Stepfamilies founded our nation. George Washington, the Father of Our Country, was a stepfather. When he married a young widow, Martha (Dandridge) Custis, in 1759, he took on her two small children, Jackie, six, and Patsy, four. When seventeen-year-old Patsy lay gravely ill with tuberculosis, her stepfather prayed at her bedside for her recovery. Jackie, at times a challenging teenager, stood at his stepfather's side when the British surrendered at Yorktown, though he died soon thereafter. Washington then offered to raise Jackie's two youngest children.[1]

The only portrait of the first, first family, titled *The Washington Family*, appears to depict a first-marriage family with children, and yet the Washington family was another kind of "traditional" American family altogether, a stepfamily. Edward Savage painted a large canvas of the domestic scene between 1789 and 1796. Washington displayed a print of the image in his dining room at Mount Vernon. Numerous companies made copies of this popular painting for sale. The children are George Washington's step-grandchildren: George "Washy" Washington Parke Custis, and Eleanor "Nelly" Parke Custis. Washington sits relaxed with his arm resting on his step-grandson's shoulder. His step-granddaughter stands by her grandmother with William Lee, one of Washington's slaves, in the background. Washington proudly sits in his military uniform looking over the plans of the new city of Washington while a view of Mount Vernon serves as a backdrop.[2] He is the quintessential slave master, plantation owner, military leader, husband, and step-grandfather. In other words, he appears as the patriarch of a family he has not sired. The first, first family was a stepfather family.

Washington was not the only founder who was part of a stepfamily. Benjamin Franklin was the child of a second marriage. The audacious young man ran away from his apprenticeship with his half brother, printer James Franklin, convinced he could open a print shop of his own in Philadelphia.[3] President James Madison was stepfather to John Payne Todd, Dolley's child by her first husband, and Madison's Virginia plantation was sold in part to pay off Todd's gambling debts.[4] Paul Revere, a widower with eight children,

1

George Washington and his step-grandchildren. Edward Savage, *The Washington Family*, 1789–96. Courtesy of the National Gallery of Art, Washington, D.C.

married Rachel Walker, who bore him eight more children.[5] These men and women were the founding stepfathers, stepmothers, and stepchildren of the United States.

Unlike today, death, not divorce, defined early American stepfamilies. Divorce, although not unknown in colonial America, was exceedingly rare, and remarriage was often not legally permitted.[6] One author from that era defined stepfamilies as "families in which death has made a breach, and which have been re-constructed."[7] The English language itself reflects the connection between stepfamilies and death. In Old English, *ástíeped*, the word from which the prefix "step" is derived, means "bereavement." A *stéopbear*, or stepchild, was a bereaved child. A stepfather or stepmother, therefore, was the parent of a child in mourning.[8] Losing a parent (or a spouse) blazed the trail to remarriage as well as stepfamily formation.

In addition, the frequency of death in early America guaranteed that everyone was in or knew someone who was in a stepfamily of one sort or another. At a time before effective birth control, remarriage almost always led to the creation of a stepfamily. And many people remarried. Studies of various locations in early modern Europe and North America have found that between 20 and 40 percent of marriages were remarriages.[9] Although the popular assumption is that many women died in childbirth, leaving more grieving men looking for new partners, these numbers are not as high as might be expected. Men also died young as a result of illness, injury, and warfare.[10] More widowed women than men remained single, mitigating any childbirth-induced imbalance between the numbers of stepfathers and of stepmothers.[11] All in all, these demographic realities assured that both families with stepmothers and those with stepfathers were a common part of the landscape.

Stepfamilies also were ubiquitous because they were necessary. Families were essentially nuclear in the parts of northwestern Europe from which many white colonists had come.[12] The couple was central to the proper functioning of these families.[13] Europeans re-created these family patterns in colonial North America as soon as demographic realities allowed.[14] An intense focus on the couple made this kind of family brittle in the face of the loss of one parent.[15] The death of a partner created a void that needed to be filled in some way so that the family could continue to function. The surviving parent could hire a servant or ask an older child to step in, but remarriage was the only permanent solution. Without two adults to run a household, this kind of nuclear family structure could simply collapse, with children farmed out to service and the remaining adult taking up residence in a relative's home or a boardinghouse.

Despite being both common and necessary, stepfamilies were paradoxically the subjects of ridicule. Prejudice against this family form has roots that stretch a long way back in time.[16] In eighteenth-century northwestern Europe and America, prejudice against stepfamilies found a new life as the Enlightenment took hold. A foil for these ancient prejudices developed in the form of the ideal "sentimental" family. Writers described this kind of family as an affectionate unit based on companionate marriage and centered on children raised with love and constant attention.[17] In addition, the members of the rising middle class in northwestern Europe began to define themselves in part by the homes they created. For the new bourgeoisie, a proper family was a sentimental one. Middle-class remarrying couples also sought this kind of family. Although burdened by prejudice, stepmothers, stepfathers, and stepchildren struggled to re-create a proper Enlightenment home despite traditional stereotypes that predicted their failure.

Beyond the white middle-class, other groups—the majority of people in early America—had different concerns and in some cases more successful approaches to the loss of a spouse. Native, African, and African-descended peoples mitigated the impact of death on a surviving spouse and children in a number of ways. A matrilineal structure, polygyny, and extended families all provided support for grieving families in a way that nuclear households did not. For example, matrilineal families included other women who could take on tasks in the absence of a wife and mother. These female-related groups lived close together or even (as with the Iroquois) in the same household. The practice of polygyny also provided an alternate maternal presence for bereft children.[18] Extended families could likewise help to close the gap left when a spouse died. Even as many native people were forced to give up their land and required to live in nuclear households over the eighteenth century, the extended family endured.[19] Most African (forced) migrants left behind elaborate kin networks but quickly worked to re-constitute them.[20] Some even began this process with their shipmates during the middle passage.[21] Slavery interfered with family development through gender imbalance and limited mobility. Slaves also could not legally marry. Slaves on large plantations and free people nonetheless worked to re-create family systems in keeping with African patterns.[22] When possible, polygyny was also practiced.[23] Both the Native American and African American responses to spouse loss proved more successful than the stepfamily strategies of their Anglo-American neighbors.[24]

Likewise, the struggle of white middle-class, American stepfamilies had little relevance to the families of the poor of all ethnicities. Households in early American communities formed to facilitate financial survival as much as familial preferences. Strangers and family members shared residences out of necessity. Nuclear families, even if they were an ideal, were hard to maintain. Marriage itself was beyond the means of many people, and partnerships often formed with no official records.[25] Also, for such "mates" struggling to keep afloat, the ideal of companionate marriage was likely not a central preoccupation when the death of a parent or spouse rocked a household.[26]

In sum, we need to think of the "traditional" American family in new ways.[27] Race, ethnicity, and class all are factors in the equation, but even the much studied American middling sorts exhibited family diversity. Stepfamilies were also "traditional." In addition, the roots of modern stepfamily stereotypes and prejudices reside firmly in early America's white middle-class struggle with cultural imperatives. Modern prejudice must be seen in light of the experiences of these founding stepfamilies.

Despite or perhaps because of stepfamilies' ubiquitousness, historians have all but ignored the unique experience of such families in the American past. Most scholars have simply folded stepfamily stories into a broader narrative of family life, while others have assumed that these families were different from "regular" families but were likely riddled with conflict, particularly when a stepmother was involved. For example, according to Peter Laslett, among English families, "The stepmother and her evil influence is so conspicuous a feature of the fairy tales and of the literature as a whole that it seems to correspond to something important in the lives of those who repeated them."[28] Similarly, historian of British North America Helena M. Wall notes, "People expected stepparents to cause problems, and their anxieties must have been as least in part self-fulfilling."[29] Such statements demand further analysis.[30]

Toward this end, when looking at experience rather than cultural perception, I focus on the much mythologized region of New England for a number of reasons. First, more has been written about the New England family than any other family system in colonial America, meaning that a great deal of scholarship undergirds this study.[31] Second, abundant archival resources survive for this region, providing the evidence needed to pursue this topic. Third, the regional interest in genealogy has helped make these abundant resources accessible.[32] In fact, genealogical material of all kinds, especially the digitalized resources available through the New England Historical and Genealogical Society, literally enabled me to find early America's stepfamilies.

In addition, the only other study of stepfamilies in early North America is an article focused on the seventeenth-century Chesapeake, where the high death rate produced a world of multiple marriages, numerous stepfamilies, and powerful widows.[33] Late colonial and early national New England was a less crisis-driven environment, with unusually low mortality rates, at least until the land filled in the eighteenth century. Stepfamilies were, therefore, common but not ubiquitous. In addition, the region featured relatively mature eighteenth-century provincial villages, towns, and cities, whereas the Chesapeake constituted a colonial frontier where life was more of a struggle and the hazards were deadlier.

Finally, the people of New England were highly literate.[34] Readers regularly bought and borrowed books, periodicals, newspapers, and other materials. A flourishing publishing industry gave New Englanders regular access to local, regional, and European publications, meaning that the robust reading public witnessed the contours of stepfamily prejudice in print culture. New England is, therefore, a useful place to begin to unravel the interplay between lived reality and cultural expectations about stepfamily life.

The book begins as do stepfamilies—with the decision to remarry and with the issues that men and women confronted as they contemplated the formation of a stepfamily, which is the subject of chapter 1. Chapters 2 and 3 look at stepfamily prejudice, describing stepmothers and stepfathers as stereotypes and examining how these images changed over time, particularly for stepmothers, as older ideas confronted sentimental family ideals. Chapters 4 and 5 then turn to the experiences of children, demonstrating how these stereotypes played out in the lives of real stepfamilies. Finally, chapter 6 examines a brief early nineteenth-century attempt to reconcile the family of sentiment and the family of remarriage.

Remarriage decisions—the subject of chapter 1—involved not only love and property (as with first marriages) but also children. The property rights of married women remained limited until the mid-nineteenth century, meaning that a woman's remarriage could jeopardize the transfer of her dead husband's property to his children. Thus, remarriage entailed financial risk. Men who had lost their wives had fewer estate-related worries but a pressing need for child care. As a result, men remarried more often and more quickly than did women. Popular culture encouraged widows to remain single, while men were urged to pick "new mothers" for their children. As the mother-run sentimental family became the bedrock of middle-class life, a stepmother needed to fill her predecessor's shoes and become a loving mother. A man had to choose a woman who could become this "new mother" even as prejudice against stepmothers predicted that such paragons scarcely existed.

Chapter 2 examines prejudices against stepfathers, which were embedded in laws, court decisions, and legal treatises. The law—written by propertied men, of course—made stepfathers powerful and potentially dangerous individuals. Lawmakers worried about stepfathers' potential impact on the financial circumstances of another man's children. What if a widow chose a new husband who was not honorable and who did not safely shepherd his predecessor's legacies to his children? What if he failed to maintain property intended for his stepchildren and thus decreased its value? Although the law required fathers to provide for their children, a stepfather had no legal obligation to support the offspring of another man, though he could choose to take on the role and act in loco parentis. In the end, marrying a widow with children gave a man financial power, few obligations, and the freedom to act the hero or the scoundrel, as his character and circumstances led him. Precautions against the worst case seemed prudent, leading to a complicated legal world that I explore using the story of one man who worked the law to his advantage.

Chapter 3 explores the roots and the development of prejudices against stepmothers. The unique American iteration of stepmother wickedness was the character of Stepmother England. The former mother country had not remarried by the time of the American Revolution; rather, she had morphed into an evil counterfeit, a stepmother country who was cruel to her colonial children. Early modern European caricatures focused on stepmothers as evil women. Like witches and scolds, they turned the world upside-down, even turning a father against his own children. As the eighteenth century ushered in new ideas about sentimental family life, these evil characterizations were joined by stories comparing idealized mothers with demonized stepmothers. The stepmother became the personification of a cruel mother, the opposite of the new mother of the rising middle class. One kind of evil stepmother did not replace the other; instead, new stories were layered on top of old. Wicked and often murderous stepmothers were joined by the emotionally abusive and neglectful stepmothers of the eighteenth century.

Chapter 4 looks at three families to find some common themes and differing responses to flesh-and-blood stepmothers. The children in stepmother families understood cultural prejudices and compared their stepmothers to their angelic dead mothers. In some instances, these comparisons overwhelmed children's ability to open their hearts to another woman; in other cases, children found ways to welcome new mothers into their lives. Regardless, stereotypes influenced the journey to becoming a stepchild.

Sibling relationships within stepfamilies, the subject of chapter 5, proved that blood was not always thicker than water. Brothers and sisters often made common cause despite inheritance laws, which predicted conflict. When a parent died, siblings often worked together for the good of the family. Fiction of the period recommended and reflected the possibility of success in sibling interactions in stepfamilies. Brothers and sisters—full, half, and step—got along or fought but did not always do so along expected lines.

Stepmothers and their families finally found some public sympathy and concern in the antebellum age of reform, the subject of chapter 6. In children's literature and women's magazines, the good stepmother appeared as a counterweight to the longtime reign of the wicked stepmother. A good stepmother could become a new mother, raising her stepchildren with the memory of their mother intact. Children and stepmothers could be taught to get along. The importance of having a mother in a middle-class family overcame the ancient prejudice against stepmothers, making them the ideal replacement, preferable to servants or overextended relatives. Remarriage for men was a positive good and a loving gesture toward children. Although this moment passed, the possibility existed for a more open-minded approach to stepmothers and their families before the Civil War.

Prejudice against stepfamilies still influences our thinking in the modern period. Today, divorce rather than death creates most stepfamilies. Despite the potential for increased animosity in the face of marital discord, the prejudice against stepfamilies looks strangely familiar. As I outline in the epilogue, stepfathers, now seen as more of a physical than financial threat, still struggle with cultural suspicion. Stepmothers are still doing battle with fairy tales. Children are still seen as potential victims. Letting go of our long-held prejudices has proved difficult. Perhaps this study can help provide the historical context to help reexamine these stubborn cultural assumptions.

CHAPTER ONE

Remarriage

Experience has taught me the dreadfull truth how:
heavy it is to live alone how hard it is.—Daniel King, Diary, 1767

In January 1786, Boston lawyer and politician James Sullivan found himself with seven children, wracked with grief, and loath to lean on his fifteen-year-old daughter. His wife had just died. Lying next to her corpse, Sullivan wrote to a friend, "For the space of nine hours illness the skill of physicians was exhausted in vain attempts to save a life dear to many, but infinitely so to me and her seven children." He worked hard to appear strong for his children, but "a life of gloominess and anxiety now awaits; and had I not now the double charge of these orphans, my earnest prayer would be to go down with her to the silent tomb."[1] Three months later, Sullivan wrote, "My dear children demand much from me, and deserve every thing—I am obliged to appear quite otherwise than I am, to keep up their spirits."[2] James Sullivan found a permanent solution to his problem in the person of Martha (Langdon) Simpson, a widow whom he married before the year had ended.[3]

Love and money entered the calculations of most eighteenth-century couples contemplating marriage, but widows and widowers had some unique needs.[4] Widows with property worried about their dead husbands' estates, since remarriage would mean that new husbands would assume ownership of the women's property.[5] Accordingly, a cautious widow who did not need the support of a husband might feel no hurry to remarry and might not choose to do so at all.[6] Widowers, conversely, felt pressure to retie the knot to provide their children with replacement mothers. By the end of the eighteenth century, for the middling sort, the quality of this care became central. Sentimental middle-class norms of the time required child-centered parenting directed by a loving mother rather than a simple caregiver.

Widows and widowers approached the idea of remarriage from different perspectives. Documents left by a man and a woman from New Haven, Connecticut, offer a rare glimpse into precisely what those inner thoughts were in colonial America. Thomas Clap, a minister, found himself mulling over the possibility in 1737, while Mary (Fish) Noyes, a boardinghouse owner whose late husband had been a minister, did the same in 1773. Both of them penned lists of what they hoped for in an ideal new spouse/stepparent. Clap's intended audience may have been his descendants. His list was appended to a handwritten biography of his wife, likely created for his children, and the style reflected his time and occupation. He focused on religion and remarriage, looking for the biblical ideal of a pious helpmeet. His biggest fear was marrying a shrew. Noyes may have intended the list for herself, but she ultimately shared it with her future husband. The list and a series of letters she wrote that touched on the issue of remarriage reflected the new sentimental style popular at the end of the eighteenth century. She yearned not only for a man who was religious but also for one with the manners to qualify him as genteel.[7] The widow's biggest fear was marrying someone who would be an unscrupulous stepfather to her children.

THOMAS CLAP, THE WIDOWER

Thomas Clap was born in Scituate, Massachusetts, in 1703. His father, a church deacon, hired a tutor to prepare his bright young son to enter Harvard and train for the ministry. After graduation and a short stint as a teacher, Thomas accepted a pulpit in Windham, Connecticut, and began looking for a wife. He set his heart on the young daughter of Windham's previous minister, Stephen Whiting. When the couple married in 1727, Mary Whiting was only fourteen, extraordinarily young for a bride at the time. The match was based on love—she came to the union with little property. By 1736, Mary had given birth six times and buried four of her children; pregnant again, she likely died of "consumption" (tuberculosis) on 9 August. Three years after her death, Clap left Windham for New Haven, accepting a post as the rector of Yale College, a title later changed to president. This move not only helped his career but also took him away from painful memories.[8] Unlike most widowers, he had difficulty contemplating remarriage and remained single, despite his familial obligations and the urging of friends, until 1741, when he wed the twice-widowed and well-connected Mary (Haynes) Lord Saltonstall.

Around the time of his first wife's death, Clap began a diary, titling it "Memoirs of Some Remarkable Occurances of Divine Providence," in which he focused on the death of his wife and his mourning process. He wrote most of the entries on the ninth day of the month, commemorating the day of his wife's passing. On 9 April 1737, exactly eight months after her death, he penned "Rev. Thomas Clap's Thoughts on a Second Marriage."

Mary's death hit Thomas Clap so hard that it came close to being his emotional undoing. According to the "Memoirs," her death "has been a very Sore and Distressing Affliction and great Tryal to me. All the afflictions which I have ever met with in my whole Life put together are small in Comparison to this. My Spirits have been much sunk and my Body Emaciated by it." By February 1737, however, he sought to control his feelings. He felt a detachment from the world that he thought a good spiritual development, but his excessive mourning had made him unfit for the sacred work of the ministry, "and therefore of late I have found it necessary to Curb and Restrain my Grief. and to Endeavour to Recover my Spirits to their Natural & Usual Order, or otherwise I should not be so Capable of Serving God and Answering the Good End of Affliction."[9]

Thomas described Mary as having been a perfect helpmeet, "a woman of . . . such Great Prudence" that she never took a "wry Step." She was "neat & Saving" and as a result "he feared no Spoil." She was "kind and Compassionate to the Poor." She dressed simply, spoke softly, and had a "pleasant and Excellent Temper and Disposition." They never fought: "neither did one Unpleasant nor so much as Short Word ever pass between us upon any Occasion whatsoever." Though they occasionally had differences of opinion on "lesser matters," after discussion she was "always free and Ready enough to fall in with the Opinion or Inclination of her Husband." If she had any fault "it was sometimes in not Insisting so much upon her own Inclination, so much as a Wife may Modertly do." When she had just cause to correct her children or servants she did so with "proper and moderate Smartness." She made her rebukes with a "few short & Pungent words" rather than "continually Fearing & Discouraging of them."[10]

Friends and family urged Clap to find a second wife and to do so quickly, not only for his own sake but also for that of his children: "Some of my Good Friends have some time ago told me that it is my Duty to entertain tho'ts of Endeavoring after a Reparation of my loss." Even his pious, dying wife had urged him to remarry. As he cried at her bedside she reminded him that "I shall be Happy" in heaven and that his loss "may be made up in another": "Get another Wife as soon as you can," she advised. According to Clap, she wanted him to ask "God to Direct You to get a K̶i̶n̶d̶ Loving and Religious Wife." She even urged him to begin their separation as she lay dying. She acknowledged that she would "envy" any woman that would be lucky enough to be his wife but now, close to eternity, "I don't want to be your Wife any longer." "A better Husband" was now waiting for her in heaven. Mary also pushed Thomas to remarry for the sake of their children. His new wife would need to "be a good Mother to the Children."[11] Thus, although Mary was a typical seventeenth-century helpmeet, her relationship with her husband and children foreshadowed the values that preoccupied the middling sort at the end of the eighteenth century.

After wrestling with his heartache for eight months, Rev. Clap determined to force "myself to entertain some some General tho'ts" about remarrying, "tho I have found it one of the Hardest things that ever I Engaged in and a Revival of my Griefs." To clarify his thinking, he listed the pros and cons of remarriage, though his "affections have been so strongly wedded to her that it seems exceeding hard for me to think of any other." He idealized his wife to such an extent that any flesh-and-blood replacement would fail to meet her example. Perhaps fittingly, then, he began with "Considerations against entertaining any Prospects of Altering my Condition." He argued first that "I have once been Entirely Pleased and Satisfied [in marriage], and it seems very unlikely that ever I should be so Please[d] & Satisfied again." Even if he found a woman with the same qualities as Mary, "she would not be the same *to me*." In fact, if the new woman deviated from her predecessor in the slightest way, "it would be a great Revival of my Grief and of the Sense of my former Loss." In addition, he considered the idea of asking for such happiness again to be expecting too much of divine largesse: "I have already had my full share of all the Comforts and Satisfactions of the married State, and why should I desire anything further."[12]

He also was emotionally scarred by the deaths of his wife and children and knew remarriage could bring a return of similar pain and heartbreak. "Tho the marriage State was designed for the Comfort of mankind, yet in this State of sin and misery there are many Troubles & Sorrows accompanying it. The care and concern for each other and for their children, especially in times of Sickness and Distress, the sorrow of losing their children of parting with each other and seems to take away or abate all that is comfortable & pleasing in the State." He continued, "If I should have another wife and should be in any measure pleased & Satisfied with her as I was with the former, I fear it would have a tendancy to bring [my] affections back into this world again." His mourning had made him more appropriately focused on the spiritual rather than the corporeal world, "but if I should have another Wife and more young children, my heart would be engaged to and for them. I should be loath to part with them." The widower also worried about stretching his financial resources to accommodate more children, wanting all of his children to have a "competency"—that is, enough money to live comfortable lives. Currently, "tho I have but a little of this world yet it may be a Competency for" his two living daughters. But if he had "another number & Stock of children I might be much more Concerned for them."[13]

Turning to "some Considerations why it might be most Convenient for me to Entertain tho'ts of marrying again in Convenient Season," Clap weighed the potential for the healing of his broken family. He reasoned that God might see fit to give him another kind companion, and perhaps he had a duty to remarry. After all, according to the Bible, "it [is] not best for man to live alone"; he needed a "help meet." Dependent on hired help, friends, or relatives to manage his household, Clap realized, "I have now a Family to take care of and none can act the womans part in it, so well as one that acts in the Relation & Capacity of Wife." Remarriage might increase the burdens of his household with new children—"I should be under much more care and Concern to Provide for them &c."—but expanding his family could also expand his joy: "The wise Author of our natures has implanted in us such an affection of love & Complacency in them, as that we are in a great measure paid for all that we do for them as we go along."[14] In the right light, his concerns could appear to be solutions to his household cares and loneliness.

Having decided to remarry, Rev. Clap set aside the ninth of the next month (and subsequent months to come) to spend the day in prayer for the strength to look for a new wife and for the good fortune to find a specific kind of woman. He asked God for a woman who had the same characteristics of the virtuous first Mrs. Clap. She should have "great Prudence" and care for his domestic affairs in such a way that his "heart may safely Trust in her." He wanted a woman whose "temper" and "opinions" perfectly "harmonize[d]" with his own and who had made the "choise of Christ for her Husband." She should be a "natural" mother to his children and "love my children for my sake, and wisely and carefully Educate and Govern them with the Authority and Tenderness of a natural Parent." He prayed "that she may always seek and rejoyce in their Good and find something of the Pleasure and Satisfaction in them of a Natural mother in them." He understood that he had set the bar high and wondered whether it would be possible to "find such a Virtuous Woman with all these Qualifications[.] I am wholly at a loss."[15]

Exhausted as he watched the sun rise, Clap ended his solicitations with a desperate plea that God not let him be "mistaken or make a wrong Choise." He worried that he might choose a shrew, even a wicked stepmother. He begged God to keep him from an "angry, Fretful" woman who would cause "jarring or Discord" in his household. It would be "better to Dwell in the Wilderness" then to be married to "a Contentious and Angry Woman." He concluded, "Lord thou Knowest my Temper & Disposition" and how much he wanted to be "joyned" to an "agreable Consort." If he married "a Disagrable one," it would be hard for his "nature to bear it." He let his tears mix with the ink of his document, demonstrating, he said, his fragile state more clearly "than words" could. He had ended his day of devotions by "overwhelming myself with Fears."[16]

More than three years passed before God answered Clap's prayers in the form of an experienced mother from a politically well-connected family. Mary Saltonstall brought six children to the marriage as well as a considerable estate. Although love rather than money had determined Clap's choice of his first wife, his second wife was a wealthy widow. He left no record of the role that her money played in his choice, and that marriage produced no children, so his worries about the further subdivision of his estate proved groundless. There is also no record of how the new Mrs. Clap treated her stepdaughters.

MARY (FISH) NOYES, THE WIDOW

Mary Fish was born in Stonington, Connecticut in 1736, to the Reverend Joseph Fish and Rebecca (Peabody [Pabodie]) Fish. Joseph Fish was the minister of the North Society in Stonington and ran an Indian school there, while Rebecca was descended from some of the first families of New England. Mary married John Noyes, a Yale graduate and minister, in 1759, and the young couple lived in New Haven with her in-laws. Over the next six years, John and Mary had four children, but John was unable to lead a church because of his poor health, and he died of consumption and "fits" in 1767, leaving Mary a widow at the age of thirty-one. She and her children continued living with John's parents after his death.[17]

John left Mary with a comfortable estate, and she had no shortage of suitors, but she was cautious about doing anything to jeopardize her future and that of her children. She received her first marriage proposal in 1769, turning it down after some hesitation. Three years later, Naphtali Daggett, formerly an assistant pastor at the church where her father-in-law occupied the pulpit and now the president of Yale, asked for her hand. Though his status should have recommended him, she nonetheless declined. He did not respond well, refusing to accept her rejection and labeling it simply "female Play" in a letter to her father. As a result, Mary turned him down again, this time more forcefully. Apparently prompted by this ugly incident, Mary sat down in August 1773 and wrote out her thoughts on second marriages. She already had enough money: she needed to overcome her loss, to find a loving but cultured gentlemen for herself, and to find a loving, honest step-father for her children.[18]

In the document, Mary Noyes layered sentimental requirements and language on top of the traits articulated by Clap: she wanted not only a religious companion but also an affectionate late-eighteenth-century gen-tleman. She began, "If heaven ever design me again for the married state, O grant me a kindred Soul, with with which mine shall mingle, mutually tasting the refin'd joys that flow from friendship; yea that ardent affection which is excited by merret, and ever growing from the fertile soil of real worth." She then elaborated on the "particulars" of what she saw as an "ac-complished man." First and foremost, and perhaps essential given that both her father and her first husband had been ministers, she wanted a man of faith, "one who has the fear of God allways before his eyes." At the same time, he needed to be refined, "genteel in his address, and exquicetly deli-cate in his actions and words." She wanted him to be a generous host, "may he love to see his table be spread with the bounties of Gods providence, not only with the necessaries, of life but sometimes, with the comforts and deli-caces; as his income will allow." He must teach her children religion but do so gently: "And above all let him take care to aillivate their minds; instruct-ing them in the grand principles of religion, and see to it that his example corresponds with his the precepts of the same. that he be kind and tender, which will leind them to obedience, when the severe treatment would excite in them not a fillial, but slavish fear." She, like her enlightened contempo-raries, believed that such parenting resulted in better-behaved children.[19]

But in addition to seeking these personal qualities, Mary Noyes needed a man who would fairly shepherd her children's estate. When women mar-ried, they became *femes coverts* (covered women)—that is, they lived under the legal umbrella of their husbands. Husbands assumed ownership of any property their wives brought to the marriage, including any land or goods they had inherited outright from previous husbands. Goods earmarked for later dispersal to children needed careful tending to keep their value intact. A second husband, therefore, needed to watch over a child's inheritance in loco parentis—that is, as an interested parent would, rather than in the role of a self-interested stepfather. As Mary Noyes wrote, "May he *indeed* be a father to my fatherless Children; ever anxious to promote their good on every account! may he look on the inheritance of their Father, as sacred, never to be converted to the a[u]gmenting of his own estate. let him put it under the best advantages to be profitable, as well for Their future advantage, as present education." A good stepfather, like a good father, would build an inheritance; an evil stepfather would line his own pockets. Finally, like Clap, Noyes mourned and glorified her dead spouse, ending her meditation with a confession: "But a word with you my heart. dost thou not look for too great perfection in this imperfect state? No, I once knew a dear man, that was the happy possesor of all those accomplishments." She, too, sought someone in the mold of her previous spouse.[20]

Mary Noyes had yet another failed courtship in October 1774, but at the end of the year, she met Gold Selleck Silliman, a lawyer and leader of the Connecticut militia, who persuaded her that she had found her ideal. She presented Silliman with her list of qualifications: not surprisingly, he found her requirements daunting. But he told her that he hoped he could live up to them, a response that Mary felt "plead in his favor."[21]

Mary nevertheless continued to worry about her children—an issue Selleck referred to as the "grand Difficulty." Selleck fretted, "I feared—from a visible Alteration in your Countenance that You was unwell: You then hinted to me that the Importance of the Subject on which we were conversing produced that Appearance." He was upset that his hopes for their happy future together caused her "anxiety," but he acknowledged the truth in her concerns: "I freely own there is a Risque in it." He even thought he knew what she was thinking: "But ah Sir, how do I know that you would ~~behave~~ treat me and my Children in this kind Manner, if You had us in your Power I have Nothing but your Word for it?" Selleck also shared some of his motivations for the marriage, writing, "I have a Child that I hope would find in my Dearest Mrs. Noyes another Dear & tender Mother; so that on the whole my Love You have some Security beside my bare Word." But his son was a married adult, while her three surviving children were still minors; moreover, only her children's financial futures were at risk. For all his sympathy and understanding, he could not share her "anxiety."[22]

Mary also wanted Selleck to understand that her children would remain her priority. She quoted to Selleck from a letter in which her parents fretted about her intention to marry: "O the dear dear Children—. . . in their present situation and stage of learning.—Where their shelter, who their protector, watcher, Counseller guide—in the midst of Snares, & temptations to go astray, at an age the most susceptable &c &c." Selleck responded with his own expectations, reinforcing the importance of Mary's maternal role. "But the Dear Children tis askt where shall be their—Shelter, their Protector, their Guide, their Counseller? give me Leave to say their Shelter shall be where their Dear Mamma's is if she pleases to accept the proposed One. Their Counseller, their Guide, their Protector shall still be their Dear mamma still assisted by One who will delight to make her and them happy." He assured Mary that she would remain in charge of her own children.[23]

Mary also worried about becoming a stepmother. She assumed that Selleck's son would resent her because his wife had died less than a year earlier. She imagined William Silliman's thoughts on their first meeting: "Here comes one to possess the place of my late dear indulgent *Mamma!*—Did I think, on that fatal day, never to be forgoten; that my dear Pappa, would ever think of another. *My* wound is *recent*, why does it so soon close with *him*! can it be, that another finds a place in his affections, as did *she*, I shall always lament? Ah, he may imagine his loss made up; mine never will be." To Mary, the risk to her children and the hurt feelings of Selleck's son portended an unhappy outcome. Selleck responded by sending William to Mary's home, where he took her aside and "genteely introduc'd the Subject, most interesting to us all, expressing his entire approbation."[24] Her children safe and her future stepson content with his father's choice of a stepmother, Mary married Selleck. He remained true to his word, taking care of her and her children, and they had a happy marriage.

THE POPULAR VIEW

Women considered remarriage carefully, even often forgoing the option, but the culture as a whole also pushed them to think twice. In fact, literature read on both sides of the Atlantic frowned on widows in search of husbands. Writers wondered what widows could gain through remarriage that would justify the risk to their husband's legacies; only a selfish need for sexual companionship could explain such potentially perilous behavior. In the public imagination, the awakened sexual appetites of formerly married women forced them to seek out inappropriate partners as soon as possible. Unfortunately, such lusty haste inevitably led to poor decision-making. The widow often fell on the first attractive man she found, despite his youth, poor estate, or both. The estate she inherited from a husband shamefully landed in the pocket of a wastrel. One scholar has labeled this common trope the "widow's tale."[25]

Typical is an epistolary essay from the enormously popular *Spectator*, a magazine published by Joseph Addison and Richard Steele.[26] This series of satirical essays was very popular not only at the time of its initial publication in 1714 but also when it was included in later collections that circulated widely on both sides of the Atlantic. In one essay, a presumably fictional correspondent posed a problem for the editors to consider: the oversexed widow. The writer expressed his concern about a new secret London association, the "Widow-Club." The author claimed to be a young "widow-hunter" who had discovered the club and was eager to warn his fellow sportsmen about the widows' cabal. According to the correspondent, "This Club consists of nine experienced Dames, who take their Places once a Week round a large oval Table." All of the members had been married multiple times, and they were always in hot pursuit of new conquests. "Mrs. Medlar," for example, had married twice and then indulged herself with a young "gallant." Although she was now married to "an old Gentleman of Sixty," her new husband's poor health allowed her to continue her membership. The "Widow Quick" had "married within a Fortnight after the Death of her last Husband," while the "Widow Wildfire" went through lovers at a speed that justified her moniker. Although a member had suffered through a marriage at the age of fifteen to a man of "threescore and Twelve," she had been freed by his death and had acquired the title "Lady Waddle" from her new, elderly, and oversized knight/husband. She eventually had her revenge when he died, and at age fifty-five she married "a Youth of One and Twenty." These women supposedly met to plot their conquests, and their greed was such that "the principal Rule, by which the whole Society are to govern themselves is this, To cry up the Pleasures of a single Life upon all Occasions, in order to deter the rest of their Sex from Marriage, and engross the whole Male World to themselves."[27] Widows on the loose, without male caretakers, were unable to make sensible decisions leaving them open to "widow hunters" looking for wealth. Her estate, inherited from a dead spouse, was the prize.

A much less common topic was the remarrying widower. There was no equivalent "widower's tale," although men, widowed or not, could be both teased and admired for marrying a younger woman. In the later eighteenth century, one essay did propose a "widower's tale" of a sort, following the outline of *The Spectator* in both format and satirical voice. The author simultaneously teased the lonely widower who married a young woman out of vanity and shamed him for picking a poor replacement mother for his children. The author was Timothy Dwight, a minister and writer and eventually president of Yale College, who outlined his concern about remarrying widowers in the *New-Haven Gazette, and the Connecticut Magazine* in 1786 and 1787. Under the pseudonym James Littlejohn Esq., Dwight published fifteen "miscellaneous essays" that addressed topics "in which most persons feel themselves interested." He titled this series "The Friend."

In one of these essays, Dwight began with a letter from the fictional "Mr. Alby" about a foolish, fifty-year-old, newly widowed man aptly named Littlechild who intended to marry an eighteen-year-old woman. Alby had been shocked when he saw his old friend in a local tavern and barely recognized him, since Littlechild was dressed in the highest fashion—for a man half his age. In the dead of winter, "instead of the furs and flannels, which I felt to be necessary for him, he was ornamented with a fine white cloth, and a thin, cotton underdress." He had done his hair in a "long queue" (ponytail) rather than his usual "manly curls." In one hand he held a "wand" with an ivory, amber, and silver head; the other hand held a silver chain at the other end of which was a small dog with a belled collar. The elderly man announced in one long breath that he had lost his wife and would soon be remarrying. Alby archly asked whether the young woman found Littlejohn as attractive as he found her: Alby thought it more appropriate that his friend adopt her as a daughter.[28]

This precipitous and unequal marriage highlighted Littlechild's vanity. He invited Alby outside to see his new horse, an Arabian, purchased to replace his former pony. When Alby asked whether Littlejohn could mount his new horse without a platform known as a horse block, Littlejohn sneered, "A horse-block!—a pretty figure a man of my age wou'd make on a horse-block!—I believe you think me a hundred years old! A horse-block, truly!—I would as soon mount the gallows." Littlejohn had been a sensible man, according to Alby, but this ridiculous courtship had "turned his brain."[29]

Dwight argued that such marriages not only were ridiculous because they were unequal and not well thought out but also totally disregarded the needs of motherless children. He even blamed "the unhappiness of families, under the government of stepmothers," on "their husbands." "Instead of looking for a good mother to their children," imprudent men preferred a "young, inexperienced, giddy girl, whose beauty may gratify their amorous views, and whose youth, and choice of them, may gratify their vanity." Such women had their appeal, but youth and inexperience frequently led to troubled households. "The unfortunate wife is introduced almost in a state of childhood, into the arduous station of mother to a numerous family, and into the difficult employments of providing for their wants, instructing them in governing their tempers, and regulating their conduct. It is impossible that such a mother should not do a thousand foolish, improper things." A man "warmly engaged in the pursuit" of such a new wife might ask, "What course shall I take? must I live a single life, in solitude, and melancholy, the remaining part of my days?" Of course not, answered Dwight, but such a man needed to find a woman who would do more than satisfy "your vanity, your lust, or your avarice." She needed to be a "kind and prudent mother to your children, a skillful directress of your domestic concerns, and a sensible, pleasing companion to you." Most important, "you ought to marry for your children, as well as for yourself; and that, in the character and conduct of your wife, their happiness is at least as intimately concerned as your own."[30]

To Dwight, a poor choice of a wife victimized and ultimately ruined children. Stepchildren, "irritated by a treatment wholly contrasted to that of their own mother, take little pains to obey, or to please her, observe all her mistakes, magnify her faults, and (if any of them, as is frequently the case, are grown to adult years) tell them with bitterness to her face." Such disgruntled children even complained openly to neighbors and relatives, ruining the reputation of the family as a whole and of their father in particular. When a new stepmother inevitably had her own "numerous offspring," they "swarm upon a house that was before filled." Quarrels broke out when the young stepmother naturally "favours her [own] children." The result is "enmity, jealousy, and jangle."[31]

According to Dwight, if a man chose poorly, his initially kind wife could even transform into a wicked stepmother. "The government of her children is rendered peculiarly troublesome, because she is wholly untried, and unskilled in the arts of governing." Her inexperience would make her wonder whether her stepchildren were peculiarly misbehaved. "She is naturally induced to believe that her children have more, and greater faults than others; . . . because she had never before at all concerned with the faults of children, or even led to attend them." As a result, she governed her stepchildren "with a dislike and rigour, conformed to such imputations." Although Dwight acknowledged that "the cruelty and odiousness of stepmothers, and the unhappiness of the families where they exist, are proverbial," not all stepmothers were cruel. After all, "it cannot be imagined that so many more bad women happen to be introduced into that station than in any other." In fact, "for many women in this character are as much beloved, as free from censure, and as happy as were the real parents of their families."[32]

His advice to a remarrying man, in sum, was first and foremost to take his time in finding a wife. He needed to look among women his own age— perhaps the friends of his deceased wife. She should be a good mother who could handle domestic concerns and be a reasonable companion, who would honor the memory of her predecessor, show respect for her husband, and garner respect from her stepchildren. Men needed to marry for their children as well as for themselves. Any reader foolish enough to disregard such admonitions would find that "MISERY is at the door, and will enter in the train of your bride."[33]

THE NEW "NEW MOTHER"

As Dwight's essay suggests, once the sentimental family became the one of choice for the middling sort, the issue of stepmother fitness emerged as a peculiar concern. A new wife needed to become a "new mother" to her stepchildren and to do so in such a way that she stepped into her predecessor's shoes. She needed to transform herself into the mother of the household to guarantee the continuation of her husband's ideal, middle-class family. A stepmother needed literally to become a "new mother," facing the nearly impossible task of reconstituting a family. Middle-class men felt increasing pressure to pick women who could perform this miracle as the eighteenth century progressed, and doing so became essential as the nineteenth-century version of this ideology, domesticity, took hold.

Mather Byles, a minister and exiled loyalist in Nova Scotia, realized the enormity of the task in 1787, at the death of his second wife, who had embodied the idea of the "new mother." He wrote to his sisters in Boston, "On the 22nd of February, about two oClock P M, her Soul took Wing for the eternal World. She was an amiable Woman, an affectionate Wife & a most exemplary Mother to my Children. Seldom, very seldom, is a Family so happily united in a second Marriage." Although her death had brought all the children home, "the Pleasure to see my Children once more all together at my Table" was "but alas!" overshadowed by "a Seat vacant, not easily filled."[34] Byles thought he had been unusually lucky. Perhaps, but it is also likely that the woman he chose for his second wife understood her new responsibilities and worked hard to repair his broken family.

Widower William Woolsey, a merchant in New York and New Haven, William Woolsey, also chose well. His careful editing of an 1816 letter to his brother, however, demonstrates his initial fears that his second marriage, to Sarah Chauncey, might prove detrimental to his children: "The connection which I have formed is one which I have not a doubt will ~~greatly promote~~ ensure the mutual happiness and welfare of Mrs W[oolsey] & myself, and ~~every member of my family~~ every one of my children." He understood the need for a good mother for his children and hoped that his children would be receptive to Sarah, as he hinted to his son, Theodore, who was away at school: "In your letters home do not forget to write to your Mama occasionally, her love to you calls for a return of attachment & attention."[35]

Theodore followed his father's advice and received a warm letter back from his stepmother in which she thanked him for his kind "remembrance of me." She went on to assure him that "my wishes and desires for you, my Son, are far from being moderate, I would not only have you distinguished for your intellectual endowments, but for the qualities of your heart, and eminent usefulness in the world—all this, the affection of a mother, fondly anticipates." She signed the missive "your truly affectionate Mother." A year later, she reminded him again, "Remember you are writing to a Mother tenderly interested in all that concerns you."[36] Sarah had indeed embraced the role of "new mother."

Likewise, famous eighteenth-century Boston minister Benjamin Colman put finding a good mother for his two daughters at the top of his list of qualifications for his new wife, before even a meaty dowry. His dead wife, "a loving and careful Mother," would not be easy to replace. He began his search explicitly looking for "the Person to make me and my Children most happy, if I married again." He thought he had found a fine substitute in widow Sarah Clark, who already boarded with him and knew his children well, having developed a "natural Love, (long since) to my Children, and theirs to her." He claimed that her maternal skill mattered more to him than her "small worldly Estate."[37]

Even relatives of a dead wife urged a man to remarry for his children's sake. The devastated Eliphalet Pearson, president of Phillips Academy in Andover, Massachusetts, hesitated to remarry after his wife died in childbirth in 1782. His dead wife's sister, although pleased that Pearson thought her sister so hard to replace, urged him to find "another Parent" for his infant daughter, Maria. "I wish for your own sake, that *you* could; for I think your famaly and domestic affairs would be in a much more eligable situation, and yet I own there is a pleasure in finding you cannot, how unaccountable! . . . I am persuaided that could you convirt your feelings over to a different channel and give Maria another Parent."[38] Although he, unlike most widowers, resisted for a few years, Pearson eventually married again, choosing Sarah Bromfield, who proved to be the loving mother his young daughter required.

Mary Hubbard, mother-in-law of Boston merchant Gardner Greene, lost her daughter, Betsey, in 1798, and although flattered that her son-in-law was hesitant to remarry, she reminded him that he must do so. Like Pearson's sister-in-law, Hubbard not only wanted Gardner to be happy but also had deep concerns for her grandchildren. She prayed: "That you may make a good choice & select a mother that will be kind & attentive to your children . . . is the fervent wish of your Friend & Mother." He chose Eliza Copley, daughter of famous colonial painter John Singleton Copley, prompting Hubbard to write to the new bride to express "the perfect confidence I have that you dear Eliza will be a tender & Affectionate mother to my dear [grand]children." That confidence "has made me resign them to your care with a pleasure I never expected to experience tis with sincerity I assure you that I am perfectly satisfied with the choice Gardner has made."[39]

Harrison Gray Otis, a Boston lawyer and politician, mused in an 1820 letter to his wife about Israel Thorndike's likely inability to find a replacement for their wonderful granddaughter, Sally. "In due time I shall be glad to see him united with a fit companion for himself and mother for his children—But with his recollections of what She was, and the little likelihood which exists of his ever finding such another mirror of angelic piety, disinterestedness and tenderness of heart; the chances would seem to be much against his ever being happy in another connexion."[40]

Some men had such confidence in their choice that they thought that even their first wives would have approved. Eliphalet Terry of Hartford, Connecticut, imagined he had found such an ideal mate in Lydia (Coit) Terry, and when she died on 2 September 1831, he told relatives of his first wife, Sally (Watson) Terry, that he hoped the two women would meet in heaven. According to Sally's brother, William Watson, he and members of his family "rode in the procession to the burying ground," where Terry "said to me, with tears in his eyes & his lips quivering, that, if friends were permitted to meet in the other world, the first thing my sister Sally would say to Mrs. Terry would be 'I thank you for your kindness to my daughter.'" Terry believed that Lydia had indeed been a new mother to his child.[41]

MARRYING A WIFE'S SISTER

By the end of the eighteenth century, one way to replace the irreplaceable mother was to marry her sister.[42] Who could be more familiar and loving to a widower's children than their own aunt? As one young Connecticut girl wrote in her diary around the turn of the nineteenth century, she looked up to mother's sister "as a second mother."[43] But such marriages were illegal on both sides of the Atlantic until the 1780s, when a cultural rethinking began that revolved around a number of issues, including the possibility of finding a loving replacement for a dead mother.[44]

Most of the debate centered on biblical tradition versus new ideas about personal liberty as the new nation struggled with the implications of a free society.[45] When a minister refused to marry one man to his sister-in-law, the would-be groom blustered that "his liberty" apparently "was to be judged of another man's conscience."[46] It therefore might come as no surprise that the law concerning incestuous marriages changed first in the revolutionary hotbed of Massachusetts in 1786, with Connecticut following suit in 1793. The law changed but the debate continued, particularly among the clergy, although even critics of the law had to acknowledge the motherly qualifications of a sister-in-law. As one pamphlet argued, "None are so likely to take special care of our affairs, particularly of our children, as near relations." This author had heard "a gentleman assert in a publick company that, 'for this reason, if his wife was dead, he would chuse to marry her sister rather than any other woman; for who, said he, would be so likely to take care of my first wife's children as her sister, or their aunt.'"[47]

In 1792, Jonathan Edwards, the son of the famous minister by the same name, urged his parishioners to oppose the new law, but embedded in his argument was the admission that such a choice might benefit the children. For Edwards and other old-fashioned Puritans, the question was not "who is most likely to be kind to the motherless children, but what is the law of God?" Edwards acknowledged that some would argue "that no person is so suitable to come into the place of a deceased wife, or so likely to be kind to her motherless children, as her own sister." Nonetheless, he also suggested that such relatives could prove to be some of the cruelest: "It is said, that orphans have been more frequently murdered by uncles and aunts, than any other persons."[48] He resorted to such extreme and perhaps overstated claims in an attempt to silence what had become a compelling argument.

The New Yorker who published under the pseudonym Domesticus in 1827 countered Edwards and other critics by making the case that a wife's sister not only might already know and love her nieces and nephews but also might already be acting the part of a surrogate mother. Some spinsters found the home of a sister a way station between their natal home and marriage. Domesticus reminded the more educated readers to whom he addressed his treatise the Latin term for "aunt" was *Matertera*, or "a sort of Mother." The lucky offspring in such a household already "have two mothers." With proximity, "it not seldom happens, her heart takes such deep root in the little spot in which Providence has transplanted her,—so completely do her interests become identified with her sister's, and those of the little prattlers, whom she has watched over and warmed in the bosom, so long, that she has almost forgotten they are not her own,—that she refuses the most brilliant offers of an independent establishment, to live and die with the objects of her affection!" The author even suggested that some women, when contemplating their own demise, recommended their sisters as potential wives: "The dying wife must be presumed to love her sister, *tenderly*,—to put *entire confidence* in her as one who will faithfully discharge the duty of Mother to her babes."[49]

In 1797, another pseudonymous New York pamphleteer, Citizen, argued that marrying a wife's sister could ensure "domestic felicity." A wife's sisters "in a peculiar manner, interest themselves in the welfare of his children, and probably secure them from the tyranny and abuse of a cruel and unfeeling step-mother." Aunts' familiarity with children as well as with their brothers-in-law made them good choices: "A woman who takes the place of her deceased sister by marriage, we may expect, will be excited, not only by her matrimonial engagements, and her attachment to her husband, but by a consideration that those orphans, now committed to her care, are the offspring of her beloved sister, to a faithful discharge of the duties, not only of a wife, but also of a parent." The children would also appreciate the choice and behave accordingly, having "special motives for obedience and submission, when they consider her past as well as present attention to their welfare." Finally, this prior relationship might mitigate the inevitable consequences of popular prejudice: "When a woman is married to a man who has children, strong prejudices and groundless suspicions often make her unhappy, and destroy her influence" with her new charges.[50]

People married and remarried for love and money but remarriage meant overcoming grief and considering your own needs as well as the needs of your children. For both men and women, the decision could be wrenching. The safekeeping of a husband's legacy, given the legal handicap of marriage, loomed large for women. Over time, men, however, felt an increased pressure to consider their children's needs as central. By the end of the eighteenth century, a mother was an essential part of the new, middle-class, sentimental family. When she died, her husband needed to find a replacement to reconstitute his family. A new wife needed to be more than a companion; she also needed to be a "natural" or "new" mother to her stepchildren.

CHAPTER TWO

Stepfathers in the Law

The Case of Silas Deane and the Webb Family

Connecticut jurist Tapping Reeve acknowledged a man's reasonable concerns about a stranger raising his children in his famous treatise on domestic law, *Baron and Feme*. "If a man makes a will, who has children, and being desirous that the children may not go into the hands of a stranger for education, leaves a legacy to his wife to be void if she marry."[1] If losing the property her husband had provided was not enough to convince a widow to stay single, at least a man might rest assured that such a provision would prevent his estate from falling into the hands of another man. The judge in one Connecticut court case saw such provisions as an appropriate way to "encourage" widows with children to remain single. "It would seem very reasonable, that a man leaving a widow with seven children, as in the present case, should be permitted to encourage her, by suitable provision in his will, to remain single, and not subject his own offspring to the probable evils of a step-father."[2]

Anglo-American law, particularly inheritance law, outlined the contours of cultural prejudice against stepfathers. Propertied men—those who wrote, implemented, and commented on the law—saw stepfathers as potentially powerful. When propertied men contemplated their own mortality and the circumstances of the families they would leave behind, they understood that stepfathers would need careful monitoring.[3] In fact, stepfathers were not legally fathers. A father's ability to be a provider, to take care of his family's economic needs, even after his death, defined his place in the early modern world. A stepfather had no such legal obligation. Historical literature on fatherhood, too, has omitted stepfathers—perhaps rightly so.[4]

Even if not legally required to act the part of a father, a stepfather had access to a dead man's attempt at posthumous providing. It was hoped that when stepfathers joined fatherless families, they would honestly steward their predecessors' estates. Estates were vulnerable because women were legally vulnerable. All women gave up control of their property when they married; the law labeled them *femes coverts* (covered women).[5] A married woman's worldly goods became her husband's; in return, she received a promise of support. When propertied widows remarried, they usually brought their "widow's third"—one-third of the personal property from their first marriages, which they owned outright, plus one-third of the real estate from their first marriages, which they owned only during their lives.[6] A widow could use the real estate—live in the house, run the farm—but when she died, that property would go to her dead husband's children. The idea was to provide for her needs and those of her fatherless children both before and after her death.

This chapter focuses on a specific stepfather, Silas Deane. As a Wethersfield, Connecticut, lawyer and the administrator of his dead predecessor's estate, Deane had the legal wherewithal and desire to exploit the inheritance system to his advantage. Deane was not a typical stepfather; rather, his story, placed alongside the relevant laws, exposes both the legal stereotype of stepfathers and the way the law could be manipulated to disadvantage widows and orphans.[7] Not all stepfathers lived up to their sinister reputation, but Silas Deane was not all stepfathers.

Deane was born in Ledyard (formerly part of Groton), Connecticut, in 1737, the son and grandson of blacksmiths. His family did well enough to provide Silas, the oldest son, with a college education, and he graduated from Yale in 1758. After a short stint as a teacher, he became a lawyer, moving to Wethersfield to set up his practice. There he met Mehitable (Nott) Webb. She had been born in Wethersfield, Connecticut, in 1731, to Gershom Nott, a sea captain, and Sarah (Waterhouse) Nott. In 1749, she married Joseph Webb, the owner of a large merchandizing business. Joseph Webb died in 1761 at the age of thirty-four, leaving her a wealthy widow with six children under the age of twelve: Joseph, Sarah, Samuel, Mehitable, John, and Abigail. Webb had neglected to write a will, perhaps because he had died young, and the court tasked Mehitable with settling the estate, a job for which she hired a lawyer, Silas Deane. Silas and Mehitable married in 1763, and Silas took over his predecessor's business, ultimately leaving his legal career to focus on the West Indian trade. He and Mehitable had one child, Jesse, born eight months after their wedding. She was, therefore,

Silas Deane at around the time of his marriage to Mehitable (Nott) Webb in 1763. Deane subsequently turned from law to the more lucrative West Indian trade, symbolized by the ship in the window behind him. Attributed to William Johnston, *Silas Deane*, ca. 1766. Courtesy of the Webb-Deane-Stevens Museum, Wethersfield, Conn.

perhaps pregnant when she wed Deane. In 1767, thirty-five-year-old Mehitable died and was buried next to her first husband. Two years later, Silas married again. His second wife, Elizabeth (Saltonstall) Evards, was a member of the prestigious, politically well-connected Saltonstall family; her grandfather had been a governor of the colony. Deane then became a politician and diplomat, representing Connecticut in the Continental Congress and serving as a negotiator with the French at the start of the

American Revolution. Elizabeth died in 1777. Deane's subsequent political career was marred by an accusation that he had used his diplomatic position to his own advantage, and he died in 1789 at the age of fifty-two, still working to clear his name.[8]

THE LAW: REMARRIAGE AND AN UNSETTLED ESTATE

When a woman needed to settle her husband's estate and she remarried before the job was done, she jeopardized her inheritance and that of her children. According to Connecticut jurist Zephaniah Swift, "when a man marries a woman that is an executrix [if her husband left a will], or administratrix [if her husband failed to leave a will], he becomes jointly concerned with her, and they must join in all matters that respect the settlement of the estate. The husband acquires no property in the estate the wife holds by such right, but is equally accountable with her as though he had been executor or administrator himself."[9] In other words, a new husband took on the liability but not the substance of the estate. This reality ideally acted as a kind of safeguard against embezzlement and weeded out the less than honorably minded new husband/stepfather. Collecting debts, paying debtors, dividing the proceeds, and even receiving a small percentage of the estate as payment for services as an executor/administrator seemed too much power for one man to have over the estate of another. The law wanted to keep stepfathers at arm's length. Laws requiring a husband's liability for his wife's debts did some of this work when estates were unsettled at the time a widow remarried.

OUR STORY

This safeguard did not work for Mehitable Deane and her children. Silas Deane helped her with Joseph Webb's estate before her death and was appointed administrator of his predecessor's estate after Mehitable's death. In other words, he had access to the substance of the Webb patrimony. His position as a husband, lawyer, and administrator allowed him to circumvent the legal system designed to protect a widow and her children. Mehitable Webb had taken a great risk in marrying Silas Deane before her dead husband's estate was settled, trusting that Deane would settle Webb's affairs in a way that was fair to her and her children. That she was aware of the risks is evidenced by the fact that she signed a prenuptial agreement a month before her wedding.[10]

THE LAW: PRENUPTIAL AGREEMENTS AND
MARRIAGE SETTLEMENTS

A prenuptial contract was one of the few ways a woman could protect her property, and widows, who had previous experience with the legal pitfalls of marriage, were more likely than women marrying for the first time to insist on these legal instruments.[11] These arrangements could overcome the legal handicap of marriage for women, although the impact of such agreements in New England is unclear. For example, marriage settlements in England were normally adjudicated in a Chancery Court, but neither Connecticut nor Massachusetts had such a court.[12]

Similarly, marriage settlements ideally provided a way for women to ensure that children receive their fathers' inheritances. In some cases, formal agreements were written and signed before marriage; in other instances, second husbands simply had to appear in court to post bonds guaranteeing that their stepchildren would receive their fathers' legacies in the future. In early modern England, prenuptial agreements, broadly conceived, were common. In particular, probate marriage settlements (when a bond was posted rather than an agreement spelled out) were popular, in part because they guarded against unscrupulous stepfathers. If a man put down a bond, or surety, and agreed to pay the children's share of their father's estate, a widow could enter a new marriage with some sense of security.[13] These kinds of arrangements appeared in the legal records of both England and New England.[14]

OUR STORY

Mehitable's prenuptial agreement failed to safeguard her interests or the interests of her children. Although the document's wording initially sounds generous, a close reading indicates that the document favored Deane. Deane may well have spent a good deal of time and used his superior legal knowledge to create an agreement that seemed fine to the cautious widow but in fact privileged his interests.

The agreement began fairly enough, with provisions that required an inventory of the widow's property and that the parties keep their estates separate, sharing only profits earned after their marriage. But then came the caveat: "except what is hereafter excepted." Because the Webb estate had not been inventoried, let alone settled, Silas's and Mehitable's properties were never really separate. Although Deane was the lawyer for the estate, he had never recorded an inventory of Joseph Webb's property, though the law stipulated that an estate had to be inventoried within less than the two years that had passed since Webb's death. Deane's negligence raises some questions. If the estate had declined in value over that time, the inventory outlined in the prenuptial agreement would have masked any mismanagement by Deane. Conversely, if the estate had increased in value, Deane would receive his share of the profits before his portion was reduced by debtors' claims and legacies. Failing to complete a timely inventory offered Deane a win/win strategy if he indeed was nefarious enough to calculate the costs.

According to the prenuptial agreement, once the inventory of the widow's property was completed, Deane would receive one-third of her real property and her personal property outright. Mehitable might have seen this provision as generous, since by law, a new husband could absorb his wife's entire estate. But because Joseph Webb's estate had not yet been distributed, the agreement gave Deane one-third of the entire Webb estate, not one-third of Mehitable's share of that estate (the widow's third). Mehitable's share of a settled estate would have been much smaller, since it would not have included any real estate, to which she would only have had rights during her lifetime. The prenuptial agreement thus gave Deane a portion of what should have been the Webb children's property after their mother's death.

The provisions in the agreement that specifically mention the Webb children also can be read as beneficial to Deane. Though Mehitable retained two-thirds of her estate, she could not use these assets as she pleased; rather, she could only give them to her children. If Joseph Webb's estate had been inventoried and settled, the adult children would have shared two-thirds of their father's estate after the creditors were paid. But under the terms of the prenuptial contract, Mehitable kept her children's two-thirds share. She might have seen this provision as benefiting not only her but also her children because it meant that creditors of the Webb estate would not have access to those funds. However, the agreement also said, "always Understood Notwithstanding that any Loss, in Misfortune in Business, sustained by the s[ai]d Silas during the Life of the s[ai]d Mehitable is first to be Deducted 2/3d of it out s[ai]d Estate." This provision exposed the children's share to the creditors of their new stepfather. Silas in effect created his own slush fund. If the two-thirds had been in the hands of Webb's creditors, Deane would have had no access whatsoever to this property. By putting the two-thirds into Mehitable's hands, he not only cut out the Webb estate's creditors but established a fund to pay his own debts.

In the case of Deane's death, Mehitable could again have seen the pre-nuptial arrangement as generous, providing her with more than the law allowed. If Mehitable and Silas had no children, she would receive the use of all of Deane's property for life, and all his personal goods would go to her outright. By law, a widow normally received only half of her husband's real estate for life if the couple had no children. If the Deanes had children, however, Mehitable would get what the "law directs if he dies Intestate. otherways. he shall by his last Will & Testament direct." If a man died intestate a widow with children would receive her widow's third. At the time of her marriage to Silas, Mehitable was likely already pregnant. Unless this child died, the seemingly generous provisions regarding a childless union were irrelevant, so Silas was only agreeing to give her what she would have received through the regular probate process.

When completed, the prenuptial agreement was given "to the Care of Mrs. Ruth Belding to be kept untill ye Death of Silas Deane or Mehitabel his Wife after which to be broken open & Copys given to their Survivors." If Belding predeceased the Deanes, the document was to go to her brother, "George Wyllys Esqr. for the Purpose above."[15] But according to a note on the back of the agreement, it was not "broken open" until 25 September 1773—six years after Mehitable's death and about the same time that Deane considered embarking on his risky career as a revolutionary. The Webb children knew about the document—in fact, Joseph Webb Jr. had witnessed its signing. Because they knew its contents, they had no reason to open it to read it. It only became important when the siblings began to consider the consequences of their stepfather's actions for their father's still-unsettled estate.

Mehitable Webb knew that marrying her lover and lawyer risked her financial health, and she thought that her seemingly generous prenuptial agreement would mitigate that risk. She probably signed it with a sigh of relief. Her pregnancy may have forced the issue of marriage, but her assets and those of her older children would be safe—or so she thought. But she had unwittingly signed a document that assured Silas of the lion's share of the Webb assets.

THE LAW: STEPFATHERS AND WASTE

When a man married a widow with children, he in a legal sense became a tenant of his stepchildren. Like any person who occupied the property of another, he had to treat the house and land as the owner would or face legal action for waste. The kinds of familial tenants who could commit waste varied, but two of the most common were a "tenant in dower" and a "tenant in curtesy." A tenant in dower was a widow or a former widow and her new husband, who had a life interest in the real estate in question. If the former widow and her new husband had a child together and she predeceased him, he could remain on the property as a tenant in curtesy. The condition of the property (house and land) after a potentially long period of tenancy resulted in large part from the care the former widow and her new husband took as tenants.

What exactly did wasteful tenants do? Eighteenth-century English jurist Sir William Blackstone explained that "waste is a spoil and destruction of the estate, either in houses, woods, or lands; by demolishing not the temporary profits only, but the very substance of the thing; thereby rendering it wild and desolate." Waste was "either voluntary, or permissive; the one by an actual and designed demolition of the lands, woods, and houses; the other arising from mere negligence, and want of sufficient care in reparations, fences and the like."[16] Waste, therefore, involved long-term destruction and could be purposeful or simply thoughtless. Blackstone gave some specific examples: "removing wainscot, floors, or other things," "to cut down such trees, or top them, or do any other act whereby the timber may decay, is waste." Any changes to the land, even if potentially beneficial, were prohibited: "To convert wood, meadow, or pasture into arable; to turn arable, meadow, or pasture into woodland; or to turn arable or woodland into meadow or pasture, are all of them waste." In a similar way "to open the land to search for mines or metal, coal, &c., is waste."[17] Blackstone's description clearly explains that tenants were to keep the land and property as it was prior to their occupancy—in the case of a stepfamily, as it was at the time of the father's death.

Many of these ideas about waste had parallels in the English colonies and in the new nation. American jurist James Kent argued that tenants could have wood "for fuel, fences, agricultural erections, and other necessaries" but "must not destroy the timber." They were entitled to the "profits of the growing crops" because "he who rightfully sows ought to reap the profits of his labour," but this applied only to the "products of the earth, arising for the annual labor of the tenant"—that is, "it applies to grain, garden roots, &c., but not to grass, or fruits, which are the natural products of the soil, and do not essentially owe their annual existence to the cultivation of man." The outline of what constituted waste in America remained based on English law into the nineteenth century; a tenant added labor and reaped the appropriate reward, but in the end he needed to leave the property as he had found it.[18]

Stepfathers were one class of the tenant that preoccupied these legal commentators and lawmakers. A woman's labor, aided by her children or hired help, might avoid the deterioration of the property to some extent, but these treatises focused on the work of men. Men could destroy the value of land, and only waste laws and good luck kept the children's share intact.

OUR STORY

Silas Deane went beyond wasting his stepchildren's estate—he stole it. According to the courts, the Webb estate suffered at the hands of Silas Deane and after his death at the hands of his administrator, his only son and heir, Jesse. Silas apparently collected debts owed to the Webb estate and bought land with the proceeds. These properties should have been held in trust for the Webb children, but only some were. When the Webb children realized what had happened, they initiated a legal battle that ultimately went all the way to the Connecticut State Assembly, which assigned a committee to investigate the Webbs' claims. According to the committee's report, "Silas Deane during the Life of his said Wife with the monies and Chattles belonging to the Estate of the said Joseph deceased purchased . . . the several Lotts of Land mentioned in said Petitions . . . received Deeds in his own Name." He "did not purchase or hold said Lands as a Trust for the Heirs of said Joseph deceased." The assembly "accepted and approved" the committee's report on 26 August 1797.[19]

The court followed a complex trail of property transactions that implicated various members of the community as well as Deane and his son, Jesse, in the wrongdoing. For example, Silas had sold one property, gained through Webb funds, to Charles McEvers "in satisfaction of an Execution against him"—that is, to pay Deane's personal debt to McEvers—even though McEvers "had notice of the Claim of the [Webb children] to said Estate." In other words, McEvers knew that he could not legally buy the property yet did so anyway. McEvers also subsequently resold the property to unsuspecting buyers, and when the matter came to court, the innocent buyers were permitted to keep the property since they were "utterly ignorant of the Claim of the Petitioners."[20]

As administrator of his father's estate, Jesse Deane continued Silas's pattern of using the Webb properties. Jesse boldly sold as part of the Deane estate even property he knew was held in trust for the Webbs—the property for which Silas Deane had properly accounted. One parcel had been under contract when Joseph Webb died, and Silas Deane properly completed the transaction, recording the property to "hold in Trust for the Heirs of said Joseph deceased." But Jesse took this property and used it as if it was Silas's outright, selling it to John Williams although "both Vender, and Vendee were w[e]ll acquainted with the Said Trust." In this case, Williams was ordered to give the land back to the Webb children.[21]

Beyond real estate, the Webb children should have inherited a portion of their father's personal property. The law often described such goods as "moveables"—items that literally could be moved, such as clothes and furniture as well as debts owed to the estate. The actual amount of the debts, credits, and other goods of Joseph Webb's estate, however, never appeared in an inventory. According to his children, Joseph Webb Sr. left an estate worth more than forty-three thousand pounds.[22] Deane carefully avoided quoting a figure but claimed that the estate was deep in debt when he took on the task of settling it. According to Deane, Webb owed more than thirty thousand pounds in New York alone.[23] And because Deane never filed an inventory, no definitive answer to the question could be determined. The members of the committee assigned to untangle this mess threw up their hands, reporting that they were "ignorant how the personal Estate of the said Joseph deceased . . . hath been applied."[24] Joseph Webb's personal property had disappeared into the mist.

No one ever suffered the legal and financial repercussions that should have accompanied the failure to file the inventory. The form signed by all administrators at this time in Connecticut required them to "make, or cause to be made a true and perfect Inventory of all and singular the Goods, Chattels, Credits & Estate of the said Deceased," imposed a series of deadlines for the steps in this process, and imposed steep financial penalties for the failure to do so. The document Mehitable Webb signed on 27 April 1761 required her to create an inventory by 27 July 1761 and to produce an administrative account outlining the distribution of the goods and real estate left after debts were paid by 27 April 1762. She and the other administrators of Joseph Webb's estate agreed to pay two thousand pounds if they were negligent in this regard. Yet no financial penalties were ever levied. Deane took over the administration of the Webb estate after Mehitable's death but did not file the required paperwork until six months later. In keeping with standard practice, Deane then promised to produce an inventory in three months and to settle the estate in a year, agreeing to pay a thousand-pound fine if he failed to comply. Once again, although no inventory was produced, there is no record that a fine was paid. In this case, the legal process for safeguarding an estate clearly failed. Silas eventually produced an administrative account on 6 April 1775, when he attempted to settle the estate on the eve of his departure for his second term in the Continental Congress. The court did not accept the document until 1783, and then only with corrections. Deane had failed to list a number of Webb properties, an oversight—perhaps intentional—that ensured further delay. He tried to settle the estate in earnest only later, when he was strapped for cash in Europe and desperate for funds.[25]

A timeline of Silas Deane's political fortunes juxtaposed with a timeline of his family life reveals an unsettling pattern. Deane appears to have used politics to escape his family obligations after the death of his first wife, arguing that public duty prevented him from settling the Webb estate, parenting his son, and even attending his second wife's funeral.

Deane took his first political post a year after Mehitable's death, taking the post of deputy to the Connecticut General Assembly in 1768 and holding it until 1775. His marriage to Elizabeth Saltonstall Evards brought him political contacts that he used to further his ambitions, and his star was on the rise as he set off for the first Continental Congress.

His return for a second term in Congress in 1775 prompted Deane to settle his affairs with the Webbs, but his professional and personal fortunes soon took a turn for the worse. He had begun to wear thin among his colleagues and his constituents, and the Webb children balked at settling an incomplete estate. Although he was not chosen to return to Congress after his second term, he received a plum consolation prize—selection for a secret 1776 mission to France as a commercial and political agent for the fledgling United States.

The Webb estate remained an unsettled mess, but Deane covered his actions with the loincloth of patriotism, telling his stepson, Samuel, "it is not a Time to dispute, about property, when Liberty and Life are attacked."[26] To a friend he explained, "I keep ever in my mind the motto *De republica nil desperandum* [do not despair of the republic]. I counted the cost, when I entered the lists, and ballanced private fortune, ease, leisure, the sweets of domestic society, and life itself, in vain against the liberties of my country; the latter instantly preponderated, and I have nothing to complain of, though much to grieve at, occasioned by the miscarriage or delay of my full powers, for open and public application."[27]

Even Elizabeth Deane's death on 9 June 1777 failed to distract Silas from his course. He wrote to his brother, Barnabas, from Paris a few months later, "You are well acquainted with my sensibility, & therefore must have some Idea of what I feel on the late affecting loss I have met with." But he also reported that he had heard the news "first in the Publick Papers" and vowed not to reflect "on the subject; at best they serve principally to amuse the mind & lull it into a soft insensibility of its suffering." In his "situation Publick distresses & calamities take the Place of every thing private." The rest of the letter was filled with plans to have twelve-year-old Jesse travel to Europe, a task that had taken on new urgency with Elizabeth's death. Silas ended with an apology for his brief epistle: "I'm too much hurried in getting away dispatches to Congress to add more than to desire my Complimts. to all Friends, & that I am, &c. Silas Deane."[28] Three years later, he exhibited the same emotional distance and lack of interest in Elizabeth's grave, writing, "I suppose my late wife was buried near my first. I desire you to erect a table to her Memory, of the same fashion as the first; and when you do it acquaint the [Saltonstall] family, and let them direct the inscription; as I shall be absent, it will be more proper for them to do this last office for one whose memory is equally dear to them and me."[29] He did not even know where his wife was buried let alone demonstrate an interest in composing a proper epitaph. Instead, he focused on the arrival of Benjamin Franklin, John Adams, and Arthur Lee in France about the same time. He became part of a team charged with negotiating a treaty with England's archenemy, France, that became one of the turning points in the American Revolution. Deane no doubt hoped that his role in concluding such an important agreement would bring him the political success, recognition, and riches he so desperately sought.

Just as Deane reached the pinnacle of his political career, however, his son's arrival in Europe demanded his attention. Deane summarily dispatched of the problem by packing Jesse off to a boarding school, but the incident coincided with the start of a prolonged and quite public battle with Lee, Deane's mercurial fellow commissioner. Lee penned angry letters to Congress complaining about Deane's extravagance and possible corruption. In response, Deane was recalled, and for the rest of his life, his mission to clear his name eclipsed all other aspects of his life.

As Deane's political and financial fortunes declined, he tried more urgently to settle his affairs not only with Congress but also with the Webbs. In 1779, Congress offered to reimburse him for expenses incurred in France, but he declined the offer, hoping to receive additional compensation for the private funds he had used as a commercial agent. Some members of Congress responded that Deane had used his position to further his own mercantile business. Seeking to prove his good intentions, Deane returned to Europe in 1780 to gather paperwork concerning his financial dealings in France. At around this time, he wrote to Joseph Webb Jr. about his father's estate: Deane described his Wethersfield holdings as a "pittance" that he deserved to retain given his service to the family.[30] He spent a year in Paris, searching in vain for evidence that would support his claims to Congress. He admitted to his brother at this time that he had "not seen his only son for four years."[31]

Deane's situation seemed to be looking up in 1783. The revised administrative account for the Webb estate was finally filed in court, meaning that the matter finally seemed to be coming to a close. He also submitted his final paperwork, such as it was, to Congress. But no doubt to his dismay, neither action resulted in a replenishing of his funds. The Webb children continued to oppose him in court, and Congress continued to go over every detail of his accounts with a fine-toothed comb. He saw himself as the victim of ungrateful stepchildren and an ungrateful country but focused on his public problems more than his domestic woes: "I ventured at the hazard of my life, at the most critical period of our affairs, to solicit succour for my country in Europe; and though unsupported by Congress, who never remitted me one shilling, I obtained those arms and stores which in 1777 prevented my country from submitting to the enemy, and rendered them victorious. What has been my reward? To be branded as a traitor, a peculator, &c. . . . what a monster is human nature when it looks out in an ungrateful form!"[32] In 1784, he was still awaiting payment from Congress and hoping that Joseph Webb Jr. would agree to a process that would close the books on his father's estate.[33] Four years later, he had entirely given up on getting funds either from Congress or from his complicated holdings in Connecticut. He was sick, dependent on friends, and destitute, and he died the following year while preparing to return to America.[34]

From Deane's vantage point, as a stepfather, he had helped an orphaned family by managing their dead father's estate, and Joseph Webb's estate was certainly complicated. He, like other merchants, conducted much of his business on credit. Merchants were notoriously cash poor, and according to Silas Deane, Webb was no exception. In addition, Deane alleged, Webb had made some poor business choices: "He had given a most unlimited Credit, and to bad subjects." As a result, his creditors were settling for "five Shillings on the pound," realizing that full restitution was unlikely from a potentially bankrupt estate. Only after "the Sale of Vessels & Cargoes & the Transfer of Notes" were the debts finally paid off. Thousands of pounds in credit had been extended to individuals who Deane believed "really never ought to have been indebted to the Amount of Ten pounds." In Deane's view, he had taken on the time-consuming and expensive task of settling Webb's estate as a selfless service to the Webb family, and, the attorney claimed, he had left "every paper, and every Security" with Joseph Webb Jr. when Deane took up his post at the First Continental Congress in 1774. "I made out an exact Inventory of every thing in my hands, and brought all Your Accts. Into a State for closing." When he sailed for Europe, he gave Joseph "a power to Settle the Accts. of the Estate, and that it might be done in Equity [fairly], I proposed that the General Assembly Should appoint Auditors or referees with full power To do Justice to all parties."[35]

According to Deane, therefore, his stepson had the accounts and terms for settling the Webb estate but inexplicably refused to implement Deane's plan for legal closure. In the spring and early summer of 1780, Deane wrote to his brother, Barnabas, that Joseph Webb Jr. "continues to refuse to accept the terms I offered." Although Silas "would willingly suffer much to settle and close" the estate, he did not want to play the fool: "I am sorry to find [Joseph] thinks himself intitled to all I ever have or may hereafter labor for, or, what is the same thing, that it should go into his hands in a hodge podge, common stock way. I pray I may be mistaken; but I think, after figuring away awhile, and blowing up his brethren with the notions of fortune and quality, all will be dissipated, disappear, and then he will amuse the world and gratify my enemies by laying all on me."[36] Deane painted Joseph as the villain.

A few months later, Deane adopted the pose of a hurt parent in another letter to Joseph. Deane had not heard from his stepson since their falling out but nevertheless assured Joseph that "with great sincerity . . . that my friendship for you, and wishes for your prosperity and that of your family, have never abated." Deane then gave his wayward stepson a way back into his good graces and revealed his true feelings. "Your rejecting my proposals, refusing the power I sent you, and dissatisfaction at my refusal to put everything in the world which was mine when I left Wethersfield unconditionally into your hands, gives me ground to apprehend that you have lent your confidence to men who, wishing neither of us well, are aiming to draw you into a dispute with me, and thereby strengthen the hands of those who mean me ill." No evidence survives of such a conspiracy; Joseph acted alone.

Deane believed that his proposals "will justify me, and be esteemed generous ones by every disinterested and informed person in the world" and reminded Joseph that he had "once acknowledged" as generous Deane's plan for settling the estate. Finally, Deane took on the mantle of martyrdom: "I am now under the necessity of going into a voluntary exile, without funds to support me, and wounded with the ingratitude of those whom I have not only served faithfully, but saved from destruction."[37]

In fact, Deane argued, he had resisted the temptation to enrich himself. "In the course of my management, had I attended strictly to keep only within the letter of the law, I must have made a very handsome fortune; what the consequences would have been, everyone acquainted with the circumstances of the estate at the time know little or nothing could have been left, if in reality the creditors would have been paid." He thus claimed that his delay in settling the estate had helped the Webb children's financial circumstances, since they would have ended up with nothing if he had simply paid the creditors. Heroically, Deane claimed, "I sacrificed my personal emolument to the interest of an orphan family, afford me in reflection infinitely greater satisfaction than any which can result from the possession of wealth." From his perspective he had "done not simply legal Justice toward them, but had treated them with parental kindness."[38]

In Silas's account, the real culprit in this family drama was Joseph. Deane confided to Samuel Webb, "Before I left America I saw with pain the extravagant course into which Your Brother was going, & I am sorry to learn that he has pursued it, it is a delicate subject, but Necessity forces Me to say, that I find him disposed, to impute his ruin to Me." Joseph "has labored to persuade himself & others, that You were entitled to an immense Fortune and he has lived up to the reality of it, though merely Ideal." In other words, the problem was not Deane's handling of the Webb estate but Joseph's spending.[39]

Deane urged the level-headed Samuel to examine the paperwork for himself and make his own judgments. "It gives Me extreme pain to Trouble You on this Subject, but I think You to be both honest, & brave, and therefore that you will take measures for doing Justice to Yourself, as well as to Me." He continued, "I spent near Ten Years of the prime of my Life, in the Service of Your Family in settling The Accts. & in superintending Your Education, That I secreted nothing, that I left in Your Brothers hand every thing of which I was possessed, That I did not bring away with me, One Shilling of effects of any kind, how then can I be your Debtor?"[40] A month later, Silas similarly complained to his brother, Barnabas, "The expence of the prime of my life I saved the estate from bankruptcy, and educated the family, who now treat me with the basest ingratitude, with being their debtor, with having embezzled their effects."[41]

THE LAW: IN LOCO PARENTIS

Stepfathers were not required to support their stepchildren but could choose to do so. According to one English judge, the child whom a stepfather "held out to the world as part of his family" deserved support.[42] Swift argued that if a man chose to take on the mantel of father/provider, taking "his wife's children by a former husband into his house, and they become part of his family, he shall be deemed to stand *in loco parentis*, and be liable."[43] Reeve acknowledged the "received opinion, that a husband in Connecticut is obliged to support his wife's children by a former husband, if he be of ability to do it, whether she was able at the time of the marriage or not, to support her children."[44] By the mid-nineteenth century, one Massachusetts judge argued that if a stepfather wanted the best for his family, he needed to provide for his stepchildren and in so doing "encourage an extension of the circle and influence of the domestic fireside." Using the romanticized language of the mid-nineteenth century, he claimed, "In this commonwealth it is quite common, upon second marriages, that the wife's children are received into the [stepfather's] family as members; and such an arrangement must tend to promote the happiness of the mother and the welfare of the children."[45] Writing in 1832, Kent opined that if a stepfather "takes the wife's child into his own house, he is then considered as standing *in loco parentis*, and is responsible for the maintenance and education of the child so long as it lives with him, for, by that act, he holds the child out to the world as part of his family."[46] In Massachusetts, according to Nathan Dane, a lawyer and politician, a stepfather had no obligation unless "he adopts them into his family &c.," in which case he becomes "liable to maintain such children."[47]

In other words, if a man took on the role of father, he took on the obligations as well. A 1799 English case, *Stone v. Carr*, became the starting point for most judicial arguments in New England about the obligations of in loco parentis status. In this case, a sailor married a woman with property, a business, and children. He moved into her house and took on the parental role, "and the children were suffered to live with him as part of the family, and provided for by him, while he was at home." While he was at sea as the "gunner of an India ship," his wife opted to send her children to school, but upon his return, the sailor refused to pay their tuition, arguing that a stepfather had no legal obligation to provide for his stepchildren. The judge agreed that "there was no doubt, if a man married a woman having children by a former husband, he might refuse to provide for them. . . . [H]e could not be compelled to do it." In this case, however, the man "did not so refuse to entertain them, and took the children into his family"; as a result, "he then stood *in loco parentis* as to them." By stepping into the role of father, the sailor had made a legal contract to pay for the education of his stepchildren.[48]

The first American case to address the issue of in loco parentis status and a stepfather's obligations was adjudicated in Massachusetts and involved the normal right of all fathers to the wages of their children in exchange for supporting them.[49] In *Freto v. Brown*, the stepfather of James Freto sued his stepson's former employer, John Brown, for his wages. In 1805, Freto "lived in the family of his father-in-law [stepfather], and was maintained by him; but was a fisherman in the defendant's fishing schooner for the season." The stepfather claimed that he was entitled to Freto's wages because he had maintained Freto for the year. The court ruled in the stepfather's favor, finding that "the father-in-law may recover against [the employer] for necessaries."[50] Voluntarily taking on the role of provider earned a man the right to his stepson's wages.

Although family disputes in court cases often made a stepfather's support of his wife's children seem forced or unremunerated, an English case, *Copper v. Martin*, suggested that some stepfathers could be generous, even overly so. A man named Copper married a woman whose husband had died insolvent; in fact, Copper sold his own estate to pay off his predecessor's debts. The new stepfather then used his own funds to support his minor stepchildren. The court found that Copper "had brought up the children and given them boarding in a manner suitable to their expectations, but beyond what could have been expected of him," and awarded him compensation for his expenses as a stepfather from his stepchildren as they came of age.[51]

OUR STORY

Joseph Webb's children saw things differently. They had trusted and loved their stepfather. When they became convinced he had abused his role as administrator of their father's estate, they felt betrayed. Their enmity following this discovery extended to their stepbrother, Jesse, as well, and when he became the administrator of Silas Deane's estate, they confronted him in court.

The Webb siblings argued that their mother had known "for a long time before his decease . . . in what manner s[ai]d Silas had conducted business" and had worried that her children "might suffer material injury" from her husband's actions. She "expressd great anxiety and concern and was extremely urgent and solicitous that s[ai]d Silas should execute deeds of conveyance to s[ai]d minor children." She finally convinced him to give "ample warranty," giving her the deeds "for their security benefit and advantage." According to her children, she believed that the estate would soon be settled and that it would be better to divide the assets as a lump sum than to do it piece by piece. She therefore held onto these papers physically but left them "unrecorded."[52]

On her deathbed, Mehitable was still clutching these deeds. Very ill, and with Joseph, her oldest son, away in New York, she called her eleven-year-old daughter, Sarah (Sally), to her side. Although Sally was "very young and inexperienced," her mother had no choice but to turn to her for assistance. She gave Sally the deeds and other papers, "enjoining her in the most strict and solemn manner to keep them safe and secure and not to deliver them to any person whatever except to the s[ai]d Joseph." But after Mehitable's death, "Silas applied to the s[ai]d Sarah to know if any papers had been left with her by the s[ai]d Mehitable the elder and the s[ai]d Sarah placing the utmost confidence in the s[ai]d Silas whom she considered her Father and Protector was prevaild upon by s[ai]d Silas to deliver to him s[ai]d deeds and papers." Subsequent testimony made Deane look even more despicable: in the revised version, Silas "insisted that [Sally] should deliver [the deeds and papers] to him assigning as a reason that they might contain directions for her [mother's] funeral which could not otherwise be attended." Once Silas procured the deeds, he kept them "secreted" and "out of view." The Webb children alleged that he had the "intention to deprive s[ai]d heirs unjustly of s[ai]d lands and reserve them to his own benefit." He also "received into his hands" about forty thousand pounds, "a great part of which has, never been accounted for by s[ai]d Silas." The court documents demonstrate more than anger at an unscrupulous stepfather, however; they reveal the betrayal felt by the Webb children at Deane's mishandling of their dead father's estate.[53]

Legally, Deane was guilty of mismanaging his stepchildren's estate, but the Webb children received scant financial reward for their efforts to hold him accountable. Jesse Deane was forced to pay off his father's obligations as well as compensate his half-siblings for his own misdoings but paid only a penny on the dollar and even charged the estate for the legal expenses he incurred. The Webb children joined a list of creditors clamoring to squeeze blood from a stone. The estate was finally settled in 1802. At the bottom of the document listing the final disbursement of the Webb/Deane estate, the word "End" was written with a flourish. The ordeal was finally over—forty-one years after Joseph Webb's death, thirty-five years after Mehitable Webb Deane's, and thirteen years after Silas Deane's.[54] Though the Webb children obtained little in the way of property, they did get official acknowledgment that their stepfather had abused their trust. Deane eventually took his place, at least officially, among those who had made the American Revolution a success. His early work securing French financial aid for the fledgling country had helped assure the war's outcome. He was never exonerated, however, for his treatment of the Webb children.

Silas Deane was a married man's nightmare. Propertied men hoped that the law would protect their widows and orphans. The law did provide certain safeguards against the potential danger and contradiction of male economic power in remarriage. For example, estates had to be settled in a timely manner, prenuptial agreements and marriage settlements could be negotiated before remarriage, waste laws kept an estate intact, and provisions for in loco parentis status for a child taken into a stepfather's home forced him to provide. Nonetheless, problems could arise when one man controlled the estate of another. If savvy about the law and bold enough to take the chance, a stepfather could deplete a widow's estate and that of her children. Legally disempowered, as a *feme covert*, a remarried woman could do little to prevent such an outcome. Mehitable (Nott) Webb Deane did what she could, even insisting on a prenuptial agreement, but in the end her children lost their father's financial legacy.

CHAPTER THREE

The Wicked "Step" mother

In one early nineteenth-century popular writing manual, a remarrying father assured his intended, "as to the common objection against being a step mother, I think it may be easily answered, when I tell you, that my children will treat you with all manner of respect." This fictional gentleman acknowledged that a more general concern about becoming a stepmother could cause her to hesitate: "As for the odious appellations usually thrown out against step mothers, they can only be considered, by a lady of your sensibility, as the effect of prejudice, operating upon vulgar minds, occasioned by the conduct of some inhuman wretches, who are a disgrace to society." The "Lady" responded to his dismissal of her worries by saying that such prejudice infected more than a few "vulgar minds." She wrote, "Your answers to the common objections made against step mothers, are altogether rational; they are what reason will at all times dictate, . . . but you will excuse me if I tell you sincerely, that even in the opinion of the thinking part of the world, the life of a step mother is far more disagreeable than you endeavour to persuade me." She believed that such women suffered under constant, suspicious scrutiny: "All eyes are upon them, and even their virtues are often construed into faults." The "Gentleman" chided her for what he saw as her exaggerated concern about "public censure," quipping, "Indeed, I think you have carried your objections against being a step mother, rather too far." He clearly understood that hurdles would have to be overcome, but he did not see them as insurmountable. The Lady ultimately accepted the Gentleman's marriage proposal, but she feared that society would relegate her to the role of a "nominal mother to your children." She explained, "I say nominal, for, although I should on all occasions consider myself obliged to act with humanity to your children as well as my own, yet I may be still named" as a stepmother.[1]

Popular culture warned one and all that stepmothers were a problem, but precisely how these women were represented as troublesome shifted in tandem with new representations of motherhood in the eighteenth century. Stories about cruel stepmothers were not new in this period; such stereotypes appear in Western tradition as far back as ancient times.[2] Rather, a new version of stepmother wickedness appeared alongside and combined with earlier stories as the eighteenth century progressed. Characterizations of stepmothers as poor substitute mothers joined descriptions of more familiar stepmother cruelty. Because the mothers of the new, middle-class families were the "natural" mothers of the Enlightenment, both loving and child-centered, the behavior of "bad" mothers found no purchase in this new ideology.[3] Maternal paragons were by definition neither cruel nor wicked. The negative aspects of motherhood were simply transferred to stepmothers, leaving them with more arrows in their quiver of cruelty and mothers free of weaponry.

Although this shift occurred on both sides of the Atlantic, in the British North American context, this juxtaposition of cruel stepmothers and loving mothers emerged most vividly during the revolution with the characterization of the former mother country as Stepmother England.[4] Proper mothers in revolutionary America were paragons of republican virtue, teaching their children to be good citizens of the nation.[5] In contrast, Stepmother England mistreated her colonial children. The mother country had not remarried, even metaphorically; rather, her behavior toward her former children awarded her a new moniker. England was compared to her former self, the supportive mother country, and found lacking. Although the revolution has been represented as a patriarchal battle between father and child, the evidence presented here suggests that stepmothers and stepchildren were also at war.[6] As William Williams, Connecticut's agent in London noted during the taxation debates, America now had a "Step mother country."[7] Likewise, John Adams enthused to Abigail after the signing of the Declaration of Independence, "Farewell! Farewell, infatuated, besotted stepdame."[8] In the soon-to-be United States, stepmothers were the personification of the revolutionary enemy.

During the Stamp Act Crisis of the 1760s, one writer warned his countrymen that their, new wicked Stepmother Country would stop her unjust behavior only after she had "STAMP[ed] on thy bowels." Her colonial children, conversely, had "patiently submit[ted] to the almost intolerable burdens; suppressing even their murmurs, they struggled against the stream; loath to impute severity to the country from which they gloried to have sprung." The Stamp Act exposed the true stepmother country, as she "cast off the mask" of an indulgent mother. She had become a "cruel step-mother, unbounded in her malice," who had clearly "resolved to *stamp* them to the earth." The colonies, now cast as "insolent, undutiful and rebellious" step-children by their formerly supportive mother, suffered as their inhuman, vampire-like stepmother drained their "vital blood."[9]

Even though England eventually repealed the Stamp Act, "Step-dame" Britain showed no signs of letting up on her stepchildren. The citizens of Boston, at the center of the gathering storm, dumped their favored drink into the harbor, making the "sacrifice of TEA to the public Welfare."[10] New Englanders subsequently boasted that they had evolved from colonial children to full-fledged adults and that if war must come, they were ready. "We do assure the Public, That there has been manufactured in this Colony," plenty of the necessaries for gunpowder—"ONE HUNDRED THOUSAND w[eigh]t of good Salt Petre" to be exact—"so good Step-Dame need make no further cringing Supplications to foreign Powers not to supply her *rebellious* Subjects with that Commodity."[11] The victimized children of America had become determined to free themselves from the tyranny of their cruel stepdame.

In a 1776 attempt to end the hostilities, English commissioners arrived to treat with loyalists in the colonies, prompting Stepmother England to reappear. "The Watchman" argued in one Pennsylvania newspaper that negotiating and reaching agreements with these commissioners would not prevent the inevitable raping and pillaging by soldiers, who would "lay waste your villages and cottages without distinction." In addition, "neither the persons of your wives nor your daughters would be sacred, but would soon fall prey to those avengers; whose greatest glory is in the violation of virtue." And colonists would not simply stand by and be "cruelly used by our step mother." Indeed, he was "confident [that] every impartial person" could see the fruitlessness of "a constitutional reconciliation with our cruel and unnatural Step Mother."[12]

Even after the war, the new nation struggled with the implications of independence. Some commentators argued that for colonial children to be truly free of their abusive stepmother, they had to cut the cord of trade. More than one pundit described the need for Americans to awaken "from their sleep on the lap of their step mother" and proclaim "by their industry, and economy, that they were an independant people."[13] One account of Stepmother England depicted her as a vindictive harpy: "'You saucy rogues,' (says she) 'I'll teach you to rebel against so righteous, so mild a parent. Independence you wanted—well, with my consent, you have it—but it shall prove a curse.'" She then threatened to beat her wayward stepchildren with a brine-covered cudgel, warning, "As a reward for your insolence, you shall have none of my excellent Jamaica spirits—no, you rogues, nor a grain of my sugar and coffee—no, no you rogues . . . not an article of mine shall you have to grow *fat* upon."[14] She threatened both bodily harm and withdrawal of her imperial breast.

Prior to the American Revolution, England had limited "all manufacturing industry in the colonies," obliging North American residents "to purchase every article" in England. Similarly, after the war, American merchants complained England flooded the American market with cheap goods, stunting American manufacturing and trade, and "in these respects" continued to be "a step mother to us."[15] One commentator saw a possible solution in the intervention of America's revolutionary friend, the Marquis de Lafayette. France had agreed to buy some whale oil from the new republic, tax free. The normal tariff on foreign oil was 20 percent, but with this deal, the writer crowed, American oil would light "the city of Paris and all the other cities of France." In exchange, the United States would receive French manufactured goods "on terms infinitely superior to any we can expect from our old rancorous step mother, Great-Britain."[16]

Later, as Americans began to shape the history of their country's founding, the former mother country continued to carry the tainted name of stepmother. In 1796, one oration commemorating the twentieth anniversary of the Declaration of Independence summed up the war as the blessed escape of American stepchildren from their imperious English stepmother's whip: "To my nation, there cannot be an event of greater importance, nor one which merits more regard, than its final establishment, and particularly if that establishment rescued the people from the actual or intended imposition of tyranny or despotism." The writer continued, "The ever memorable Fourth of July, Seventy-six, was such a period—it brought us forth on the theatre of nations, and it saved us from the impending lashes of an ungracious step mother."[17] In a similar 1809 oration, Isaac Gardner Reed, speaking in Portland, Maine, recalled the colonial period as one of great "prosperity" until "Britain, forgetting the duty of a parent, became a cruel stepmother, and protected us from others only that she might enjoy the plunder without division."[18]

The metaphor of stepmother country remained powerful as the passing of the last veterans created a new wave of patriotism in the 1820s and 1830s. One author put to verse an imagined conversation between Benjamin Franklin and Lord Howe, the revolutionary British military leader, demonstrating the familiar characterization of Stepmother England.

According to the verse-spouting Franklin, God, not England, had planted the colonists in the wilderness of North America and helped make "the desert bloom." "Step-mother Britain," however, "left us to our fate, When war and famine lower'd o'er our heads." As soon as "our skies grew bright, and fortune smil'd," she "Usurp'd o'er us despotic domination, And pluck'd away our heaven-descended rights." When the colonists took up arms to defend their rights, intoned Franklin, England sent "hireling butchers of a savage prince"—the Hessians—to quell the rebellion. Such were the "tokens of [her] maternal care." In this reimagining of the hapless stepchildren of 1776, their celestial parent vanquished their cruel stepparent.[19] The passage of time had transformed England from a previously frightening wartime visage to a less intimidating, defeated old stepmother.[20]

Why did popular culture in the colonies find the trope of Stepmother England so compelling? The answer to this question takes us back in time and across the Atlantic to the mother country itself. Around the time of the early English colonization of North America, stepmothers, like all women, were suspect simply because they were women. Starting in thirteenth-century France but taking on new life among early seventeenth-century Englishmen, a literary campaign, later dubbed the Querelle des Femmes, worked to discredit womanhood itself.[21] In addition, scolds or rough-speaking women were increasingly persecuted in England between 1560 and 1640.[22] Supposed witches were regularly prosecuted, including a large number in Salem, Massachusetts, in the late seventeenth century.[23] Women were seen as both inferior to men and potentially powerful, even dangerous, and needing careful management to keep them in line. Stephen Collins, a historian of the English stepfamily persuasively argues that "if a stepmother caused trouble, it was her fault because it was in women's nature to do so."[24]

The English language itself reflected the conflation of evil women and stepmothers. The most negative of the terms for a stepmother, "stepdame," originally referred to all wicked mothers.[25] For example, Henry Goodcole, in a collection of lurid criminal stories from 1637, identified stepdames as "unnatural mothers," but not all of the women so branded actually had married men who already had children. *Natures Cruell Step-Dames; or, Matchlesse Monsters of the Female Sex* included two gruesome tales of murdering mothers: widow Elizabeth Barnes stabbed to death her eight-year-old daughter, "the fruit of her owne wombe," while Ann Willis gave birth to a "Basterd-child" and then threw her live newborn down a "vault [cistern or privy] in *Rosemary* Lane," where it was found dead.

The book dubbed both women "stepdames" because of their "unnaturall," murderous behavior.[26]

In a 1590 book, *Newnams Nightcrowe: A Bird That Breedeth Braules in Many Families and Housholdes*, John Newnham used these familiar tropes of generalized female wickedness to describe his stepmother. She sounded like a scold and acted like a witch, initiating a "monstrous transforming of the Father" of the household and "inchanting" her spouse. She cawed like a crow, whose call predicted bad times ahead. According to Newnham, his stepmother, like other evil women, had succeeded in the "turning of al[l] upsice downe."[27]

Newnham also suggested, however, that stepmothers had some distinctively wicked ways. Based on the actions of his stepmother, Newnham argued that "stepdames prevaile much in bringing their iniurous purpose to passe, by forging faultes in their husbandes children." They poisoned their husbands against their own offspring by "backebiting, lying . . . and false accusing." Such verbal treachery, he generalized, was "seldome separate from stepdames." Moreover, these women subverted their stepchildren's interests by producing additional children. Newnham's inheritance was threatened by a stepmother who "perswadeth as much by night as by day." He explained that she performed her "night worke so well, that she will raise uppe new plants and fruite that will soone be ripe." Newnham believed that he had been stripped of his birthright, raging that anyone who "enricheth a stepmother, helpeth a stranger and hindereth his owne."[28]

In his 1611 play, *Cymbeline*, William Shakespeare created a wicked stepmother character similar to Newnham's nemesis. The Queen, who is King Cymbeline's wife, works to gain power by manipulating her husband at his child's expense. She convinces the king to force his daughter, Imogen, to marry her son, but Imogen thwarts the plan by marrying her lover. Outraged by his daughter's boldness (and the poverty of the man she chose), her father banishes her new husband. Imogen understands that her father's behavior is linked to her stepmother's plotting, lamenting "a father cruel, and a step-dame false." Cymbeline eventually imprisons Imogen to keep her from her husband, but the Queen frees her stepdaughter as part of a plot to put a permanent end to her marriage, offering false reassurances: "No, be assur'd you shall not find me, daughter, After the slander of most stepmothers, Evil-ey'd unto you." But the cautious Imogen remarks, "How fine this tyrant Can tickle where she wounds!" In the end the stepmother's twisted scheme is revealed, the lovers reunite, and the treacherous stepmother is punished.[29]

Robert Stapylton, a political pamphleteer and playwright famous for his royalist leanings and support for Charles I, presented the stepmother as the master of her infatuated husband in his 1664 play, *The Step-Mother: A Tragi-Comedy*. As the play begins, a tutor warns his former student, Filamor, "Your envious and imperious Step-Mother, Who rules your Father," is now plotting to "ruine You." The stepson laments his father's blindness about Pontia, the stepmother: "Since he marry'd This Woman, she has master'd both his Courage And Reason: she governs his very Soul, He cannot live without her." When he was sixteen, Filamor had said to his father "that Wives should not rule their Husbands," and he now repeats this injunction after returning home as a young man: "'Tis not fit your wife should govern you." His father laments, "Ever since I marry'd *Pontia*, I've serv'd under her." For her part, the evil stepmother complains to her son, Adolph, that her stepson is "disempowering me to rule my Husband," and she plans to have her husband and her stepchildren killed and sent "to Hell." She hires men to carry out all the killings except for that of Filamor, whom she will kill herself: "None shall revenge *Pontia*, But *Pontia*." Her plan unravels and she quickly stabs her adversary, only to discover that she has mistakenly killed her own son.[30]

Wicked stepmothers who manipulated their husbands also appeared in popular English broadsides, with lurid descriptions of sensational crimes.[31] Most stepmothers in this genre killed their stepchildren, either directly or indirectly. In *Newes from Perin in Cornwall*, a "covetous Step-mother" encourages her husband to kill and rob a sailor who has come as a boarder to their home. The sailor turns out to have been the man's long-lost son by his first wife. The author explains that the father was "rul'd" by his wife, and in the end, he kills both the evil stepmother and himself.[32]

Such stories retained currency in the eighteenth century in England as well as in its colonies. Nicholas Rowe, a landed gentleman and poet, crafted a very popular play, *The Ambitious Stepmother*, featuring his contribution to the already familiar stepmother trope. Ametris, the title character, tries to undercut her stepchildren's claim to the throne of Persia by promoting her own son. In this drama, unlike in Shakespeare's similar story, she manipulates the situation to her advantage, but her son refuses his mother's prize. In the end, her son ascends to the throne but does so on his own terms.[33]

In all of these tales, regardless of the format in which they appeared, stepmothers corrupted fathers to the point that they lost sight of their obligations to their own flesh and blood. Although these wicked women/

stepmothers were punished in the end, they had the initial power to turn the world upside-down, subverting the patriarchal order. The popular culture version of stepmothers reflected contemporary fears about women as a threat to male power.

The etymology of the word "stepmother" suggests that by the end of the eighteenth century, stepmothers were perceived not just as evil women but also as inferior replacements for mothers. In *A Dictionary of the English Language*, the first standardized English dictionary, Samuel Johnson noted that "for the Saxons," the word "step" was used only in reference to a "stepmother," a "stepdaughter," or a "stepson" (not a stepfather). Johnson reported that although all these variations had previously been common, the prefix "step" was "now seldom applied but to the mother." Johnson also indirectly revealed that the term "step," when used to refer to a stepmother, had taken on an added meaning: "It seems to mean, in the mind of those who use it, a woman who has *stepped* into the vacant place of the true mother."[34] By the early nineteenth century in the United States, the word "stepdame" had become synonymous with "stepmother" and was used only in that context. When Noah Webster published the first dictionary of American English, *A Compendious Dictionary of the English Language*, in 1806, he included entries for "stepchild" and "stepfather" but substituted "stepdame" for "stepmother."[35] To Webster's mind all stepmothers were stepdames.

In keeping with the changing definition of the word "stepmother" in popular culture, authors contrasted stepmothers to the newly sentimentalized mothers of the rising middle class. A ghostly but angelic mother appeared as a savior in *The Cruel Step-Mother; or, The Unhappy Son*, an anonymous English broadside from 1760 that enjoyed multiple reprintings through 1810 on both sides of the Atlantic. The husband in this story tearfully promises his dying wife that he will not remarry after she begs him, "For the child's sake, wed not again, my dear, For if you do, I cannot rest, I fear. Let no step-mother my dear child abuse, Whom I so tenderly did love and use." A mere two months later, he breaks his promise, and as predicted, his new wife is "cross, and very proud." His five-year-old son suffers, becoming a servant in his own home. When the hapless boy receives an unanticipated gift from his uncle, the greedy stepmother makes her husband believe that the child has stolen from him. Infuriated, the father beats his son mercilessly and then sends him away to sea. The stepmother chooses the boy's new master, who sells him into slavery in Jamaica. In the end, he is saved by the ghost of his mother, who keeps her promise and haunts her faithless husband. When her spirit exposes the stepmother's plot, the angry father turns on his new wife, taking his estate out of her hands. Because of his guilt at his unfair treatment of his son, the father hangs himself. The boy is ransomed by a timely legacy forwarded by his father's lawyer and returns to claim his due. He takes his stepmother to court and wins a five-hundred-pound judgment against her.[36] This story showed the mother and stepmother side by side for all to compare.

Older stories were also revised to fit this new pattern. One reinvention of an old English tale created an idealized mother figure out of whole cloth. In the original story, Geoffrey of Monmouth, most well known as the recorder of the Arthurian legend, blamed an evil stepmother for the Saxon invasion of Britain. In *The Historia Regnum Britanniae*, Geoffrey outlined the tale of Vortigern, the king or head chief of the Britons. Vortigern puts away his wife in favor of a beautiful Saxon maiden. The king of England, now literally married to England's traditional Germanic enemy, inspires opposition among his own people, led by the eldest son of his first marriage, Vortimer. Although Vortimer overthrows his father, his stepmother makes sure his reign is short by poisoning him. Geoffrey claimed that Vortimer's goodness quickly stirs up the enmity of his devil-possessed stepmother: "The demon, entering into the heart of his stepmother Rowen[a], excited her to contrive his death. For this purpose she consulted with the poisoners, and procured one who was intimate with him, whom she corrupted with large and numerous presents, to give him a poisonous draught; so that this brave soldier, as soon as he had taken it, was seized with a sudden illness, that deprived him of all hopes of life." Rowena's husband then resumes the throne.[37]

A late eighteenth-century version of this story added an additional character, the discarded first wife, Edmunda, her loving self-sacrifice now contrasted with Rowena's treachery. William Henry Ireland, a famous London forger, presented, *Vortigern, an Historical Tragedy, in Five Acts* in 1790s England, claiming that it was a lost work by William Shakespeare to guarantee a larger audience. In this version, Vortigern's son went to war against his father but did so in part to champion his humiliated mother, Edmunda, a grieving and pitiful figure who became the tale's sentimental heroine. One scene between this loving mother and one of her daughters emphasizes the emotional connection between an ideal mother and her children. In a failed attempt to lift her mother's spirits, the girl begs,

Oh! my beloved mother!
Turn, turn those tear worn eyes, and let one smile,

The Wicked "Step" mother 53

One cheering look of sweet serenity,
Beam forth to comfort my afflicted soul!

Her mother responds,

Oh! heavens! . . . would I could!
But this corroding pensive melancholy
Most venom like, destroys its nourisher.
Oh! Vortigern, my lov'd, once loving husband,
Why rend this bursting heart with cold disdain,
E'en the poor culprit brought before his judge
May boldly plead his cause; but alas!
Most innocent, and ignorant of my fault,
Must bear the weight of judgment.

At the conclusion of the play, the stepchildren have the satisfaction of seeing their stepmother imprisoned and ultimately dead, righteously proclaiming that her "wicked soul has taken its flight."[38] As in Geoffrey's version, Rowena was cruel, but by the end of the eighteenth century, she had an antagonist in the sentimental, loving mother Edmunda.

Similarly, on the other side of the Atlantic, the Reverend Thomas Worcester of New Hampshire compared one mother and her successor in a 1798 sermon delivered on the occasion of his brother's remarriage. Worcester warned his new sister-in-law that she could never take the place of her predecessor: "Room has been made for you to be here, by the death of an amiable woman, a woman who will never be forgotten. Her piety, modesty, gentleness, kindness, prudence, and helpfulness, have left an impression on many hearts which must and will remain. You are in the place she left; but you cannot be the same person." Thomas also lectured the new bride, "Your Marriage has connected you with children, who cannot be expected, in all things, and at all times, to feel toward you as towards a natural mother." Only self-sacrifice could motivate such an undertaking. "Benevolence . . . has inclined you to step into a station which is not without difficulties." Regardless, "these things you have doubtless considered; and as they did not prevent your undertaking, let them never sink you in discouragement." She should "endeavour always to feel happy in the consideration, that the more difficult your station is, the more opportunity you have to know yourself, to display the most amiable Christian virtues, to the glory of God, and the benefit of your generation."[39]

The anonymous author of "The Step Mother," a story printed in the *Providence Gazette* in 1825, lamented, "How momentous a thing, it is to introduce a wife, who is not the parent of her husband's family, into it." Emotional chaos inevitably followed: "What jealousy! what injustice! what strife does not occur from such a union! how many struggles to alienate prior affection, what poutings and strivings." The author suggested that a "man and woman ought to think thrice, before they give a nominal mother to motherless children." The "Slighted" stepchildren, ignored as the unwelcome remains of a previous marriage, inevitably ran "headlong to ruin and despair[;] take to idle habits and a vicious life; imbibe at an early age, the poison of envy and hatred." Children unfortunate enough to have a stepmother naturally "pine in the wasting agonies of sensibility wounded by neglect." They suffered "the tyranny of a strange woman, placed in usurped authority" over them. The author concluded that all stepmothers deserved the title of "Injustaque noverca"—an unjust stepmother—"it depends on her alone to merit a better name." When one curious man asked another at the conclusion of this diatribe, "What is a stepmother?," his surprised friend responded that of course, a "Stepmother is a step toward being a mother, and yet no mother at all, at all."[40]

In a series of letters between a stepmother and her stepdaughters published in a Boston advice column in 1820, the disgruntled stepdaughters openly compared their stepmother's behavior to their sainted mother's perfection. The two stepdaughters explained, "Our mother—our own mother—is dead.—Our mother in law is—a mother in law." She "scolds, raves," she watches them like a hawk, she is a "severe governess." Remarked the columnist, "Mothers, especially step-mothers, by being *over* scrupulous and watchful, may occasion indiscretions in their daughters." In others words, attempting to take on a maternal role assured a stepmother that she would fail. For her part, the stepmother tried to defend herself against these "ungrateful" "girls" who even "insulted to my face." From her viewpoint, "In fact my daughter[s] in law are—daughters in law." They acted as if she was "only a servant in the family." She assured the editor that she was no monster.[41]

Other authors made less direct comparisons between mothers and stepmothers, simply casting stepmothers as monstrous mothers. One song about a stepmother, *The Lady Isabella's Tragedy; or, The Step-Mother's Cruelty*, which first appeared as an English broadside in 1670 before undergoing various revisions, presented the inheritance-seeking stepmother of the seventeenth century as the sentimental villain of the eighteenth century. This song inspired a play of the same name that was performed in Baltimore in 1783. In the early version, the daughter has a "cruel Step-Mother [who] Did envy her so much, That Day by Day she sought her life Her

Malice it was such." The stepmother convinces her cook to kill the girl: he butchers her and bakes her remains into a pie, which the stepmother serves to her husband. Before he can take a bite, however, the scullery boy, who has witnessed the crime, reveals the truth. The father decrees that the stepmother be burned at the stake, the cook be thrown in boiling oil, and the scullery boy be the heir to his estate.[42]

The eighteenth-century version of this story took into account the sentimental predilections of the period, adding gruesome descriptions of body parts and the unsuspecting father sitting down to supper that were no doubt designed to inspire a strong emotional response in readers. This edition also included an addendum, "Their Lamentations," with the last words of both villains. The Cook "pour'd forth many a Tear," admitting he had "destroy'd the Innocent." But the "worst of all Step-Dames" simply admitted she had broken the law and "shall have my Reward."[43] The perverted mother received the infamous title of stepdame for her lack of tears.

Writing in the *Connecticut Courant* in 1825, one man described his stepmother as indifferent toward "the tender complaints of hapless children" and speaking "to wound the heart." She engaged in "angry clamouring," "petulant scolding," "malicious threatenings," and "haughty commands." She expressed her (not very well) "suppressed malice" toward her stepson with fearsome facial expressions, turning her "fiery eye-balls . . . with vengeance" on her victim. Her "vengeful brow of malice," "fierce grimace," and "dreary scowlings" no doubt had their intimidating effect.[44] Another feckless stepmother dismissed her unfortunate stepchildren with the wave of her hand, saying, "Go away you troublesome thing[s]." The author explained that "wounded by neglect," these stepchildren "pine[d] in the wasting agonies of sensibility."[45]

Around the same time, the *Farmer's Cabinet* of New Hampshire printed an anonymous story, "The Tombstone," that bemoaned the fate of a young girl who suffered first the loss of her mother and soon thereafter that of her father, leaving her alone with a greedy and uncaring stepmother. Eager to inherit the orphan's estate, this stepmother acted so cruelly that her stepdaughter died. "One cold and gloomy night," after the girl had dared to visit the graves of her parents without permission, "she was locked out in the yard alone." This episode, combined with other incidents of poor treatment, led her to contract an "unnatural sickness" that killed her. Completing her perfidy, the stepmother then buried the girl without even a tombstone, a travesty remedied by "some friends" who collected money for the purpose. Bringing his story to a sentimental crescendo, the narrator claimed that while he was weeping over the message on the simple marker, "the splendid carriage of her stepmother" drove by, "and the dust from its wheels almost covered the inscription."[46]

Over time, stepmother wickedness evolved in English and Anglo-American popular culture. In late eighteenth-century British North America, revolutionary fervor created a unique version of the wicked stepmother. From the colonists' perspective, the mother country had become abusive and neglectful, the opposite of a good sentimental mother. England, through her cruel behavior toward her colonial children, therefore, earned the title, Stepmother England. At the time the English North American colonies were settled, English stepmothers were associated with the evil behavior of all women, particularly those attempting to usurp patriarchal authority. By the end of the eighteenth century, however, the term "stepmother" itself implied an inferior replacement for a "real" mother. Whether a new story or a new iteration of a familiar tale, stepmothers were cast as the opposite of idealized mothers. Stepmothers had become both wicked women and wicked mothers.

CHAPTER FOUR

Through the Eyes of a Stepchild

When seventeen-year-old Dolly Murray heard the news of her father's 1762 remarriage, she cried.[1] Dolly struggled with what she saw as her father's slight of her sainted mother.[2] Her relatives encouraged her to remain open-minded. Her aunt, Elizabeth (Murray) Campbell, a successful Boston merchant, enthused, "Yours of the 3d Jan gave me the greatest pleasure, first, to hear of your wellfare what adds vastly to that is the Charactar you give of your mama. My Dear Child you are Blest beyond the common run of mortals I dare say you must be sensible of it & will make a good use of the opportunity that you now have the example you have is scar[ce]ly to be equaled."[3] Dolly's aunt assured the girl that if she had a good stepmother, she was indeed very lucky. Dolly's uncle, himself widowed and remarried, urged her to accept her new stepmother even though she had "lost a Most Worthy Mother." Her new stepmother, Margaret (MacKay) Thompson Murray, had an "amiable Character" and might even become a "female Friend to advise you."[4]

Despite such encouragement, Dolly never fully accepted her father's wife. After a short visit at home, she quickly returned to live with Elizabeth Campbell, and Dolly married very young, in part to ensure her independence from her father and his household. Five years after her father's remarriage, Margaret Murray hinted at the quality of her relationship when she urged Dolly, "If you can't write to me as a mother then write to me as a friend."[5]

How did stepchildren in early America see their own circumstances? Although the sources that provide such answers are rare, some voices of stepchildren survive.[6] This chapter examines three families with stepmothers in late-eighteenth- and early nineteenth-century New England. In each case, cultural prejudice played a role. For some stepchildren, kinder feelings prevailed despite cultural expectations; nonetheless, prejudice specifically

58

against stepmothers had a hold on children's imaginations and made their ready reception of a "new mother" far from certain. As in popular culture of the time, all of these stepchildren compared their stepmothers to their idealized dead mothers, and in some cases, the comparison became an insurmountable impediment to their relationships with their stepmothers.

THE BYLES FAMILY

Mather Byles lost his beloved wife, Rebecca (Walter) Byles, in 1775, the same year that events at Lexington and Concord shook the foundations of British North America, the city of Boston, and Rev. Byles's congregation. As a royalist leading an increasingly independence-minded congregation, Byles realized his need for a new position, but before he could find one, the war had made him an exile. By May 1776, he wrote to his Anglican superiors in England not from Boston but from English Nova Scotia. He described the days leading up to his departure in part through the lens of his personal family crisis, his loss of a partner, and his children's loss of a mother. He had prepared himself for "close confinement, scarcity of provision, and even cannonading and bombardment . . . but I must confess I had not the least suspicion that the army would ever have evacuated Boston." Caught up in the resulting chaos, he found himself unable to "bring away my furniture, or anything I possessed, but a couple of beds, with such articles as might be contained in a few trunks and boxes." Within a few days, he was in Halifax, a city overrun with other loyalist refugees. His situation was dire, "pent up in one wretched chamber, in a strange place, together with my five motherless children, one son and four daughters" aged five to thirteen. Byles's letter precipitated action: he was awarded the position of chaplain for the garrison in Halifax. He also found a partner to mend his broken family. Sarah Lyde, another refugee from Boston, became his wife by midwinter 1777.[7]

Ten years later, the same year that the U.S. Constitution dictated the contours of the nation the family had left behind, Mather Byles again found himself a widower. Again he looked to repair his family, which now included seven children from both his first and second marriages, the youngest of whom was nine. In 1789, he married a childless widow, Susanna (Lawlor) Reid, giving his two youngest children their first stepmother and his five oldest children their second.

Members of the Byles family in Nova Scotia and in Boston corresponded during and after the American Revolution, and their letters provide a remarkable account of stepfamily life through the eyes of the Byles children. Two of

Mather Byles's unmarried half-sisters, Mary and Catherine Byles, as well as their father, Mather Byles Sr., remained in Boston. The Byles sisters kept their nieces and nephews up on events in the city they had left behind, while the Byles children provided stories about the loyalist community in Nova Scotia. Both sides also focused on more intimate domestic affairs, the health of the aging family patriarch, and the growing ranks of the Byles stepfamily.

From all accounts, Sarah (Lyde) Byles was an exemplary "new mother" to the first five Byles children. Less than a year after Mather's second marriage, a family friend informed Mary and Catherine that "your Brother & sweet family are well, I[t] would Charm you to see the Sweet Olive Branches round thire Mother, & indeed invi [even] must say she do[e]s the dity [duty] of a Parent by them, this I know will mack you happy in hearing."[8] The children unerringly referred to their stepmother as "mama," and when twelve-year-old Elizabeth Byles shared with her aunts the news of a new baby, she wrote proudly, "I have got a little Sister namd Louisa," and "mama is got abroad again."[9] Two more children, Belcher and Samuel, followed in quick succession, prompting Elizabeth to write to her aunts, "It is with not a little pleasure that I inform you, of the Birth of another Brother, & I would be glad to know, if you don't think it is almost time for some of us to begin to look out. Especially as Mamma intends to have as many *Boys*, as there is *Girls*."[10] Elizabeth clearly had a comfortable and playful relationship with her stepmother.

In 1784, Rev. Byles sailed for England, leaving his new infant son, Samuel, and still recovering wife to the good care of his children. His precarious finances made his visit necessary, as his son, and namesake, Mather, explained to his aunts: "You ask the reason of my fathers voyage—It was to obtain a compensation for the property he left in New England. . . . [T]he Board instituted to examine the Claims of American Loyalists would grant nothing without a personal application." Of course "he had other motives.—His income here was small—inadequate to the support" of a family that now included eight children. Moreover, "his situation as a Clergyman was disagreeable": having had conflict with his congregation, he was hoping for a new assignment. And he felt that he had no "opportunity to exert his talents and render himself useful to Society" in this outpost community and believed that "in England all these *Desagrémens* might be rectified." Rev. Byles clearly enjoyed his time in England but worried about his loved ones, writing to his father, "I should be much happier than ever I was in my Life, if I had BUT my Family with me.—A monstrous great BUT that tho' it 'corrodes & leavens all the rest.'"[11]

Sarah was having difficulty recovering from Samuel's birth: according to Rebecca, "Mama is very poorly, she has never recover'd her Strength cince she lay-in." She was unable to nurse the baby, and he subsisted on a kind of gruel or pabulum. The other Byles children watched over Sarah with real concern. In April 1784, Mather Byles III told his aunts, "My good Mother, has been something better these last few days—but is in a very bad state of health" in general. The following December, Rebecca remained worried but optimistic: "For my Mothers Health, so lately restablished I fear'd a dangerous relapse, thank Heaven! I have nothing to fear from that, she still remains on the recovery, and is well enough to be out and abroad."[12]

In the fall of 1784, however, baby Samuel received an inoculation involving the live smallpox virus, the common method used at the time. This approach often resulted in a milder form of the disease, but Samuel developed a severe case. His brother Mather reported to their aunts, "Sam has had the smallpox it is just turning—he is remarkably well—but severly peppered, and looks like a fright: We reckon he has about two thousand pock, large, and distinct; which on so small a surface make no inconsiderable show. But don't be frightened—he won't die—take my word for it." Mather went on to paint a verbal portrait of a happy, loving family, beginning with his oldest sisters, Rebecca and Elizabeth: "Tis a pity one of them isn't married[. They] are already women; of course I dare not mention any thing about them. A woman you know never alters after she is a woman the same forever or until she is married—in Youth, Beauty, and Accomplishments." His next two sisters, Anna (Nancy) and Sarah (Sally), "grow handsomer every day, and with a little attention will become very fine women[.] The former will be I can't find a word that exactly suits me something more than *Agreable* the latter will be lovely. One will be *captivating* the other *fascinating*. Do you find any difference between these two words? I think there is a great deal. Both are *lively* Both have *sensibility* Nancy has most of the former the *latter* predominates in Sally. You may call this a Brothers portrait—But I am not partial; it is a just one." And Louisa and Belcher "are almost two young to judge of—the one bids fair to be a *fine lady*; the other will be—*a Man*[.] You may laugh at that character if you please—I affirm it is a good one. It conveys my idea and tho' short is expressive." And Samuel "closes the list. I believe he will be a quiet good sort of an animal—If he should happen to get a wife like Nancy, she would twist him round her little finger, and laugh at him for letting her."[13]

But soon thereafter, baby Samuel died after suffering febrile seizures, forcing Mather to again take up his pen to break the sad news: the funeral had "greatly affected me." and his only consolation was his belief that Samuel's "spotless soul" had ascended to heaven. The baby's death also added to Mather Jr.'s concerns regarding his stepmother, who "bears the loss with fortitude. I am anxious lest it should affect her health, which is yet hardly reestablished; but at present I have no reason to apprehend a relapse."[14]

Rebecca had nursed her half brother during his last illness, and at first her "head and Heart were both too much agitated to think of composing myself to my Pen, for the Dear Ascended innocent I felt scarcely any Passion moved, except a degree of Envy, at a comparative view of his situation with my own, nor could I avoid repeating while I held his little clay cold Hands in mine. Happy Infant: early blest! / Rest, in peaceful slumbers rest / Early rescued from the cares, / Which encrease with growing Years. / No delights are worth thy stay, / Smiling as they are and Gay; / Lasting only and divine. / Is an innocence like thine." Writing to her aunts, Rebecca, shared her fears about how her father would take the news, "tenderly attached as I know him to be to his Children." "I have often sincerely prayd we might all be restored to him on his return alive, and in Health, yet an alwise providence had otherwise ordained." She fretted that Rev. Byles's instinct would be to "bitterly regret" his absence, though she believed that "every thing was done that could have been, had he been here." Composing the letter to her father took her "a whole Day" until "at last . . . I wrote him as circumstantial an account as I could possibly give."[15]

By March 1785, at least some of the joking, good humor had returned to the Byles household. Rebecca provided her aunts with an inventory of the "family Group" in which she described her brother, Mather, as "*very studiously employed* in his Chamber, surrounded with Maps, Dictionaries, & Compasses, I fear he will leave us in the Summer, but I dare not trust myself to think of it." Elizabeth, who suffered from epilepsy, appeared to be "out growing her Interesting complaint, the returns are much less frequent, and much less alarming," and she remained Rebecca's favorite. Nancy continued "*lively* sprightly *sensible* and *Gay*, want only a few years to make her a fine Woman, at present she is to me a perfect Plague, wither me with the most Sarcastick attention, puts forced constructions on all I say, and do, & tho pleased with her humor I am often vexed at being the Object." And Sally was "*agreable* and *engaging*, *modest* and *totally unaffected* grows extremely handsome, I think Beautiful, . . . she is a truly lovly Girl, and my Affection for her is unbounded." Rebecca deemed eight-year-old Louisa "*pretty sensible*" but also "*affected* & vain," while Belcher, "except a little warmth of disposition, which only wants direction[,] is almost Faultless, a finer a more *promising* Boy both in *Person* & *Mind* I never saw."[16]

In 1785, Rebecca Byles married William James Allmon (Almon), a Rhode Island–born loyalist physician who served with the British army during the revolution and set up a practice in Halifax after the war. After their first child was born, Rebecca's stepmother was an invaluable help, and in 1786, as Sarah prepared for a visit to Boston, Rebecca told her aunts, "We are a going to loose for some time, a part of our family, which I shall greatly miss worthy Mother." Rebecca continued, "Should it be in your Power to call & see her, you will greatly oblige me, she has ever treated me with the Affection of a Parent, & I am under great Obligation to her, I have scarcly known since I was married the cares of a Family, owing to her kind assistance."[17] Neither Mather nor Rebecca paid attention to the intricacies of blood relationships in assessing their family members.

Rev. Byles returned to Halifax in 1785 having obtained the compensation he sought in England and resumed his life among his tightly knit family. In February 1787, however, the Byleses suffered another blow with the death of their matriarch, Sarah. She had apparently recovered from Samuel's death, and her passing was so unexpected that her grieving husband insisted on an autopsy, which was performed by Rebecca Byles Allmon's husband and revealed that her death had been caused by overcorseting. Writing to her aunts about the "death of my Mother," Rebecca took comfort in the fact that although "a Death Bed is a scene of gloom and distress, yet hers had great alleviations, the calm composed resignation with which she died, is a great consolation to her surviving friends, my dear father bears the stroke like a Christian, yet he deeply feels the loss, God grant he may long be continued the *support* the *pride* of his family." A few months later, Rebecca reported that the older children had resigned themselves to their terrible loss, but their father's depression and lack of a partner left their younger half-siblings lacking proper management: "Louisa & Belcher are capable of mak[ing] fine Children & when Pappa recovers his spirits enough, which he is doing gradually, enough to attend to them, I have no doubt of their being every thing we wi[sh for] them."[18]

Elizabeth Byles, the eldest of the Byles children still at home, took up the responsibility for her half brother and sister, partly to help her father but partly to honor her dead stepmother. She lamented to her aunts in May 1787, "What a scene of distress, I have experience'd. The loss of a valuable Mother, & the Unhappy, distress'd Situation of a fond, endearing Father has unfit me for writing, or anything else; twice has he been bereft of the fond faithful partner of his Bosom; he lays it greatly to Heart.—Aunt my Heart achs!" She also felt her own loss keenly. "I miss my poor Mother greatly, every Day I meet with something or another that brings her fresh to my Mind. She was an Amiable Character, & was Exemplary in her Conduct to us: She deserv'd every Mark of Gratitude, & filial Affection that we could possibly shew her. I hope we were not remiss in it." Elizabeth believed that she could not "recompence" her stepmother "for her kindness & Attention to us, more, than by returning it upon her own two little Children, whose grief was but momentary, they are not old enough yet poor things to know what they have lost."[19]

Again in need of a replacement for a beloved partner, and this time pushed by his family, Rev. Byles chose Susanna (Lawlor) Reid as his third wife. In August 1788, an enthusiastic Elizabeth announced to her aunts that her father was remarrying: "Our Family is soon to be increas'd: Pappa is shortly to be married to a smart widow; or Mrs Reid. She is a Charming Woman, & we are much pleas'd with the Connexion. She appears much Attach'd to us, & I have every reason to believe that she will prove a Blessing to us all." Her brother, Mather, concurred, writing cheerfully to the Bostonians that when his father traveled to St. Johns, Nova Scotia, where he was considering taking up a new pulpit, "there were two or three ladies there making up new caps, but it is whispered that they are too late, a certain matter being agreed upon before leaving Halifax, the particulars of which time will discover. If so I think the purchase money of the gauze and ribbons ought to be refunded—for if a man passes for a widower when by a mental reservation he is no widower—the law will admit it to be a deception & actionable." In a subsequent letter, he referred to the wedding preparations as "the great family revolution" and expressed his "great and I think rational confidence" that the arrival of a new stepmother would not cause "any interruption to the chearfulness & unanimity of the family." Moreover, Mather hoped that "this new connection" would give a "spring" to his father's "spirits," especially in light of "the chearful aspect which seems of late to be given to his affairs."[20]

Nancy, too, chimed in approvingly, telling her father's sisters in November 1788, just a few weeks after the wedding, that she, Sally, and Elizabeth had served as "Brids Maides," and that all was well: "We have the sources of enjoyment within ourselves, & need not look abroad for that happiness, which I believe is seldom to be found but at home, especially when a family is united in its self; & strongly attachd to each other, as I can with pleasure say ours is." In Nancy's estimation, "My Father is married again to a worthy, amiable Woman, who appears disinterestedly fond of *him*, & of us *all*, & in whom I doubt not, we shall find an agreeable companion, & a faithful friend, she appears to study our inclination & happiness in every thing she does, &, I am sure I can answer for my Sisters, & my Self, that our utmost endeavours will not be wanting, to make her situation agreeable." Already "Pappa seems happier than I have seen him for sometime, & I sincerely hope, that the conversation of a sprightly Wife, will restore his wanted chearfulness."[21]

The confidence expressed by the Byles children was not misplaced. In early 1789, a few months after the wedding, the reverend wrote to his sisters, "My wife . . . is a most excellent Woman, & delights in diffusing Happiness all around her. She is dear to me, & beloved by my Family; which exhibits the curious Spectacle of two Sets of Children, & a third wife, all living together in the most perfect Harmony & Love, without one jarring String, or the least Mixture of Coolness or Jealousy." He was both pleased and surprised that his family had defied the cultural expectations regarding conflict within stepfamilies: "You cannot imagine how happy this circumstance makes me, or with what Pleasure I view them at this Instant, as they are sitting in Tranquility about me." A year later, Elizabeth was still content, reporting that her father "is also Bless'd with a truly Amiable & beloved wife, whose whole study is to make him & every one about her happy. She is a Charming Woman, & every Day convinces me more & more of her worth."[22] Despite the trials the members of the Byles family faced and the cultural expectations regarding stepfamilies, domestic harmony prevailed.

THE NORTON FAMILY

In the winter of 1811, Elizabeth (Cranch) Norton was suffering from a "disorder of the pleurisy kind." As she struggled to breathe, her husband, Jacob, a minister in Weymouth, Massachusetts, prayed for her and for his crumbling family: "O god prepare her,—prepare me & the children whom thou hast graciously given me for the work of thy wholly will." As her condition worsened, he and his mother-in-law watched her descend into a "bewildered state of mind" and then finally, in the early hours of 25 January, find relief, "without a struggle or a groan." Devastated, Jacob prayed that God would "sanctify" this "heavy dispensation" to himself and his "motherless children." Elizabeth had been "a companion . . . most faithful & affectionate" and "a mother most kind tender & vigilant." He buried his "dear deceased companion" with many friends and neighbors in attendance, each carefully listed in his journal entry of that day. When the ceremony ended, Jacob retreated to his house and his journal, noting, "My friends left me in the evening & I *felt* what it is to be *alone*."[23]

Hard on the loss of his wife, the lonely preacher had to find a solution to his domestic circumstances. His fragile nuclear family, which included eight children, five of them still at home, lay in tatters. His financial situation as a small-town minister was also precarious: "A considerable part of this period I have been in a[n] unsettled state in making preparations for discontinuing house-keeping & affecting it in selling off furniture at auction—in taking a family into my house (Capt. Copelands) with whom I expect for some time to board." Sixteen-year-old Edward became "an apprentice to the Cabinet business," while his brother, Jacob, age eighteen, became "an apprentice to the book binding business." The Nortons' three youngest children—Elizabeth, nine; Mary, seven; and Lucy, five—went to live with Elizabeth Norton's parents, Mary (Smith) Cranch and James Cranch, in Quincy, Massachusetts. And thus, as Norton recorded in his journal, he was truly "left alone." Having provided for his children's safety, he could do nothing more except pray, "My dear children I desire humbly to commend to the divine protection guidance & mercy." But that was not the end of the Norton family's suffering. Before 1811 had ended, both of Elizabeth's parents had also died, again leaving her daughters bereft and meaning that they moved yet again, taking up residence in the home of their mother's sister, Lucy (Cranch) Greenleaf and her husband, James Greenleaf.[24] For the Cranch family, caring for the Norton girls ensured that they would remember their mother and think of her as still watching over them from heaven. Mary Cranch's niece, Abby Shaw, explained in a letter, "I have lately been reading the Pleasures of Memory and my attention was much arrested by a few lines which I thought bore a strong resemblance to the character of your dear departed Daughter." That sentimental 1792 poem, written by Englishman Samuel Rogers, described the comfort memory could bring by telling the story of the poet's dead brother, who continued to watch over his loved ones from heaven. Shaw quoted that section of the work but substituted "mother" for brother, so that the poem read, "An angel's pity with a Mother's love, Still o'er my life preserve thy mild control, Correct my vices, and elevate my soul." Shaw also suggested Elizabeth Norton might memorize the lines.[25]

After two years of a makeshift life without his children, Jacob Norton found another wife. In the spring of 1813, the forty-nine-year-old widower married Hannah Bowers, a forty-seven-year-old spinster. He recorded in his journal, "This morning was united by Rev. Dr. Cummings to Miss Hannah Bowers by the most sacred & enduring . . . bond of union after remaining in a single state for . . . more then two years. . . . May it be mutually happy to us—O let its consequences to us to our connexions & to others be desirable for time & for eternity." At first, Norton's prayers appeared to have been answered. "It is now more than three weeks since my marriage with my wife—in whom I have found a help meet & much satisfaction & comfort. I desire to Bless go bless god for this happy connexion—O may the connexion never cease to be a happy one." In August, he wrote, "In the beginning of May I was married to Miss Hannah Bowers of Billerica—who has been truly a help mate for me—& with whom I have lived in the utmost harmony—friendship & love."[26]

On 2 August 1813, Jacob began the process of reuniting his family, recording in his journal, "Took tea with Mrs Norton & our little girls" at the Greenleafs. Having given his new wife and his daughters a chance to get acquainted, Jacob happily reported that on 18 August, he "call'd at Mr. Greenleaf for our little girls." Jacob opened 1814 by noting, "My children who are with me have been a comfort to me."[27]

Letters written by the Norton girls as young adults show that they loved their stepmother and were close to her. In 1824, Jacob and Hannah Norton intended to move to Vermont, Jacob losing his pulpit at Weymouth, Massachusetts, due to his increasingly Universalist leanings. As Elizabeth noted, she and her sisters were sad to "leave the place where so many of our happy hours of childhood has been spent." In addition, however, they worried that their stepmother would overexert herself to move the household: Elizabeth reported, "Last sabbath I was at home, found Mama without any help, the girl was obliged to go home; Papa expected to commence his journey soon." The Norton girls came to their stepmother's aid. And in late December 1827, Elizabeth wrote a long, chatty letter to Mary that concluded, "Mother wished to write but her eyes were so weak and her fingers rheumatic, she thought she could not.—'but tell my dear Mary I exceedingly regret her so long absence, & can only be reconciled to it by supposing that it is for her interest & happiness. . . . Assure her of my unabated affection & earnest desire of her reunion with the family whenever it shall accord with her convenience & inclination.'"[28]

Nearly two years later, Mary penned a lively account of her life as a schoolteacher to share with her stepmother, "though you might perhaps be best pleased were I to come and relate my adventures by word of mouth." Mary related her nervous anticipation about her students' first public recitation and then crowed, "After all was over, I received the applause of the trustees and they said that my scholars appeard the best!!!—There! Don't you think I have cause for triumph." Mary expected her stepmother to be both pleased and proud.[29]

And in one 1829 letter, Elizabeth encouraged Mary to take a teaching job at Haverhill Academy by enthusing, "Haverhill is a delightful place, and I think it probable you will meet with some who were once friends of our mother, who you know used in her youthful days to visit Haverhill." Here, "our mother" was the late Elizabeth Norton. But young Elizabeth closed the letter with the words, "Tell mother not to exert herself too much in moving." Perhaps the Nortons planned again to move to Vermont having only gone as far as Billerica, Massachusetts in 1824. This "mother" was Hannah Norton.[30]

Mary, too, used "mother" to refer to both of her father's wives. She told her sister, Lucy, that she had met "a number who were formerly acquainted with Mother, and Aunt Greenleaf" and that one of these people suggested that "as they were formerly acquainted with Mother they must claim me as an acquaintance also." Later in the same letter, Mary reminded Lucy that Hannah had good-naturedly recommended against one particular suitor: "Mother said he had no heart, or if he had There was no avenue to it."[31] Their stepmother and mother filled similar places in the young women's lives and hearts.

But Richard Norton had decidedly different feelings about his step-mother. Unlike his sisters, he let his prejudice against stepmothers in general color his view of his father's new wife, whom he never met. Richard was living in Washington, D.C., and studying law with his maternal uncle when he learned in March 1813 that Rev. Norton was planning to remarry. Richard responded by telling his father that regardless of her merits, no one could ever replace the mother "that gave him birth." After the wedding, Richard recorded in his diary, "Recd a letter from my father informing me that he had entered into the matrimonial connexion which he has long contemplated, & that he is happier than he has been before since the death of my ever dear & honored mother." He continued, "may his happiness & that of his companion continue to increase with time & be completed in eternity—My father tells me that my sister[s] are very attached to their new mother & she to them." Nevertheless, he sent his father the expected congratulations: "I rejoice, my dear Father, to find that you are so happily situated—May Heaven shed its choicest blessings on your head, may you enjoy, in the bosom of your family, that domestic tranquility & happiness to which you have so long been a stranger."[32]

In keeping with propriety, Richard also wrote to his new stepmother, beginning his letter formally with "my Honoured Mother" and asking her to "permit me, though a stranger to you personally, to address you by that endearing appellation." In contrast to his earlier statement to his father than no one would ever take his mother's place, he told the new Mrs. Norton, "May you never have reason to be ashamed to acknowledge me as your son.—I hope & confidently trust that I shall never be wanting in that filial duty and respect which is due to my mother." He expressed his pleasure at the marriage and the joy he hoped it would bring to his father and sisters, and he urged her to provide a suitable role model for the girls, "a mother who, like that dear departed parent who gave them birth, will be solicitous not only for their temporal welfare, but in a particular manner for the infinitely more important concerns of their immortal souls—May you find a pleasing employment in forming their youthful minds to piety & virtue, & in bringing them up to those domestic habits which will make them useful in their day and generation—which will make them dutiful daughters, faithful & affectionate wives, loving & tender mothers, & ornaments & blessings to society in whatever situation they may be placed." He apologized for writing to her "before receiving my communication from you," as etiquette dictated, but explained that he was "anxious to become acquainted with my second mother." And he closed by saying that he "anticipated with pleasure the time when I shall have the happiness of a personal acquaintance," though "when that will be it is impossible for me to say, I hope however ere another year elapses—but in this world of uncertainty we can make no confident calculations—I shall see you & the rest of my friends whenever the Supreme Disposer of Events sees fit that I should." A month later, Richard had received no response.[33]

For several years, Rev. Norton hoped that the relationship between his oldest son and his stepmother would thaw, repeatedly asking Richard to do what he could to improve the situation. However, a blunt 1817 letter from Richard put an end to Jacob's entreaties: "I regret that my supposed neglect or inattention on my part with regard to Mrs. N. should have occasioned you any uneasiness. I assure you I asure you I feel for her the most sincere respect &, an affection as great as I ever felt for one whom I never saw, & with whom I had no personal acquaintance." But he "candidly confess[ed] that I cannot feel for her that filial love & affection which a son ought to feel for a mother—I consider the name of mother as sacred—as comprehending in its meaning the warmest affections & tenderest charities of the heart, & to apply the title where these sentiments do not accompany it appears to me a kind of hypocrisy—as a term indicative of respect & affectionate regard I can conscientiously use it." Richard made no secret of his feelings: "I wish my mother to know my sentiments on this subject, that if she has considered me guilty of inattention or disrespect toward her I may no longer lie under such an imputation."[34] Though he called Hannah Norton his mother, it was clear that she did not occupy the same place in his heart or his life as his true mother.

Thus, the Norton children had vastly different responses to their stepmother. Perhaps the daughters were simply younger and less jaded, less unwilling to accept a replacement for their departed mother. Perhaps their personal knowledge of a kind and loving Hannah Norton overcame any cultural predispositions for hostility toward a stepmother. But however pleased Richard Norton was that his father and sisters were happy, Hannah could not be his mother. His mother was dead.

THE SEDGWICK FAMILY

Writing her memoir at the age of sixty, Catharine Maria Sedgwick, by then a famous novelist, concluded that her experience as a stepchild had followed a predictable storyline. After the death of her mother, Pamela (Dwight) Sedgwick, in 1807, her father, Massachusetts lawyer and politician Theodore Sedgwick (1746–1813) "felt the solitarity of his home—He was the sort of Man to whom the companionship of a woman is a necessity." He married "again a little more than a year after my Mother's death," choosing as his new bride Penelope Russell, "a Boston woman—of a highly respectable family and agreeable exterior & an attractive vivacity." The speed of his remarriage and his choice of partner answered his needs but not necessarily those of his family. Recalled Catharine, "The poor lady was put in a life for which she was totally unfitted—She knew nothing of the business of country domestic life & her ambition to shine in it was simply ludicrous to us—onerous to her. She fluttered gracefully enough throt the inanities of town drawing-rooms—but the realities & simplicity of our country life was insupportable to her." In addition, according to Catharine, "like most second marriages where there are children it was disastrous." However, the Sedgwick stepfamily did not involve young children. The oldest two girls, Eliza and Frances, were married, while Theodore Jr., Henry, and Robert were working or at school. Only eighteen-year-old Catharine and her brother, Charles, two years younger, remained at home.[35]

All of the Sedgwick children disliked their stepmother, calling her "Mrs. S" or "Mrs. Sedgwick," never "Mother" or "Mama." They constantly compared her to their mother and found Penelope lacking, although life with Pamela Sedgwick, who suffered from depression and was a longtime invalid, had been difficult. Moreover, Theodore Sedgwick was often absent, pursuing his political and legal career, and the Sedgwick children already had a substitute parent in Elizabeth "Mumbet" Freeman, a former slave whom their father had helped to freedom and who remained a constant in their lives.[36]

Penelope Sedgwick came to her new role seeking to please her new stepchildren and fearing that she might not. As her new husband explained to his son, Henry, "she is infinitely anxious as to the impression which her character may make upon the family." Theodore expressed similar sentiments to his son and namesake, Theodore Jr.: "She has but a single source of anxiety—that she will not be as acceptable to the children as she is sure they will be to her." He urged his children to give her a chance. "I hope and pray that [her reception] may be just and favorable. My heart is full of this, and I shall not be happy untill my hopes are realized." But he also wanted his children to know that despite what they thought of his speedy marriage to a Boston gadabout, he still tried to find an appropriate "new mother" for them: "Had I imagined it possible that the harmony of the family could have been disturbed by this event or the happiness of my dear children impaired I would have preferred death to it."[37]

Theodore's children, however, loved their home in Stockbridge and feared that their father might move to Boston to please his citified wife. After learning of his father's plan to marry, Theodore Jr. lamented to his brother, Henry, "To tell you that I was astonished and afflicted is unnecessary—I was totally unprepared to hear of such an event, as I had not the slightest expectation of it." He could not "disapprove the measure . . . at present" since he did not know "the Lady," but what he did know made him apprehensive: "To me personally however it is a misfortune, which I have hardly the courage to think of—as I see in it the certainty of the breaking up of the family and your removal to Boston.—That Miss R[ussell] will not live in S[tockbridge] is I think certain & that the Judge will be little disposed to remain there is as much so—I see at once the whole extent of the misfortune and cannot but feel it most severely." As long as the family remained in Stockbridge, Theodore Jr. "entertained a hope (perhaps a vain one) that it would be in my power in the course of events to have you near me—Now I fear that we shall be separated forever—With regard to Catharine I have entertained the same hope—But that is gone too—Perhaps I am selfish—Indeed I know I am—But upon this subject, it is impossible for me not to be so. . . . My heart is so full that I hardly know what to write." He cautioned his brother not to "let Papa know that You have written me upon the subject, for then He will ask what I say about it—You had better burn my letter for fear of accidents." Theodore Jr. was much more circumspect in a letter to his father, writing, "In Nov[embe]r you will I presume be married—In this connection I hope you may realize your fondest wishes and that as you have been to us the best of Fathers, she who is to stand in so near a relation may be the best of Mothers—I am sure there will be on our part every disposition to make her happy, and if she makes you so, every wish of ours will be gratified."[38]

Visiting her sister in New York when her new stepmother arrived at the family home, Catharine received a letter from Henry with his impressions of their new stepmother: "Perhaps of the whole family I am the 'most' competent to give You a detail of small minute events & circumstances separately unimportant, but from which continued You might form an idea in what manner our happiness is to be affected by this new connexion." He acknowledged that Penelope had "a strong desire to initiate our affections, and to conform to our wishes in every respect." The children were doing their best as well, "partly by forcing our feelings and partly by yielding to the impression naturally made by the social a[nd] festive qualities which Mrs Sedgwick iminently possesses." Of course, used to Boston society and city life, she was extravagant in her tastes. "Family oeconomy she would not be expected to understand, and I believe she does not at all. Our household expenses must be considerably increased by the new establishment." He could tolerate these failings but could not bear to see his father with a woman other than their mother: "The only unpleasant circumstance which I had not precisely anticipated, in the very form & shape in which it has occurred, was to see our revered father caressing a woman with any other sentiment that that of paternal affection. This however was not altogether unexpected neither has it occurred frequently or offensively, & perhaps it is to be attributed to the particularity of my feelings that I have been at all affected by it." The effort to please this suspicious brood was already taking a toll on the new Mrs. Sedgwick. Although "generally cheerful," Henry explained, she "has had turns of depression, which however she has endeavoured to conceal by retiring into her room."[39]

Penelope Sedgwick's withdrawal and a vague stomach complaint, medicated with alcohol and laudanum (morphine), a combination prescribed by a Boston physician named Danforth, gave the children a focus for their discontent. In 1812, Eliza told Henry that she did not see "the least prospect of [Penelope] ever being well." According to Eliza, "She lives upon both laudnum and disappointment and her flesh and strength are constantly

wasting." As her unhappiness turned to addiction, her visits to Boston became not just a psychic relief but also a physical necessity. Charles reported,
"Mrs. S. was sick when she left home, but I believe the last view of the man-
sion restored her. It is a little strange that a long season of continued dissem-
bling cannot divest love of its blindness. It would have been to shameless for
Mrs. S to pretend that it was on Papa's account that she accompanied him &
so the absolute necessity of seeing Doct. Danforth obviated every difficulty.
She even went so far as to say, but without his knowledge that if he did not
go soon she should go without him. Self preservation is the first requsition
of nature & this was her pretended justification." Four years into the marriage, Penelope's stepchildren saw her as a hopeless addict and wondered
at their father's continued devotion. Noted Catharine in 1812, "Mrs S. has
behaved much better for three or four weeks"; however, "nothing but the
power of Heaven" could "change her."[40]

Because the Sedgwick children considered their father's remarriage
financially imprudent, they began a campaign to get him to consider
writing a will, though they denied that their opinion of their stepmother
played a role in their concerns. Theodore opened the painful conversation with their father in 1809, writing, "That your Children all think
M*rs* Sedgwick generous noble and disinterested is most true—That they
feel towards her no jealousy is as much so." Theodore claimed that "nothing but a sense of duty enables me to mention" the subject "at all" and that
he hated to think about an event that would "deprive fond and affectionate children of the kindest and most excellent of Fathers." Nonetheless,
compelled by "all the family now at Stockbridge," he thought it his duty
to address the issue.[41]

Theodore Sedgwick was not persuaded of his children's benign intentions and considered the possibility that they wanted to commandeer their
stepmother's estate. Henry now made the case for his siblings, protesting to
their father, "So far am I from wishing to do any thing . . . to the prejudice
to Mrs Sedgwick that I have proposed to submit this letter to her. But in
this I have been overruled." He, too, described pursuing the issue as "my
duty," and he refused to "believe it possible that in so doing I should have
incurred your displeasure." Theodore Sr. remained unconvinced, explaining to Henry, "There are many considerations which ought to impress cir-
cumspection upon me. My own comfort it is my duty to regard. There is no
probability that I shall long continue in my present office, and an old man
straightened in his circumstances who has been used to care is among the
most miserable of human beings. I know not how long, nor to what extent,

you & Robert may want support; Catharine is unprovided for; Charles is yet wholly dependent, and to Mrs Sedgwick I must be just."[42]

Catharine then weighed in, excoriating her stepmother in an 1811 letter to Robert: "Meanness & malice cannot have any triumph that we need dread over true nobility of soul[.] After all when my resentment subsides I can pity the tumults of a conscience that never whispers peace, & the conflict of a heart that has no sacred rest for virtue—The miserable half gratification of an insatiate vanity, & the bustle of impertinent trifling make up the sum total of Mrs. S's happiness." Catharine went on to compare her stepmother to her idealized mother: "Let us Together my dearest Robert, thank our God, that that purity which is now sainted in Heaven, shed its blessed influence on the formation of our characters, & early taught us to love the light of virtue & the favor of Heaven. May the memorial of her excellence the treasured recollection of her patient endurance of every evil preserve us from even a momentary forgetfulness of our filial duty, that duty must be paramount to all earthly ones, & it is made easy & delightful to us by the parental virtues of the best of Fathers." The Sedgwick children needed to focus on their father, not their stepmother: "*If we* do *right* Mrs. S. cannot invade the sacred circle of our happiness, but my dear Brother in order to attain this great end, we must place our *chief dependence* on the guidance of that Power that will assuredly save those from temptation, that pray to him for this preservation *Forgiveness of injuries* is the first precept of that Gospel which is to bring peace to the world; let this be our peace, and the blessing of God will rest upon it." Robert responded in kind, writing, "I have often thought it almost a miracle, that in the Providence of God, I have such Sisters, and Brothers, that we have still such a Father, & that we have had such a Mother. *Our Mother is in Heaven.* God grant that *we may all meet her, as a family there.* But while we remain on Earth, let us never waste a single particle of that invaluable treasure, which we have in each other's affections."[43]

In 1813, Theodore Sedgwick died, prompting Henry to confide to his brother, Theodore, "I trust he is now with our sainted mother" and Robert to reflect to Catharine, "Our dear departed Father has gone to join the blessed family above, and is reunited to our sainted Mother."[44]

Though Theodore Sedgwick had indeed written a will, he bequeathed part of the Stockbridge house to his wife and part to his son, Charles, a common arrangement that provided both a widow and the selected child with a home and provided a caretaker for the widow as she aged. In this case, however, Charles and his siblings wanted Penelope out of their family

This portrait of Theodore Sedgwick became a source of conflict between the Sedgwick children and their stepmother. Gilbert Stuart, *Theodore Sedgwick Sr.*, ca. 1808. Courtesy of the Museum of Fine Arts, Boston.

home. The Sedgwick children began negotiations with their stepmother's lawyer, offering her a generous share of the rest of the estate—equivalent to what she had brought to the marriage—if she would relinquish her claim to the house. The amount they offered was greater than the widow's third to which she was legally entitled, but as Robert wrote, "I would sacrifice half I am worth than have her take up her abode at S[tockbridge] or even be there any portion of the year." The children also wanted to hold onto the only surviving portrait of their father, viewing themselves as their father's only "real & sincere mourner[s]." Penelope Sedgwick wanted the portrait, and according to Catharine, if the children "would believe that Mrs S was, sincere in her professions it would be cruel not to grant her so precious a favour." But they did not believe her.[45]

The Sedgwicks eventually reached an agreement with their stepmother, but not without damage to their reputation and hard feelings. Henry wrote to Catharine, "I really & sincerely pity Mrs. S. She has lost all that could preserve her respectability. . . . [C]onsidering her wants, her helplessness, & her extravagance, she is poor. Besides, she has placed herself in our power by her misconduct." Catharine responded, "I confess it grieves me very much, that we must suffer in the opinion of the good—I would make many personal sacrifices to remove the odium which the stories of disappointed malice, have thrown upon our characters, but my dear Harry if they can only be refuted by the exposure of the vices and follies of our accuser had not we better rationally suffer—She is so poor in the esteem of the world that I cannot bear to take from her the little she has: We can (thanks to the nurture and admonition of our sainted Parents afford to spare something— When the world leaves Mrs S. she will find that she has leant upon a staff that will pierce her she has no comforter in her own bosom—I think we have many friends in Boston that calumny cannot take from us." Catharine saw Penelope as "the slave to a degrading appetite, and the victim of vanity and folly—She finds too late that misery cannot be parted from sin. I forgive her freely the hours of vexation, sorrow and solitude that she has caused us and most fervently pray that the God of forgiveness may have mercy on her." Frances had less sympathy: "This Woman ought to be the subject of unmisced justice as respects her own demerits—and I have no doubt that the Chalice of even handed justice will still be emptied to the very dregs by this pitiably bad woman."[46] Penelope Sedgwick ultimately gave up the house and the painting and returned to Boston. After a stay there, perhaps unable to reclaim her good social standing, she left the country, undone by her sojourn as a stepmother. Her stepchildren erased her from their lives as quickly as they could.

Looking through the eyes of a stepchild of the late eighteenth and early nineteenth century meant looking though a prism of cultural prejudice. Nonetheless, good relationships between stepmothers and stepchildren did exist, as demonstrated by the Byles family and to a more limited extent by the Nortons. The Sedgwicks, however, exemplified the situation predicted by cultural norms, in which the addition of a stepmother created a hostile atmosphere.

CHAPTER FIVE

Brothers and Sisters

Elizabeth and Samuel Epes came to live with the Holyoke children in 1742 when their mother, Mary (Whipple) Epes, became the third wife of Edward Holyoke, longtime president of Harvard College. Eight-year-old Sammy and six-year-old Elizabeth instantly became part of a very large family—eight stepsisters and stepbrothers ranging in age from one to fourteen. Two years later, the birth of Mary Holyoke—the half sister of all the children—further increased the brood. When Elizabeth died in 1759, she was predeceased not only by Mary but also by two stepbrothers and a stepsister. She still had her brother, Samuel Epes; her eldest stepbrother, Edward Augustus Holyoke; and four stepsisters, Margaret, Elizabeth, Anna, and Priscilla Holyoke. In her will, she did not distinguish among them, calling all of them her sisters and brothers.[1]

Elizabeth Epes bequeathed most of her estate to her mother, not just for her own sake but to "keep . . . [the Holyoke] Family together, and in some Measure return to them the many Kindnesses I have received from their Father." Edward Holyoke had been "the best of Fathers to Me," but his "benevolent Heart, will I am sensible never permit him to lay up much Treasure on Earth." If her mother was widowed she would "not to be able to do that for his Children, w[hi]ch I am sure she wou'd be inclin'd to do."[2] Elizabeth thus hoped to provide for her stepsiblings by leaving the resources she had inherited from her father, Symond Epes, to her mother.

Similarly, when Samuel died sixteen months later, he, too, provided for his stepsiblings through his mother. After settling his business affairs and debts, he left his real estate to his mother and three-quarters of his personal estate with the proviso that after her death, what remained of his personal estate would go "to my Belovd. Brother Edward Augustus Holyoke, Anna Holyoke and Priscilla Holyoke Equally to be divided Between them." Samuel appointed Edward the executor of his will and charged him with caring for his mother. Edward took on both responsibilities, settling Samuel's estate and watching over his stepmother's portion until her death thirty years later. The Epes family's fortune nurtured the roots of the Holyoke family tree.[3]

Although inheritance law emphasized purity of blood in sibling relationships, in legal practice, literary culture, and personal correspondence, the step-, half-, and full-sibling relationships in stepfamilies followed less predictable patterns.[4] Fictional representations of stepfamily life, with a nod to stepfamily prejudice, actually depicted positive relationships between siblings of all kinds. In addition, real stepfamily siblings acknowledged but did not dwell on blood distinctions. Older brothers and sisters cared for their younger siblings regardless of blood ties. They often worked together for the welfare of the whole family.

In early America, "half sister" and "stepsister" were not pejorative words like "stepmother"; rather, they carried a specificity of relationship that most people felt rarely needed naming. Siblings of all kinds, regardless of blood relationship, were most often simply called "brother" or "sister."[5] For example, a survey of 8,082 issues of the *Boston Newsletter* and *Connecticut Courant* between 1704 and 1850 found no references at all to "stepbrothers" or "stepsisters" and only four references to "half sisters" and eight to "half brothers."[6] Dictionaries of the time also avoided these terms. Samuel Johnson's 1755 English dictionary had no entries for "half brother" and "half sister."[7] Daniel Webster's 1806 dictionary of American English had no entries for "stepbrother," "stepsister," "half brother," and "half sister."[8]

The absence of such labels created complications in inheritance law—or simply when calling someone for dinner. For example, distinguishing between children was a challenge for the Lay family of Lyme, Connecticut. John Lay married twice and named his eldest son of both marriages John. Parents in colonial New England commonly reused names to honor dead children, but in this case, both Johns were alive and well. John Lay père distinguished between these sons in his will by labeling them "My son John which I had by my former wife" and "John whom I had by my present wife."[9] Peter Lay, who was the full brother of one John and half brother of the other, wrote a will in which he left legacies to both brothers, distinguishing them as "John Lay, my younger Brother," "my brother John Lay Junior," "my Elder brother John Lay," and "John Lay Senior."[10] Even when blood-specific terms would have provided clarity and been more succinct, they were not used.

This phenomenon does not mean, however, that such distinctions had no value. They clearly mattered in inheritance law. In eighteenth-century

England and New England, blood-based distinctions created a legal hierarchy of siblings in stepfamilies. When a father's estate passed down through a stepfamily, half siblings had fewer rights than full-blood siblings, and stepsiblings had no rights at all. The term "half-blood" never appeared in family correspondence but was regularly used in legal sources to refer to an inferior heir. William Blackstone addressed this issue of half-blood rights in his *Commentaries on the Laws of England* using the word "only." If one was "only" the heir's "brother of the half blood," the law clearly stated that "they shall never inherit to each other." The terms "right" blood and "worthiest" blood carried similarly negative connotations.[11] Half siblings in inheritance matters were clearly not the same as full-blood siblings. Stepsiblings were not even considered in the laws that addressed the rights of siblings to inherit from one another because they did not share a bloodline and consequently had no rights.

English legal tradition favored full-blood heirs. If the goal was to keep land within the bloodline of the original owner, the thinking was that an adult child should not leave family land to a half-blood sibling. The law came into play only when an unmarried and orphaned full-blood heir died without leaving a will outlining his desires. In such cases, property inherited from a parent descended to full siblings but not half siblings.[12] English inheritance law shunned half siblings, even when they shared the same father, in favor of full-blood siblings.[13] Blackstone reasoned that the purest blood relative should inherit because the founder of the family, in whose stead a parent stood, had obtained his land through service, usually provided to a king or lord, not purchase. Blackstone argued that "the true foedal reason for which rule was this; that what was given to a man, for his personal service and personal merit, ought not to descend to any but the heirs of his person."[14] Land earned through merit, therefore, should descend only to the full-blood relations of the original, meritorious owner. Blackstone elaborated: "The heir need not be the nearest kinsman absolutely, but . . . he must be the nearest kinsman of the whole blood." Even "if there be a much nearer kinsman of the half blood, a distant kinsman of the whole blood shall be admitted, and the other entirely excluded." This exclusion, Blackstone noted, "being almost peculiar to our own law, is looked upon as a strange hardship" by some.[15]

Although Blackstone generally agreed with the law, he was "impartial enough to own, that, in some instances, the practice is carried farther than the principle upon which it goes will warrant." He worried about the law's placement of an uncle ahead of a half-blood son and wondered why royal succession half siblings inherited from one another but commoners did not. England changed its half-blood provisions with the Inheritance Act of 1833, which was passed after the emerging manufacturing elite pushed for revisions of inheritance laws that had previously guaranteed the power of the landed gentry. Related reforms soon followed.[16]

Although Massachusetts was more forward-looking than the mother country in inheritance matters and had officially outlawed the ancient practice of primogeniture in 1692, it continued the feudal inheritance tradition designed to keep land within a particular bloodline by excluding half siblings from inheriting from full-blood heirs who died intestate. Primogeniture (the hereditary practice of leaving all ancestral land to the eldest son) and entail (a linked notion that limited the ability to sell family land) arose from a system designed to maintain landed, familial power. Like the half-blood provision, the goal was to keep land in the family. Oddly, in otherwise legally open-minded Massachusetts, the half-blood exclusion was continued and reinforced throughout the eighteenth century, remaining a part of state law until 1835.[17] One reason for this legal anomaly was the power of stepfamily prejudice and the assumption that affection followed along bloodlines in sibling relationships.

Prior to 1835, Massachusetts law concerning half-blood siblings was revisited multiple times, but each time the wording was merely clarified and the provision strengthened. John Adams recorded some of the often unspoken assumptions behind these debates. According to Adams, "The true Reason, the true Principle of Distribution, is this. The Law is to give, as the Intestate might reasonably be supposed willing to have given, his Estate in Case he had made a Will, and had not been surprised by a sudden Death." Given this reality, Adams reasoned, "Now, Is not the natural Love of a Person to his Brothers and sisters of the whole Blood, greater than that to Brothers and sisters of the half Blood, and must we not supposed a Mans Inclinations would be to bestow his Estate upon his whole Brothers and sisters in Preferences to his half Brothers and sisters?" Adams argued this point from what he considered a common cultural understanding: "I appeal to Experience, whether Brothers and sisters of the half Blood, have half so strong an affection for each other as Brothers and sisters of the whole Blood."[18]

Under the heading, "Blood. Whole Blood and half Blood," in Adams's legal papers, he noted that "a great Controversy" raged in midcentury Massachusetts. Some argued that "the half Blood shall have a whole share," while others believed that they should have "half a share." The "advocates for the half Blood" argued that the preference for full-blood siblings over

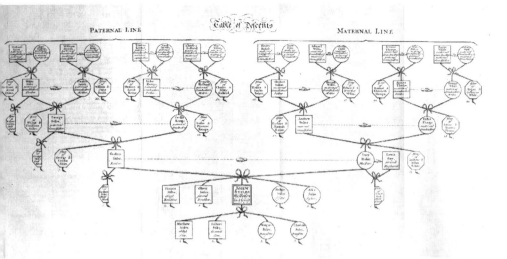

William Blackstone's view of a fictional stepfamily from the legal perspective. William Blackstone, *A Treatise on the Law of Descents in Fee-Simple* (Oxford: Clarendon, 1759), appendix. Courtesy of the Linda Lear Center for Special Collections and Archives, Connecticut College, New London.

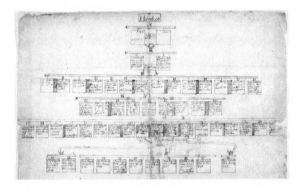

A stepfamily from an eighteenth-century child's perspective. John Holyoke, Genealogy of the Family of the Holyokes, October 1746. Courtesy of the Phillips Library at the Peabody Essex Museum, Salem, Mass.

half-blood siblings was simply a "maxim of Law"—in other words, derived from legal custom, presumably English legal custom—and that "a Brother of the half Blood is a Brother to the Intestate, as well as one of the whole Blood, and therefore should have an equall share." Adams was apparently not convinced, asking rhetorically, "Is a Brother or sister of the half Blood, in the same Relation with a Brother or sister of the whole Blood?" His answer: "I think not." Adams had no personal experience with stepfamily life but assumed that "grudges and Miffs and Misunderstandings between the second Crop of Children and the first" were the norm.[19]

Like Adams, Blackstone suggested in his discussion of the hereditary rights associated with the Founders of All Souls College at Oxford that affection followed blood: "A decent and reasonable Regard will be paid to the FOUNDER's Blood, so far as his Affection may be supposed to reach, and no farther." He continued, "Affection and Regard for his *real* Kindred: And these Motives we must suppose to be greater or less, in proportion to the Nearness to, or Distance from him."[20] Blackstone and Adams assumed that affection and blood were inexorably linked.

Blackstone outlined his thinking visually with the help of a fictional family, the Stileses, using bows, clasped hands, squares, octagons, and circles to illustrate his inheritance principles. In Blackstone's scheme, half siblings were represented by half symbols.[21] In 1746, twelve-year-old John Holyoke—a member of the Epes-Holyoke clan—constructed a similar chart that depicted the differences between familial behavior and legal expectation. Unlike Blackstone's bows, which could be untied, and hands, which could be unclasped, Holyoke used bricks, mortar, and hooks to depict solid, enduring bonds. Though Holyoke represented only his blood relations, his half siblings were visually indistinguishable from his full brothers and sisters. In Holyoke's view, his half siblings were as tightly bound to the family as his full siblings.[22]

Did blood ties determine the quality of sibling relationships? In legal practice did step and half siblings respond as Adams and others would predict? Did people think in terms of the worthiest blood? Looking closely at one Connecticut town suggests that the legal choices made by some stepfamilies (and to some extent by the courts) demonstrate a more complicated picture, following a pattern of flexibility and family survival rather than adherence to strict bloodline principles.

Saybrook was one of the first towns founded in what later became the colony of Connecticut, on the Long Island Sound at the mouth of the Connecticut River. It was unusual in that it tracked not only marriages but also remarriages. Using these records as well as other estate documents, I found 29 marriages (out of a total of 480) that clearly involved men who remarried and formed stepfamilies between 1647 and 1834. I was able to trace 19 of these men from marriage to death. The stories that emerge from these stepfamilies demonstrate that more than blood relationship motivated the brothers and sisters in these families.[23]

When Peabody Grinell (also spelled Paybody Greenell, Grenell, Grinel, and Grinnell) died in 1767, he did not leave a will, forcing the court to choose an administrator. The task commonly went to the deceased's eldest son, to his widow, or to both, but in this case, the court named the oldest son from each of Grinell's two marriages to work together to inventory and distribute their father's estate. Surviving documents indicate that they did a thorough job, completing their task within the allotted time, and that the court assumed that they would do so.[24]

In the Kirtland stepfamily, brothers of all kinds worked together to provide for their stepmother. Nathaniel Kirtland had three marriages prior to his death in 1750. His first wife, Sarah, and their only child died soon after their marriage. Nathaniel and his second wife, Phebe, had nine children, while he and his third wife, Elizabeth, had two more. Nathaniel's will awarded Elizabeth a portion of the family enterprise, part of the farm, part of the house and its contents, and produce from the farm—a common arrangement for a widow in a farming community. Nathaniel directed that his eldest son would share the house with his stepmother and would be responsible for providing for her. If he refused, his two full brothers from the marriage to Phebe would take on the task. In other words, along with possession of the farm went responsibility for a stepmother. Though the law required children to support their parents so that they would not become public charges, stepchildren had no such obligation. But Nathaniel wanted his sons to care for their stepmother.[25]

When Thomas Merrill died intestate in 1711, all of the siblings in his stepfamily cooperated to help out their mother/stepmother. His widow and his eldest son from a previous marriage settled the estate, submitting a joint bill for their care of the family farm from his death until the estate was settled—perhaps an indicator that both were living in the family house, as in the case of the Kirtland family. In addition "the widdow and children have [unani]monimosly agreed" to set aside some money to help raise the widow's two-year-old daughter by Merrill. Merrill's children wanted to care for their youngest sibling even though she was not a full-blood relation.[26]

Finally, Thomas Silliman's children agreed to provide their mother/stepmother with an annuity of four dollars a year (equivalent to less than one hundred dollars today) in exchange for her share of their father's real estate. Since Silliman was ninety-one when he died, his widow was likely also quite elderly, and a predictable payment, rather than running a farm, probably suited her circumstances. Moreover, since she only had a life estate in the farm, it would have reverted to the children at her death, so this arrangement meant that they received their inheritance early, while she received a generous settlement that provided her more than the law required.[27]

These stories of cooperation and accommodation undermine the notion that stepfamilies worked as a strict hierarchy based on blood, as the law assumed. The legal focus on half-blood rights and expectations of conflict did not predict these kinds of outcomes, nor were such legalisms reflected in the period's stories of fictional and nonfictional stepfamilies. These accounts suggest that blood relationship was just one of the predictors of sibling interactions. In fact, these accounts often assumed that siblings did—or at least should—cooperate across bloodlines, with some stepsiblings acting as surrogate parents to younger children and even compensating for poor parenting.[28]

In an 1815 story, *The Sisters: A Domestic Tale*, a girl cares for her two younger half sisters to compensate for their mother's poor parenting. When Olivia's mother dies, her father marries a much younger woman in an attempt to produce a male heir for his estate. The stepmother soon gives birth to a daughter but does "not devote any of her time and attention" to the child, behavior that "greatly displeased her husband, who had been used to see such very different manners adopted by his late wife toward her offspring." After the stepmother bears another girl, her parenting does not improve: "She was not only extravagant, but selfish to the greatest degree, as most extravagant people are," and she spends her husband's fortune on her social climbing. Olivia steps in, helping to care for and educate the younger girls by providing "constant care and affectionate vigilance." "Being ever on the spot, and influenced by the most tender regard, and the most conscientious motives [Olivia] operated as a shield to their young minds, and prevented at least a considerable portion of the bad effects taking place which might have been expected." Olivia eventually leaves home, in part to secure her half sisters a home away from their mother's bad influence, and their father considers hiring a governess, but the younger girls pine for her and complain, "Will the governess take us to see poor people, and explain the Bible to us, and tell us stories about good people, and pray with us, as Olivia does? and can we love her as well papa? will she be as patient, and as kind?" In the end, the girls go to live with Olivia, who raises them to become lovely and virtuous women, and they marry well.[29]

The sibling bond also makes up for poor parenting in "Duncan Campbell," a story by Scottish writer James Hogg. Although originally published as part of his *Winter Evening Tales: Collected among the Cottagers in the South of Scotland*, the story was also available in the United States and was widely serialized in the press. The title character is long-lost son who returns to care for his elderly father, countering the presence of a cruel stepmother and winning over a half sister. The stepmother, a former maid, has taught the girl to mock her father's age and infirmity, but Duncan arrives, dethrones the stepmother, and takes up the parental mantel. Though the stepmother weeps bitter tears, the girl is thrilled: "Contrary to what might have been expected, Duncan's pretty, only sister Alexia rejoiced most of all in his discovery. She was almost wild with joy at finding such a brother."[30]

In "The Cinderella Story," a stepbrother thwarts his own mother's wishes to protect his stepsister. The sight of the girl scrubbing the front stoop while his full sisters entertain in the parlor moves him to appeal not to his mother but to his status-conscious stepfather, pointing out that gossiping neighbors might mistake his stepsister for "a hired scullion." Stung by these rumors if not moved by his daughter's plight, the man puts an end to his wife's abuse. Later, however, the wicked stepmother convinces her husband to whip the girl, and again, the stepbrother comes to the rescue, declaring that he would "raise the cry of murder till he alarmed the whole neighborhood" to prevent her victimization.[31]

In an English child's tale, *The Step-Brothers*, two young stepbrothers parent one another. Philippe, naturally spoiled and ill-tempered, at first rejects his new stepmother and her son, Antoine, because Philippe's father has remarried without telling his son. Philippe finds his stepmother wanting compared to his dead mother: "And when I contrasted the coarse manners and person of my stepmother, with the remembrance of my own mother, who was so gentle and so amiable in every respect, my aversion to the former seemed to increase, while all my mother's excellence rose to my mind; and when I thought thereupon I wept." He and his stepmother are soon at war: "But if I hated my stepmother, she beheld me with equal share of dislike, and, by her disdainful manners, proved she had not forgotten the salutation she had received from me upon her bridal morning; and she found a thousand ways of making me feel her power, and rendering me miserable. I upbraided, but in vain. Incessant altercation took place between us. The house was filled with noise and contention." When asked by his father to welcome his new stepbrother, Philippe says, "Nothing should ever force me to acknowledge a stranger for my mother, nor the son of a stranger as my brother." In part, he hates his stepbrother because "like Cain . . . my heart was evil and his was good." Philippe tries to kill Antoine's dog but almost dies, and he is saved by the stepbrother and the dog. The rescue leaves Antoine sick, but the grateful Philippe nurses him back to health, and from his sickbed, Antoine entreats, "Philippe! dear Philippe weep no more. Forget that you have ever erred against me. Let us henceforth live as brothers—as though we both had been children of the same parents." When Antoine recovers and emerges from his sickroom, the stepbrothers enter the adjoining garden "in perfect love and confidence." Philippe goes to church with the pious Antoine, and during their absence, a tornado kills their parents, leaving them with only each other. Next comes a famine that results in Antoine's death, and the book ends with the loving and devastated Philippe at his brother's bedside, having conquered his evil nature to behave like a proper sibling.[32]

Representations of similar relationships can also be found in nonfiction sources. The well-known story of Benjamin Franklin as a runaway printer's apprentice began with an age-based rivalry between Benjamin and his older half brother, James—a tale so familiar that historians often omit the fact that the two were half rather than full brothers. Apprenticed to James, Benjamin felt that as James's brother, he deserved to be treated differently from the other boys working in the shop. According to Benjamin, "Though a brother, he considered himself as my master, and me as his apprentice, and accordingly, expected the same services from me as he would from another, while I thought he demean'd me too much in some he requir'd of me, who from a brother expected more indulgence." James, conversely, saw his role as older brother as including teaching the often "too vain" Benjamin a lesson about authority. Whenever Benjamin brought their disputes "before our father, . . . I fancy I was either generally in the right, or else a better pleader, because the judgment was generally in my favor." Nevertheless, when James Franklin landed in jail for criticizing the government in the *New England Courant*, Benjamin came to his defense, "notwithstanding our private differences." However, Benjamin also took advantage of James's absence to get his freedom. Recounting the story many years later, Benjamin acknowledged that his behavior was misdirected: "It was not fair in me to take this advantage, and this I therefore reckon one of the first errata of my life." James retaliated by discouraging other printers from hiring Benjamin, and even "my father now sid[ed] with my brother." Benjamin ultimately left Boston for New York and eventually Philadelphia, where the rest of his story is even more well known. But the incident reflects typical brotherly relations, with stepfamily dynamics only secondary in this drama.[33]

Revolutionary-era painter John Singleton Copley similarly took on the education of his half brother, albeit with less conflict. Copley's father died soon after his birth, and his mother, Mary (Singleton) Copley, remarried Peter Pelham, a talented engraver and producer of mezzotints from

John Singleton Copley's half brother, Henry Pelham, playing with his pet squirrel. John Singleton Copley, *Boy with a Squirrel* (Henry Pelham), 1765. Courtesy of the Museum of Fine Arts, Boston.

England, and bore him a son, Henry. Peter Pelham had two previous marriages and had five older children. Copley grew up in a two-room home with his mother, his stepfather, and his half brother. Peter Pelham died in 1751, when John was thirteen and Henry only two. Peter had nurtured John's talent, and the fact that his early portraits featured his adult stepbrothers seems to indicate that he was close to them as well. In 1760, Copley painted his half brother, Henry, holding up his head with his hand as he reads by dim candlelight. Four years later, Copley produced another portrait of Henry, this time with a pet squirrel. This finely crafted painting was exhibited in England in 1766 and received great acclaim, helping to make Copley's name as a painter. Copley's paintings demonstrated his pride in and love for his brothers, and he eventually shepherded Henry into a successful career as a painter as well.[34]

Copley frequently sent advice to Henry, affectionately known as Harry. In a letter written in July 1775, during the run-up to the American Revolution, Copley warned, "I would here renew my instructions to Harry not to suffer himself, for any person, or on any account whatever, to take part in the present dispute. I doubt not he will comply with my wishes." Copley's stepbrother, Peter Pelham Jr., acknowledged the quality of the painter's brotherly care of Henry when he wrote, "Please to remember me to your ingenious little Brother Harry whom I expect to see in a very respectable situation of Life by and by, owing to your great Care and Brotherly Love." And in another letter, Copley reflected that Henry "will always find in me a friend as Dear as his most sanguine wishes can suggest ever ready to do every thing for him, for he is very Dear to me."[35] Copley was thus like a father to his half brother.

Minister and loyalist Mather Byles, who went on to become the patriarch of his own successful stepfamily, cared well for his own half sisters. With the outbreak of the American Revolution, Mather Byles fled to Halifax, Nova Scotia, far from his aging father and two half sisters, Catherine and Mary, who remained in Boston. Throughout their separation, Mather Byles and his half sisters exchanged long, loving letters. When he arrived in Nova Scotia despondent and bereft, they sent him a lock of their father's hair as well as news and entertaining poems. When he wrote a detailed account of his struggle with kidney stones, they consoled him and sent him their cure, blackberry jelly. And when their father died in 1788 and Catherine and Mary wanted specific items from his estate, and Mather assured them that he would cooperate: "Rest satisfied, my dear Sisters, that in the Settlement of our Fathers Estate I have no Interest distinct from your's. Let us convince the World, by our Example, that such Matters may be easily accommodated upon the plain Principles of Equity, Candor, & mutual confidence: & Nothing, in my Opinion, can be plainer than this; that 'it would be highly unjust to blend the personal Property of our two Mothers with that of our Father.'" In addition, on at least two occasions, he asked his half sisters to come live with him. In October 1789, he wrote, "And now, my dear

Sisters, my Thoughts naturally turn to you. Happy myself, I would fain be an instrument of making you so. Inform me, what are your Circumstances, your Plans, & your Prospects? Do you wish to remain in Boston? or had you rather remove to me? Be free Agents: consult your own Interest & Inclinations: & tell me, without Reserve, what you wish, & in what Manner I can most effectually serve you. Remember, that I am your Brother, your only Brother, that I love you tenderly; that I am particularly grateful to you for your exemplary Attention to our departed Parent: & best satisfied that the fullest Confidence in me will not be abused. . . . I mention no Plan for you, because I had much rather you should plan for yourself."[36] The fact that Catherine and Mary were the children of a different mother clearly did not diminish the strength of Mather's feelings for them.

Older sisters, too, could act as surrogate parents. In 1817, twenty-year-old Amelia Russell, from Mendon, Massachusetts, traveled through Europe with her father, Jonathan Russell, and stepmother, Lydia (Smith) Russell. While there, Lydia gave birth to Amelia's half sister, Ida. Amelia was excited about the new arrival, writing to a friend beforehand, "In the course of two months I hope to have a little sister or brother to play with," and subsequently enthusing to a cousin, "I have now a sweet little sister to nurse & I am very fond of it. She is the prettiest & best child I ever saw & I am sure you will love her very much when you see her." When Lydia Russell had difficulty with her milk supply and needed to bottle-feed the baby, Amelia did what she could to help, carrying "Ida's little bottle of milk in her bosom" to keep it warm. Many years later, Amelia's nieces and nephews recalled that "her step-sisters and brother became as dear to her as her very own. She was a second mother to them when they were children."[37]

Such mothering by an older sister, as with the surrogate fathering of James Franklin, was at times unwelcome. Maria Pearson, known as Mary, helped her stepmother care for her half brothers and sisters, with mixed results. After the death of Priscilla (Holyoke) Pearson in 1782, Mary's father, Eliphalet Pearson, a professor at Harvard and later president of Philips Academy, found himself a widower with an infant daughter. In 1785, he married Sarah Bromfield, with whom he had four additional children, Sarah, Edward, Margaret, and Henry. Mary often acted as an assistant to her stepmother, and the settling of Eliphalet's estate after his death exposed Henry Pearson's resentment about his half sister's attempts at mothering him and created a breach in the family that did not reflect bloodlines. As an adult, Henry claimed that his "sister in law" had acted cruelly when he was a child, treating him like a "stepmother . . . in its most strict sense." Henry claimed to have forgiven Mary because he now understood that "her native narrowness and confined sense of duty" had been the problem. "But to forget is one a thing I cannot do; and therefore while 'memory holds a seal' in my forme, (unless indeed the *constitutional* pillars of my mind should be thrown down) I shall remember only to regret the lasting injuries done in my infancy." He had no doubt that her "native & nurtured pride" might lead her to "spurn my forgiveness."[38]

But Henry also criticized his full-blood siblings, maligning Margaret and Edward for what he saw as their mishandling of their father's estate. He excoriated Margaret, "How could you be so foolishly affectionate to [Edward's] weakness, so unjust to us all, & how could yr husband be so blind as to give yr written approbation to accounts which were at war with the plainest principles of common sense. I forgive *you* as a woman—for what do you know of settling Estates; but yr husband shd. have had the sense to examine." Margaret responded to this letter by writing to Mary, wondering "what is to be done about H[enry]." Thus, the rift did not pit full-blood siblings against half siblings but a troublesome member of the family against the others. Mary remained close to her other half siblings and served as the caretaker for her aging stepmother. Though as a married woman she could not write a will, on her deathbed, she asked her husband, Ephraim Abbott, to watch out for Edward. According to a document Abbott drafted, Mary "in the time of her last sickness expressed to me a wish, that in case her Brother Edward Augustus Pearson should ever be in such circumstances as as [*sic*] to need the assistance, which a life annuity would afford him, and should need the same more than myself should at the time want it, I should purchase for him a life annuity worth one Thousand dollars." In 1822, Abbott complied with Mary's wishes.[39]

Stepsiblings and half siblings often called each other brothers and sister, perhaps because in most ways they were. Despite the cultural expectations embedded in legal constructions of familial relationships, the ways that people used the law reflected more flexibility. Literature, too, offered representations of stepsibling relationships involving cooperation and affection that counteracted popular prejudice. Thus, in practice, stepsiblings' interactions looked very much like those among full-blood sisters and brothers.

CHAPTER SIX

Reforming Stepfamilies

The step-mother, if she performs her duty, is a *gem* in the casket of human souls.—Maria Jane Agard, "The Step-Mother's Reward," 1847

There are hearts that feel for them.—Isaac, "The Good Step-Mother," 1846

Catharine Maria Sedgwick recorded in her memoir the pleasure she had derived from reading when she was a child. Her favorite was Arnaud Berquin's *The Children's Friend*, which made such an impression on the girl that even half a century later, she could "remember the form and shade of color of the book, the green edges of the leaves, the look of my favorite pages." The collection included a children's play, "The Parental Stepmother," in which a new stepson gradually realizes that his prejudice against stepmothers has little to do with his own stepmother. Before meeting her, he laments, "I have indeed a mother; but a mother, as they say, in-law; and that, as I am told, is just as much as if one were to say, a cruel mother." Once they make each other's acquaintance, however, his real stepmother speaks soothingly to the still mourning child: "I wish I were but able to restore [your mother] to you; which I cannot do, and therefore I will take her place, poor little fellow, in your bosom. I will love you as she did, and will be a mother to you." By the end of the play, the stepson is convinced of her sincerity. "She received me with the greatest kindness, and had so agreeable a countenance, she cannot be ill-temper'd. I perceived even by her tone of voice, I should be easily induced to love her."[1] But Catharine had very different experiences with her own stepmother.

Amelia Russell, in contrast, likely read *Little Goody Two Shoes*, another story featuring a good stepmother, with her own beloved stepmother. One of the most popular children's tales in England and America, *Little Goody Two Shoes* features the story of an orphan girl who freed herself from homelessness through teaching. She lives an admirable life and is rewarded with marriage to a widower, which not only relieves her of the necessity of paid work but also makes her a stepmother. At first, her suitor "had conceived such an high Opinion of her, that he offered her a considerable Sum to take the Care of his Family, and the Education of his Daughter, which, however, she refused." He later becomes ill and asks again for her assistance; this time, she comes to the aid of the motherless family "and behaved so prudently in the Family, and so tenderly to him and his Daughter, that he would not permit her to leave his House, but soon after made her Proposals of Marriage." She carefully considers the needs of her future stepdaughter as she mulls over her future: "She was truly sensible of the Honour he intended her, but, though poor, she would not consent to be made a Lady, till he had effectually provided for his Daughter; for she told him, that Power was a dangerous Thing to be trusted with, and that a good Man or Woman would never throw themselves into the Road of Temptation." She wants her stepdaughter's considerable estate to be safe from misuse, including her own. With such actions, she demonstrates that she is a selfless and good stepmother.[2]

Amelia Russell's stepmother, Lydia (Smith) Russell, may have wanted Amelia to see her in the same light. While traveling in Europe in 1818, when Amelia was twenty, the two women visited a copper mine, donning trousers for the occasion. Lydia declared that the outfit made Amelia look "so much like *Goody Two-Shoes*." They may have been familiar with an 1811 edition of the tale whose frontispiece featured an illustration of a young person in trousers.[3] If Lydia Russell's goal was to portray herself as a good stepmother and forge a strong bond with her husband's daughter, she succeeded: the two became lifelong friends.

A new potential for stepmother kindness and even love emerged in children's books and maternal literature on both sides of the Atlantic at the turn of the nineteenth century and continued as a theme in periodical literature over the next half century.[4] The authors of these stories proposed that stepmothers were not innately cruel but rather suffered under the weight of cultural prejudice. The solution to this social problem was both to enlighten the broader community and to teach stepmothers as well as stepchildren how to behave—as one author put it, "The remedy is, for both parties to become better women and children."[5] In this view, women and children, not fathers, needed to bear responsibility for maintaining a peaceful and loving home. According to one article, "The Christian Step-Mother," a father "loved his children, but to his business he gave his best thoughts and his chief concern; returning to his family, he came home, to be relieved of care and to be made happy; he then wished to see his children bright and joyful around him." Even in this stepmother-run home, "peace, sweet peace must be dear to every family. What renders heaven so delightful and desirable a place is, the love and harmony that reigns there. No discordant note is heard there, no selfish enjoyment known, and the domestic circle should be an emblem of the love and harmony of heaven."[6] If stepmothers and stepchildren could be taught to behave properly, stepfamily homes would be heavenly. A man assured of domestic tranquility would be free to pursue the middle-class imperative of providing an appropriate income for his family. A loving wife and loving stepmother could provide the trappings of domestic life that guaranteed their class status. And the children/stepchildren could demonstrate both parents' success.[7]

These writers believed that wicked stepmothers could and indeed must be reformed. This didactic literature presented a new version of stepmotherhood designed to counter the popular view that all stepmothers were cruel mothers. If women and their children heeded this advice, they might believe that stepmothers could evolve into loving mothers. This literature provided a cultural space in which stepmothers could become the "new mothers" that widowers were supposed to find for their children. This change occurred in part as a result of the religious revivalism of antebellum America, dubbed the Second Great Awakening. This movement stressed the importance not only of emotional religion but also of personal transformation. Sinners could become saints; people were no longer predestined to be one or the other. Many of the writers of this new literature promoting good stepmothers wrote from this religious perspective. Instead of casting stepmothers as at best shadows of their predecessors, these authors argued that God's grace could enable stepmothers to transform themselves into real mothers.[8]

The middle-class imperative to have a successful family life also played a role in forcing the reconsideration of stepmothers.[9] If death made a family motherless, how was a widower with children to proceed? One author explained that as a "man of business," a middle-class father could not take on the daily care of children.[10] But leaving children in the care of hired help or relatives placed them at risk. The father in one story was "afraid his motherless babies should be neglected or hurt."[11] In another tale, the author explained that "governesses, teachers, and nurses" naturally had "home ties and affections, far warmer and dearer than any they can form for the children committed to their care." And an unmarried "female relative" would be inexperienced and therefore "seldom a fit guardian or guide," while "the chances are very great that" a married relative "has interests infinitely more clashing than those of the step-mother."[12] The father in one story remarried after realizing that neither his fourteen-year-old daughter nor a "mercenary hireling" could solve his domestic problems.[13] In another instance, a father allowed his eldest daughter to take "the care of the infant, and the oversee-ing of the other little ones, which was too much for her delicate constitu-tion, and she was prostrated under it." Her near death forced him "though reluctantly, to look about him for another companion."[14] Only a "respectable female at the head of his family, who would have a legal right to preside, and control" could foster the best "interests of his children."[15] A widower, therefore, had to remarry and had to find the right woman. What was new in this literature was his potential for success. A stepmother now could be the right woman for the job.

One author explained that the "cruel cause" for the "unhappiness" of families with stepmothers was the "prejudice of the world against" them. In fact "in all the departments for improvement and reform I do not know of one more important and that is actually suffering for the want of a re-form more than this. I have been in hopes that some persons capable of doing justice to the subject would show to the public mind that there is an interest felt upon the subject, and endeavor to bring about a reform." This writer was convinced that "a vast amount of good . . . will be the re-sult, if the public mind can be made to view the step-mother in her true light." Without some sort of change, "as soon as she enters upon her new task," prejudice would "destroy the good influence that she would have in her family, and in due time this object is accomplished—the children are set against the mother, and the mother against the children, and then it is almost out of her power to do anything for them aright." If prejudices were conquered, however, these families could improve themselves.[16] Although one author admitted that in the absence of a biological mother, "no second bond of affection can be quite so strong and pure; but surely for this reason it is folly to reject that which must in the nearest degree replace it."[17] After all, "the family needs a new head, for the honor, the comfort, the inter-est, and the spiritual welfare of all the household." The good stepmother had the potential to occupy "the important and difficult place that God has made empty."[18] If well chosen, a stepmother made "the home of the bereaved family smile once more,—as she takes the motherless children to her bosom, who have scattered among strangers, and bid them confide in her, and rejoice again in a mother's love—as she soothes their sorrows, and restrains their waywardness."[19] In short, a good stepmother could heal a broken family.

RETRAINING STEPCHILDREN

These new ideas appeared first in children's books. Literature written specifically for the young was a new genre on both sides of the Atlantic at the end of the eighteenth century. Although the first American publication of this kind appeared in 1787, European children's stories, like Catharine Maria Sedgwick's favorite, had been available since midcentury. Fairy tales, didactic literature, etiquette books, and more began to fill the shelves of middle-class children.[20] Along with the proliferation of children's literature, most of which espoused traditional notions of stepfamily life, came a new genre of material on happy families with stepmothers.

In one early English example, *The Good Stepmother* (1797), "prejudice" is overcome despite the difficulty of the task. The story was part of the Cheap Repository Series, which offered inexpensive paperbound books, or chapbooks, and had remarkable success in England and was soon available in the former English colonies. *The Good Stepmother* tells the story of a sincere and hardworking stepmother who overcomes society's prejudices through unflagging attention to the needs of her stepchildren. The tale begins with a young widower's search for "a notable good-tempered woman, who would become a second mother to his children." He finds a woman eager to make herself "useful" by giving his motherless children the care they deserve. The man's eldest daughter poses the main challenge. The girl is "untractable" because of the "prejudices she had imbibed from some weak meddling people" who have assured her that she will receive "ill treatment" at the hands of a stepmother "and such stuff, equally unjust and absurd." This eight-year-old even convinces her brother and sister that "their father's wife" is their "greatest enemy."[21]

The tide turns when the family patriarch dies. The new widow is encouraged to relinquish her parental responsibilities by giving her orphaned stepchildren to the parish. Her friends remind her that "one pair of hands" could not possibly "feed so many mouths" and that her "husband's children" had no right "to look up to you for support." Nonetheless, this good stepmother vows to "try first" to see what she can "do for all my little flock," including both her own children and her stepchildren. She becomes a seamstress and uses some of her earnings to set up her stepson in business, forgoing her own children's education. He repays her kindness by paying for his half-siblings' education, and even the recalcitrant stepdaughter comes forward to support the woman in her old age. As her stepson, William, explains, "He thought it a very lucky thing for children who had lost an own mother to have a good stepmother."[22]

Another English publication about a good stepmother that crossed the Atlantic was *Mrs. Leicester's School; or, The History of Several Young Ladies, Related by Themselves* (1809), which contained a series of vignettes about fictional boarding school students, including "Father's Wedding Day." In this faux autobiographical account, a good stepmother battles the prejudice her young stepdaughter has imbibed, in part by allowing the girl the opportunity to remember and honor her dead mother. The bereaved father has preserved his wife's memory by locking the door of her former sickroom, and his young daughter keeps a vigil outside the door, looking through the keyhole at where her mother had lain and "thinking of my mamma, and trying to remember exactly how she used to look." At first, the girl is looking forward to her father's wedding, since he conveys the news of his impending remarriage "with such pleasure in his looks, that I thought it must be a very fine thing indeed to have a new mamma," and she convinces herself that her new stepmother will even look like her mother. When the newlyweds arrive and her father joyfully announces, "Here is your new mamma," the girl bursts into tears: "I remembered my mamma was very pale; she had bright black eyes, my mother's were mild blue eyes; and that instead of the wrapping gown and close cap in which I remembered my mama, she was dressed in all her bridal decorations." Rather than being disheartened, however, the stepmother responds appropriately, opening the locked room despite the protests of the household. A childhood friend of her predecessor, the stepmother honors the dead woman's memory by telling "stories of mamma when she was a little girl no bigger than me." The girl and her stepmother become close, and the story ends with the stepmother announcing to her astonished husband that his daughter "has promised to love me, and she says, too, that she will call me 'mamma.'" The enthusiastic girl chimes in, "Yes, I will,—mamma, mamma, mamma." The woman has thus succeeded in what one author dubbed the "delicate duties" of a stepmother.[23]

Mary Pilkington's *Mentorial Tales* (1802) included "The Amiable Mother-in-Law; or, Prejudice Subdued." In Pilkington's view, "Of all the antipathies natural to childhood, that against *mothers-in-law*, in general, is the most forcibly imprest; and the little tongue, that scarcely can lisp in broken accents, is taught to express its hatred of the name." In this story, a widower chooses for his next wife a family friend and "a great favourite" of one of the daughters. Unfortunately, however, "from the moment that one of the daughters lost her amiable parent," the girl's caretaker gives "the account of stepmothers' cruelty" so that "her infant mind imperceptibly became prejudiced against the character, long before she knew what the word prejudice could mean." In fact, "the very sound of mother-in-law excited in her bosom a sensation bordering on contempt and hate." This good stepmother "pitied" the girl but "blamed" the caretaker for filling her head with such ideas and fires the guilty domestic despite her stepdaughter's protests because the caretaker's "prejudices were too strong to be easily eradicated, and therefore it was necessary she should be removed from her place." The woman's ignorance "prevented her mind from being improved, and prejudice has supplied the place of experience, and taught her to indulge opinions, which the liberal and intelligent must despise." The stepmother then begins the hard but ultimately successful work of subduing her stepchild's prejudice. Pilkington hoped that "those young persons who have unfortunately been prejudiced" against stepmothers could learn from this cautionary tale.[24]

In addition to such reprints of English texts, the idea of a good stepmother appeared independently in children's periodicals all over the United States as well as Canada and England. The core problem of "prejudice" and the idea of a stepmother as a new mother dominated these didactic tales. In "My Good Step-Mother" (1843), the author explained that "children should always try to love and respect such a one, because she assumes great responsibility, and has many trying and arduous duties to perform; and she requires much grace and patience."[25] In "The Good Step-Mother" (1848), a maternal aunt told her sister's replacement, "Receive my thanks, in the name of my departed sister, for all the good you have done her children. Who can reward you for the love you have shown these forsaken orphans? God only, and he will do it; and when you reach the next world, my sister will thank you for the maternal faithfulness, with which her children have been blessed through you."[26]

The central issue that interfered with good stepmother-stepchild relations as depicted in these magazines, as in children's books, was stepmother prejudice. The author of "The Stepmother; or, Prejudice Vanquished" (1838) opened with an anonymous quotation, "He who loosens a single link of the chains of prejudice, that great enslaver of the mind, has not written in vain," and went on to parallel stepmother prejudice with abolitionist rhetoric. Stepmothers, too, were chained, though not literally but by cultural perception. The young girl in this tale grows under the parental care of her stepmother, so that she "experienced only an accession of happiness; the object of unceasing care and judicious kindness." Not until she is twelve does the girl learn that the woman she considers her mother is in fact her stepmother. She is brought to her mother's grave, and her father explains his reasons for keeping her in the dark: "The common observations of servants, 'She is not your own mother, or such things would not be,' haunted me, and I was anxious to prevent your imbibing opinions which have so often been the bane of domestic peace; and which have caused the most generous and forbearing step-mothers to be weighed in the balance of prejudice, and found wanting." He believes that after a child is exposed to such thinking, the effects are difficult to undo: "Where once an early bias has been received, and the mental vision has been distorted, it is vain to hope that actions and opinions, the result of sound judgment and warm feelings, can be viewed in their true light." By waiting until the girl is older to reveal her status as a stepchild, the father hoped that she would bond with her stepmother, a strategy that seems to have worked.[27]

In Sophia S. Harrington's "The Stepdaughter" (1847), the girl in question, Helen Marshall, has already heard tales about wicked stepmothers and expects the worst when her father remarries. After learning of her father's impending wedding, she turns to her mother's sister and exclaims, "in a half-angry tone, 'Aunt Catherine, what do you think? Father is going to be married?'" Helen is shocked when her aunt replies, "I am very glad to hear it," explaining that she believes that the father is being "kind enough to supply you the loss of your own mother, by giving you another." When Helen protests that no one "could take the place of my own dear mother," Catherine cautions her to change her perspective: "Well, my love, instead of looking upon your father's wife as a stepmother, who will make you unhappy by thwarting your wishes, and controlling your actions, think of her as one who stands in your mother's place to you; who will teach you to fulfil your duties, and endeavor to make you what you should be, as a daughter, sister, and a disciple of Christ; in short, a true woman." The aunt then closely questions Helen to determine "who has been putting such ideas in your head about stepmothers." A friend has told the girl that "I might as well give up at once, if I was to have a stepmother; for there would be no more peace or happiness for me, and I had better set up my will in the beginning, and let her know she was not going to queen it over me." Catherine explains that Helen should "control" her "temper"; otherwise, "when your mother feels obliged to exercise authority, you may sometimes think that she has no right to deny your wishes." But Helen's "gentle stepmother" soon wins over her charge, and Helen declares, "I love you."[28]

In these stories, stepchildren often learn their prejudice from the tales of other stepchildren. At a comfortable family breakfast table, one boy explains to his stepmother that he and his brother had thought that all stepmothers were "cross and disagreeable" because one of their friends had a stepmother who was "cross to him, and gave him no peace of his life." After a man makes an analogy to an apple—just because one is bad does not mean that all are sour—the boy feels foolish. The man encourages him "to go and act like a boy of sense, and one that loved his father," by treating his stepmother with respect and kindness. And so the boy and his brother realize that their original ideas were silly, and they now love their stepmother.[29]

In "The Step-Mother.—Fear and Love" (1846), a stepson overcomes the prejudice of his companions by comparing his good stepmother to popular ideas about stepmother cruelty. The issue comes to the fore when he asks permission to go collect nuts with his friends and his stepmother kindly but firmly tells him no. His friends encourage him to ignore her wishes based on their own prejudice against stepmothers. "Won't let you! just as ugly as all mother's-in-law!," says one boy. Another claims, "I would not mind her, she is not your mother." Emboldened, the boy goes with his friends, but his conscience bothers him, whispering, "Has she not a mother's care and a mother's *love* for you?" When he returns home, the house is empty, and alone in the garden, he resolves to change his ways: "She is my mother, the boys shan't call her ugly; she loves me, she wants me to be good; I will mind her, I will; I hope she won't die like my other mother; O, I wish I had minded her, she *is* my mother."[30]

These stories depicted stepmothers as the best replacements for dead mothers. In "The Good Stepmother," the children are initially cared for by a servant, who is "unfriendly, scolded them when they made mistakes, and with a heavy hand punished them severely, when they sought to [do] any thing in self-defense. As for their cleanliness she cared little, and they often went, uncombed and unwashed, and with their finger nails uncut. Their clothes, which they had from their mother, were dirty and torn, and the servant did not see to their being washed or mended." It was clear to all "that they have no longer any mother." This treatment soon made them "unlovely toward each other, and [they] quarrelled continually." Their father saw their decline and "was sad, but could not alter it, for his business took so much of his time, that he could not possibly devote as much to his children as they required." The proper solution was to replace his dead wife with a new mother for his children. When he tells them, "My dear children, you will become quite spoiled; if you always remain without a mother; I must find you one," the children are relieved: they "fell upon his neck, and kissed him, and begged that he would do so, and so he did." He found a "young, friendly woman" who promised the children, "I will try to do for you, all that your good mother used to do."[31]

In "My Good Stepmother," the author suggests that a mother's dying prayer to preserve her children can be answered by a stepmother. One child declares, "The prayers of our departed mother were answered, inasmuch as God provided another kind mother for us." Explains the author, "I must tell my little readers that this is what is termed a *step-mother*. Children can best understand the meaning of this term, when I tell them it means her who steps in and takes the place of the one that is dead, and adopts the name of mother."[32]

RETRAINING STEPMOTHERS

These kinds of stories appeared also in early nineteenth-century adult periodicals, nearly half of which focused on moral reform.[33] By the middle part of the century, there was also a growing corpus of magazines aimed at women, in some cases with female writers and editors.[34] The increased number of literate women in the United States in this period also provided publishers with a previously untapped audience.[35] Women were praised for reading, especially useful texts that promoted the welfare of society and the family and the education of children.[36] Stepfamilies were not a common topic, but when the subject was addressed, authors overwhelmingly focused on the issue of stepmother prejudice and the need for reform. Such articles appeared in publications in all parts of the country and in major cities, smaller towns, and rural areas.[37]

Magazine authors were working in part to supplant advice books for mothers.[38] In addition, authors of periodical articles thought that stepmothers needed targeted advice for their unique circumstances. Two of the most well-known mothers' manuals—Lydia Maria Child's *The Mother's Book* and Catharine Beecher's *A Treatise on Domestic Economy: For the Use of Young Ladies at Home and at School*—provided mothers with information on the care and management of children but failed to focus on the unique challenges of stepmotherhood.[39] As the editor of *Mother's Journal and Family Visitant* put it in 1852, the "subject is one of vast importance, and challenges far more attention and sympathy than is usually bestowed upon it. As it is one properly belonging to the Mothers' Journal, we ask the attention of our readers to a few thoughts upon it."[40] Similarly, the author of "Trials of Step-Mothers" (1837) argued, "There is one class of mothers who would rejoice now and then to have a word of instruction, advice, and comfort, that seldom receive any in the numerous publications of the day; I mean, step-mothers."[41] The author of "Step-Mothers" acknowledged that such women "have reflected seriously on their duties [and] will of course seek every aid, and read every work designed for mothers, which [they] can procure"; nonetheless, "there are lessons important for [them] to learn, which a mother's book will not teach, and there are trials in [their] way which do not lie in the path of the natural mother."[42]

Many of these authors saw stepmothers as a "class of mothers," with some of the same "cares, solicitudes, and privations of the maternal lot" but often "shut out from sympathy, and regarded with a reproachful, a jealous, or, at best, a pitying eye."[43] As one author argued, these mothers deserved "as much aid and instruction as any other."[44] Another author focused on the plight of the desperate young stepmother riffling through a recently delivered "Magazine for Mothers," hoping to find some helpful advice: "Laying it aside with a dissatisfied, disappointed air," the stepmother asks, "Is there no one to give a word of advice, encouragement, or instruction to the class of mothers most of all needing it. . . . Public opinion, scandal, and even the press, are at all times ready to censure [stepmothers] for severity, unfaithfulness, or injudicious indulgence; but who will show them any good? Who measures their difficulties, regards their trials, guides their efforts?" Her needs are so overwhelming that as she speaks these words, her "lip quivered."[45]

Adult periodicals, like children's literature, followed some common patterns, focusing most prominently on prejudice but also on how women in general and stepmothers in particular could work to overcome cultural bias. Most focused on the difficulty of the task stepmothers were asked to perform, seeking to elicit sympathy for their traditionally unsympathetic subjects. These articles also emphasized the importance of becoming a new mother to motherless children without eradicating the memory of a predecessor.

STEPMOTHER PREJUDICE

According to the author of one piece, although the word "stepmother" "has indeed become proverbial, to mark an association in which one party is the victim of the other," in fact, "there is no small absurdity in presuming a necessary character in every person who enters into a particular relation in life."[46] Another claimed that stepmothers were unfairly judged: "While a mother is living, few people take the trouble to observe whether she is judicious or injudicious in her management, or to assist her in her toils by recommending to her notice suitable reading; but the moment her place is filled by another, all eyes are ready to observe, and many tongues ready to condemn on the slightest occasion."[47]

A stepmother's family could act as a buttress against this cultural onslaught, but turning to her stepchildren to find "unprejudiced minds" might also result in "disappointment." Prejudice clouded their perspective and prepared them for the worst. They likely had already heard that a stepmother "must be a usurper and a tyrant." Prepared "with an independence and self-confidence worthy of military heroes, they . . . determined to resist the first attempts at oppression."[48] Men could mitigate such behavior, since "it is, after all, in the power of a husband and a father, in a measure, to avert some of the evils, if not wholly prevent such outrages done to his family." In fact, like the famous patriarch of the Bible, "if he has self-respect, and will command his children and his household after him, as did faithful Abraham, it is believed that he can, more than any other human being, solace his wife under such oppressive wrongs, and prevent their future recurrence."[49] Nevertheless, many stepmothers continued to wrestle with heightened scrutiny and criticism even in their own homes.

And this cultural bias was firmly entrenched and had a long history: "From age to age, the poet and the novelist have excited the sympathies of their readers by portraying cruelties of the step-mother." One woman related that while teaching English history to her young stepson, she told the story of Elfrida, a queen who had her stepson killed to "procure the crown for her own son." Overhearing the lesson, the woman's older stepson remarked "in the presence of the other children, that it was very natural for a step-mother to do so." He later regretted his comment, but his first instinct was to repeat the accepted trope even in the presence of a stepmother who clearly did not fit the mold.[50] The author of "The Good Step-Mother" also acknowledged that "the step-mother has had an ill name with many from ancient poets down to modern ones." Nonetheless, she insisted, even among the "heathen families of Greece and Rome" were "bad mothers, as well as bad step-mothers."[51]

The editor of *Mothers' Journal and Family Visitant* outlined the contours of this unfair prejudice against stepmothers: "With very many, a stepmother is regarded as a kind of monster in human shape, devoid of even the common feelings of humanity; one who ruthlessly crowds herself into the sacred enclosure of a family, to do sacrilege to the tenderest ties, and whose presence is more to be dreaded than that of the grim messenger, who caused the vacancy there which she enters to occupy." The name of stepmother "means cold and heartless neglect, if not severe cruelty." At best, a step-mother was an "expedient" who might "mechanically perform the offices of wife and mother if carefully watched and guarded." Children were poisoned with these "strong prejudices" that were "instilled" into their minds and "grow with their growth."[52]

According to another author, "some of the crimes of which the persons whose case I am presenting, are presumed to be guilty" had an underlying explanation. What was frequently labeled "cruelty to children," for example, was the necessary but often painful need to provide discipline for stepchil-dren: the stepmother "occupies the place, she sustains the responsibilities, and she must perform the duties of the departed mother." Another typical accusation was that stepmothers lacked "interest in the future welfare of children," an impression often created by the newness of the stepmother's responsibilities: "Have we reasons to expect that inexperienced individuals would not shrink from the censure of the world, and hope to avoid it by leav-ing the children to their own course?" Although "jealousy of the merits of the departed mother" often arose from praising the dead mother at the ex-pense of the living one, "it is not well so to speak of the dead as to insinuate an undeserved censure upon the living." Stepmothers should ideally "cher-ish with delight the hope of meeting in heaven the mothers whose respon-sibilities, cares, and labors they have shared on earth." Even the "cold and suspicious treatment of the departed mother's relatives" might result from the biases of those relatives, who "withhold the confidence that should have been extended and reciprocated" to the new mother of the household.[53]

The "playmates" of one young child, already immersed in stepmother prejudice, warned a new stepchild about what she could expect from her new stepmother. "'Your father has got a new wife now,' said one, 'he will not be so fond of you as he was, I dare say.'" Another remarked, "'You will not have so many beautiful new frocks now, Miss.'" A third warned, "'Your mother-in-law will take you to task, Miss, if you tear your cloaths, you may depend upon it.'" This "prejudice" of her peers "took a deep and perma-nent root" in the heart of the new stepdaughter. She and her sister accord-ingly resented any attempt by their stepmother to control their behavior or discipline them. The older girl married a libertine, and the younger went to live with her sister and her new husband. When the husband literally tried to sell his sister-in-law's sexual services to the highest bidder, she ran home, where her father lectured, "I trust that now, divested of prejudice, you will acknowledge, that my wife has acted by you only as a judicious mother would by her child." The penitent stepdaughter admitted her error and hoped that her own children "should they live to be placed in similar circumstances, they will evince more humility and good sense than their mother."[54]

Prejudice could cause stepmother-family strife, creating "the very unhappiness that was apprehended."[55] One stepdaughter "knew how it would be, long before my father was married, and I made up my mind that I should not like his wife, the very first time I saw her." She had already learned the tropes of popular culture, having "heard a lady once say, she would rather a child of hers should be brought up in a convent, than by a step-mother." The girl resolves accordingly, "I would rather take the veil, or be a slave all the days of my life, than to live with one, if I could have my choice." But with proper training, this predisposition can be overcome. Two stepdaughters, one happy, and one still under the influence of popular opinion, listen to an older woman's tale of her recovery from stepmother prejudice. Her bias had caused her stepmother to become "distant and cold" and "divided" the family. Then her brother sickened, and their stepmother worked tirelessly to save him. Though she failed, he implored his sister with his last words to reconsider her feelings. The stepmother became ill soon thereafter, and this crisis caused the girl to repent, resulting at last in a "happy family." The reformed stepdaughter explains, "I had thought her unkind, because having enveloped myself in a mantle of selfishness and prejudice, she could gain no access to my heart. Once admitted there, she was ever afterward my friend and counselor, and my most intimate companion. I now *loved* her; and strove to make her happy—and so doing, effectually secured my own happiness."[56]

Similarly, in another story, the news arrived of a father's remarriage causing the two older daughters to lament that "the calamity we have dreaded of all others, should have at last come upon us,—that of having a step-mother." Echoing them, the youngest sister declares, "I will not love her. . . . she is naughty and wicked." She continues by announcing that she "will not sing to her, nor pick flowers for her, and she shall not hear me say my prayers at night." But when the disheartened stepmother sickens, she cries out deliriously, "To think I should have brought discord into your home!" The eldest daughter sees her distraught father and feels the weight of her guilt and nurses her stepmother back to health. When "she at length opened her eyes," her stepdaughter "imprinted a gentle kiss on her pale brow, and murmured softly, *mother*, for the first time." The sisters finally realize that "our unhappiness" the first few months after their father married "all arose from a foolish prejudice." They again had a "happy home" and "a mother's love."[57]

THE "DELICATE DUTIES"

With prejudice a huge impediment, a woman needed bravery, religious faith, and strength to do the hard work of replacing a mother. As one author explained to a would-be-stepmother, when "the appalling idea of 'stepmother' . . . presents itself" and the challenge is accepted, "it requires moral courage. It requires the exercise of all the Christian graces to enable you to perform the duties devolving upon you."[58] The diligent stepmother "knew she must bestow far more upon [children], than chance attention, or stray thoughts, or just the leisure she might steal from society and friends; they were duties to be studied, thought upon, prayed over, when she came in and when she went out, by the fireside and in the night watches." A good stepmother "wisely, skillfully, and earnestly" pursued her task.[59] One author urged stepmothers to "regard not the opinion of the world" but rather "press forward, my dear friend[s]."[60]

One woman wrote that she looked forward to the challenge of raising her stepchildren, even when a friend told her that the job would be harder than she thought and asked, "How *can* you marry that dull, prosy, old widower, with two children, too? You are getting yourself into business, I assure you?" But the difficulty of the task was part of its appeal for this selfless woman. She thought it the best of motives to want to "do good" to "poor children." Her stepchildren needed her, and she saw her marriage as a "providential circumstance." She taught her two stepchildren at home rather than sending them to school and reaped the reward of seeing them become happy, useful adults. Her stepson calmed his temper and became a minister. And with the woman as a kind companion to listen to her musings and encourage her, the brilliant but isolated stepdaughter became a well-known poet. This stepmother thus offered "an example for mothers."[61]

The hard work of raising children was especially difficult when the love and respect of one's charges was uncertain. Even the most sincere stepmother had trouble conjuring up the "natural affection for an own mother, which [children] cannot feel for another, however kind and faithful." Even if the family could afford servants, a stepmother and new wife still had a "laborious and anxious oversight of the household." "There must be many things done which hired help cannot do; and, how much is to be done, good mothers alone know." If "the family have no great income," the "stepmother must do the work of the household herself": "With her own hands she cooks, and scours; she washes, irons, and mends; she makes, alters, and adjusts [the children's] clothes. She attends them when sick, watches by them for many a weary hour of night. And she does this when she knows that her kindness cannot be received and appreciated as an own mother's would be."[62]

A good stepmother acted with "eminent disinterestedness" secure in the knowledge that she had "endeavoured to do her duty." And as a result, "in many cases, perhaps in most, she secures the esteem of those to whom she supplies a mother's place; and in some instances she is greatly loved, and kindly cared for."[63] The goal was selfless service. Although being a stepmother was "a trying office" when God calls "you to be a mother to a child not your own," obligations must be fulfilled with prayer and impartiality. A stepmother needed to act out of "moral obligation" if not instinct, "adopt[ing] the children of her husband as her own," learning their "characters" and "habits," and "secur[ing] their love and confidence." If she followed these precepts and looked to God for "wisdom," she would succeed. Above all, if "the mother of 'two sets' of children," she "must be as faithful toward the one as toward the other" to prevent division and strife: "He who has imposed them upon you, has given you no choice. You have no right to make any distinction." Ultimately, a family "divided against itself ... cannot stand."[64]

The stepmother's "duties are many and arduous."[65] Most people understood that "the situation of a mother-in-law is replete with care and responsibility."[66] A stepmother took on the task "without the authority of a mother, yet with all a mother's responsibility."[67] At the same time, "a family bereft of the mother is an object of pity, and she who consents to become the *wife*, does violence to the most tender relations and sacred obligations, if she refuses as completely to take the place of the *mother*."[68]

Authors of these good stepmother stories thought that stepmothers were more likely to err through overindulgence rather than punishment and cautioned that ignoring discipline could lead to additional problems: "The step-mother fears to use too much authority and restraint, and to put too much on the children under her care; and her indulgence nourishes that pride, willfulness and love of ease which are natural to the depraved heart; and consequently, her difficulties are greatly increased."[69] A "*good step-mother*" was not someone "who imposed upon them no restraint, and allows them every indulgence they ask." Some stepmothers "think this the most peaceable course, and that in no other way can they insure the love of the children, and the confidence of their friends." But such women were mistaken. The right course was to "guard with the same vigilance, control with the same firmness, and watch over" them "with the same untiring faithfulness" as would be devoted to her own children.[70] To win the love of stepchildren should not be her goal: "It is not so important for the child to love *you*, as for right habits and right principles to be inculcated."[71] One author advised, "Now is the time for you to decide upon the course you intend to pursue with the children. Require implicit obedience, and at all times maintain that calm and decisive manner which will convince them that you act from principle, and they will respect you." Understandably "you feel it a delicate subject to act upon. You have just entered the family. You fear . . . that you shall alienate the affections of the children." Nonetheless, a stepmother's duty, like a mother's duty, was to put the proper education of children ahead of the personal need for acceptance.[72]

Lacking the cultural authority that accompanied the role of mother, stepmothers had to work hard to take over child rearing. In addition, they had to display remarkable strength and courage in the face of social prejudice that predicted their failure.

THE DEAD MOTHER

Stepmothers needed to concern themselves not only with general social scrutiny but also with the ghostly presence of their predecessors. They needed to allow children to continue to love the memory of their natural mother while trying to take her place. This difficult task began with the initial meeting between a stepmother and her stepchildren. One author suggested that stepmothers acknowledge the feelings of their stepchildren by saying, "You had once a kind mother, whom, I doubt not you loved, very, *very* much. . . . You have indeed been very much afflicted. No loss can possibly be greater to a family of children than the loss of their mother." Only by paying such homage to their dead parent could stepmothers hope to find a place for themselves in children's hearts. The same author suggested that stepmothers also say, "I do not wish you ever so to love me as to forget your own dear mother; but I hope you will become attached to me by and by." Until such time, they should pledge to "try, by the grace of God, to be to you as a mother."[73] A good stepmother needed to take a mother's place without erasing her right to that place.

The body of a beloved dead mother is a physical presence in one story: "Mrs. Allston was not laid in the village churchyard, but was buried, at her own request, within an arbor, at the end of the garden." She had thought that "it would not seem that she was thrust out from her home, if the light from her own window shone out toward her grave; and that she half-believed the beloved voice of her husband, and the singing of her daughter, and the laughter of her children would come to her" in the garden, surrounded by the flowers and birds she had nurtured. The children visit the grave daily, leaving wreaths of flowers and kissing the headstone. Three years after the woman's death, her eldest daughter meets her father's new wife and then runs to the window to view her beloved mother's grave: "It was a moonlight night, and she could see the arbor and the gleaming of the white tombstone within, and she wondered sadly if her mother, lying there in her grave, knew about *this woman*, and was troubled for her children's sake." The father normally visits his wife's grave on Sunday afternoons, but he hesitates after bringing home his new bride. His wife urges him to join his children, so he finally confesses that the "arbor . . . is the place where my Emma lies buried." The new wife is "startled and somewhat troubled, but said nothing." After everyone except the eldest daughter has accepted the stepmother, the girl runs to her mother's grave and "flung herself upon the turf, and clasped the mound, and pressed her poor, wounded heart against it, and wept aloud." Crying out, "Oh, mother, mother!," she is quietly joined by her stepmother, who begins to tell the girl the story of her own life and losses. The two become reconciled, with the dead mother as a silent witness.[74]

Another eldest stepdaughter acknowledges that when her father first marries, "it seemed like sacrilege to give her own dead mother's place to another." Her brother agrees: "I just went into mother's chamber, and it seemed as if I could see her beautiful pale face pressing the pillow, and I though how kind, how good, how like an angel she was to all of us; and now, to have that ugly old maid here." The children eventually realize that their stepmother is not an "ugly old maid" but a loving substitute mother, and the daughter admits, "I have treasured so many hard thoughts against you because you were not my own mother. And you have been so kind, so tender toward me; you have never spoken a harsh word to me, and my heart has rebelled against you. Can you, will you ever forgive me?" Her stepmother understands, describing the girl's behavior as "natural, for your own mother was an angel compared to me." The stepdaughter gushes back, "Oh no; you are sister angels—one in heaven and one on earth." The author concurs: "I think the mother in heaven, with unspeakable gladness, gazed upon the mother on earth."[75]

One overwhelmed stepmother saw her predecessor in a dream. This woman was inexperienced, having not had her own children, and faced the added handicap of parenting children who had been motherless and "left to the care of such persons as their father could get to keep his house." With such familial disarray the children "had acquired habits of disobedience." She "felt like giving up in despair." Trying to get her young stepson to school one day took all her strength. He "told her she was like all step-mothers, a tyrant, and he meant to run away when he should be a little older." This exchange caused her not only to break down in tears but also to examine her own behavior. She concluded that she needed to try harder and turn to God for assistance. After praying at her bedside, she fell into an exhausted sleep, dreaming that her stepchildren were climbing a mountain with her at their side. She shepherded them away from many false steps and mistaken paths, and as they struggled, "she raised her eyes to the summit of the mountain, and saw amid the shining throng, one whom she knew to be the mother of the little ones at her side." This angelic mother bid her replacement to bring the children to her. She began the difficult ascent, "encouraged and strengthened" by the heavenly vision. The children matured, eventually staying on the narrow path without her help. When she finally arrived at the summit "to receive a glittering crown," she awoke, but for years, "when trials came she remembered the mother's outstretched arms, and the loving and anxious looks of those angel-faces which she saw in her vision, and she was patient."[76]

The successful stepmother might even receive the thanks of her child's dead mother. Promised one author, "When the angel of death shall come to bear you hence, you will seem to hear, in the soft beating of his dark wings, the voice of another mother saying, 'Dear sister, come away, your work is accomplished, our child is saved. We will spend eternity in rejoicing.'"[77] Another author thought that mothers and stepmothers would have good reason to be the best of friends in heaven: "Who can imagine the joy of that meeting, when she who bore, and she who cherished as her own those loved ones, shall embrace each other."[78]

One departed mother still watched over her replacement: "Mother, to whom are committed the children of her who once bore thy present name, thou has an important charge. Be tender to those who have now no natural mother to listen to their infant complaints. Their helplessness demands it; the yearnings of her, whose mother's heart tenderly responded to their slightest sorrows, demands it; your tacit promise demands it; religion demands it."[79] These stories depicted stepmothers and mothers as allies, working together to raise children.

Stepfamilies needed the attention of reformers. The problem of prejudice against stepmothers was a social problem that needed solving. Some felt that stepmothers deserved respect and even admiration. Some argued that stepmothers could be models for natural mothers. As a "class of mothers," they provided the essential happy home and proper, intensive, parenting middle-class children deserved and the freedom for business that middle-class men demanded. In order for these reconstituted nuclear families to function, however, stepchildren needed to be cleansed of the common prejudice against such women. At the same time, stepmothers needed to be taught to mother other women's children as their own. They needed to be surrogate mothers without replacing their predecessors. The role was challenging, but if successful, heavenly awards awaited.

EPILOGUE

In the modern United States, twenty-first-century stepfamilies struggle with negative cultural stereotypes refined and elaborated in the eighteenth century. Although death rates have declined and fewer stepfamilies are formed following the loss of a partner, divorce rates have skyrocketed, making remarriage a common part of the American familial landscape. In fact, in the popular mind, stepfamilies and divorce have become inexorably linked. This connection has given negative stereotypes a new life. I suspect, as with the "sentimental" family for the founding generation, high divorce rates have exacerbated traditional prejudices against stepfamilies. Specifically, stepfathers are still seen as sinister, stepmothers as wicked, and stepchildren as victims.

The history of divorce intersected with the history of stepfamily prejudice starting at the end of the nineteenth century.[1] Prior to that period, divorce was rare and often came with prohibitions against remarriage.[2] By the 1880s, however, divorce became so common that one out of every fifteen marriages ended in court. By 1900, that ratio was one in ten; by 1950, it was one in three; and today, about half of all marriages end in divorce, with about 75 percent of divorced adults choosing to remarry.[3] In fact, almost half of marriages are remarriages.[4] Divorce, in the words of one historian, is now an "American tradition."[5] At present, most stepfamilies result not from random, untimely deaths but from marital conflict and dissolution.

With this tradition of divorce, how do we now define a stepfamily, and how many stepfamilies are there? The most recent census defines a stepfamily as "a married-couple family household with at least one child under age 18 who is a stepchild." This definition and the way in which the census counts children in stepfamilies in general (even young children) lead to greatly underestimating stepfamily numbers. For example, stepfamilies are limited to married partners, excluding a large number of unmarried couples and their households. Since most states still do not allow same-sex marriage, the census statistics also exclude these stepfamilies. In addition, the 2010 census assigns stepchildren only one household, the household where they reside most of the time. Since children still live most often with their mothers despite joint custody arrangements, a stepfather family (a mother's home) is counted, while the same child's stepmother family (a father's home) is not. Even the U.S. Census Bureau admits that its definition "undercounts the true number of step families."[6] The 1990 census is more reliable in one way: children were allowed residency in more than one household. Based on that data, therefore, 43 percent of marriages were remarriages, and 65 percent of those remarriages included children. According to the 1990 census, 23 percent of children under eighteen lived in stepfamilies as a result of remarriage.[7] A recent report on stepfamilies from the Pew Research Center provides perhaps the most accurate estimate of the impact of stepfamilies on the American population. Of the almost 2,700 adults interviewed, 42 percent said that they had steprelations of some kind.[8]

The presence of stepfamilies in today's society, as in the past, has not stifled ongoing prejudice. For example, the loaded terms "stepfather," "stepmother," and "stepchild" are still regularly used to refer to individuals in these families. Some alternatives for "stepfamily" have been proposed, most notably "blended family." Critics argue, however, that "blended" suggests an effortlessness that rarely reflects reality. Stepfamilies have also been called "reconstituted, remarried . . . extended . . . merged, combined," or even "reorganized" families.[9] These alternatives still fail to address the naming problem for individual members of such families.[10] Labeling, therefore, remains a much debated issue that reflects the prejudice that still hounds these families and their members.

Have old prejudices simply remained intact? In some ways, stepfathers, stepmothers, and stepchildren are still burdened by stereotypes that at least echo the characterizations common at our nation's founding. Some changes have occurred as a result of the changing status of women, although the overall popular impression of these families still inclines toward the negative. Stepfathers are still cast as sinister, though physical abuse rather than bilking an orphan's inheritance is the crux of the modern characterization. Stepmothers still wrestle with fairy tales. Stepchildren are still characterized as victims not only of parents' divorce but also of their subsequent remarriage.

Popular culture still depicts stepfathers as menacing, although their sinister nature has evolved. The improved legal status of married women in the nineteenth century inadvertently revised the contours of their perceived threat. Married women's property acts passed beginning in the 1840s gave women the right to own property.[11] A new husband no longer had automatic access to his wife's estate, meaning that a woman could protect property inherited from a former husband and pass this property to her children. Stepfathers, therefore, lost their reputation as economic exploiters.

But that does not mean that American society has embraced stepfathers as substitute fathers. To this day, stepfathers remain still legally exempt from supporting their stepchildren.[12] In addition, popular culture frequently depicts stepfathers as child abusers, committing crimes against the bodies rather than the estates of their stepchildren.[13] Newspapers are full of stories about abusive stepfathers.[14] The press uses the word "stepfather" almost exclusively in negative contexts, in headlines such as "Maximum Term for Stepfather in Death of Girl," "Police Charge Stepfather in Murder of Battered Girl," "Stepfather Is Sentenced to Prison in Abuse of Girl Who Later Died," "Stepfather Gets 57 Years for Raping Two Children," "Stepfather Sentenced in Rape and Sodomy."[15] Such popular stereotypes of abusive stepfathers are reinforced elsewhere in popular culture. For example, three movies, *The Stepfather* (1987); a sequel, *Stepfather II: Make Room for Daddy* (1989); and a remake, *The Stepfather* (2009)—packaged together at a special price in a DVD trilogy of stepfather abuse by a large online retailer—tell the same story of a crazed and murderous stepfather.[16] According to some researchers, stepfathers are no more abusive than natural fathers.[17] Successful stepfathers befriend rather than frighten their stepchildren.[18]

For stepmothers, the stereotypes of the eighteenth century remain entrenched and largely unchanged from their fairy tale origins.[19] The evil stepmother stories of *Cinderella* and *Snow White* remain ubiquitous. The Disney Corporation has perpetuated these old prejudices in films and numerous consumer products.[20] Disney sells Cinderella dolls, costumes, games, and backpacks; dolls also depict Snow White's wicked stepmother as the queen and as the old hag who tries to poison her stepdaughter with an apple. Two more recent films, *Mirror, Mirror* (2012) and *Snow White and the Huntsman* (2012), update the tale of Snow White for more adult audiences, demonstrating that the evil stepmother remains alive and well in popular culture. Writes one family researcher, "The old established equation" of "stepmother = wicked" remains culturally intact.[21]

Stepmothers also continue to suffer when compared to biological mothers.[22] In part, this reality is linked to the continuing idealization of motherhood. By the mid-nineteenth century, mothers gained so much power within the family that they were seen as the appropriate parent to receive custody of their children in cases of divorce; previously, fathers had been the legally preferred parent. Legal authorities decided that children needed maternal care more than patriarchs needed the presence of their progeny. The debate over what exactly constitutes a "good" mother continues today, with modern talk of traditional "family values," women in the workforce, and abortion.[23] Today, what some researchers call the "mommy myth" continues to pressure mothers to achieve perfection.[24] Popular culture often characterizes stepmothers as "bad" mothers.[25] In the words of one researcher, stepmothers are in a " 'damned if you do, damned if you don't' situation."[26]

Meanwhile stepchildren are still portrayed as victims.[27] The word "stepchild" is still used metaphorically to describe anyone or anything that is neglected or mistreated. *Big Girls Don't Cry . . . They Get Even* (1992) and other films show children struggling to find their place within a complex stepfamily construct. Stepchildren are portrayed as suffering from their parents' remarriage despite research to the contrary.[28] One study, for example, found that inexperienced mental health professionals assumed that clients they thought were stepchildren were more troubled.[29] In another study, a group of adolescents asked to describe stepchildren portrayed them more negatively than even stepparents. According to one group of researchers, "Although *wicked* is readily associated with stepmother and *abusive* has recently been linked with stepfather, it may be that the frequent use of *stepchild* to mean poor, neglected, and ignored has had an insidious impact on attitudes over time."[30] In fact, many stepchildren describe themselves as close to their stepparents, although the relationship is often more friendly than parental.[31]

With ideas about the American family evolving toward more inclusivity, perhaps the time is right to revisit stepfamilies and their struggles in the past. Though stepfamilies are common, we still have trouble even naming these relationships without dredging up negative connotations of the past. Despite evidence of positive relationships, families continue to struggle with modern stereotypes that have a close connection to traditional prejudices. Characterizations of stepfathers, stepmothers, and stepchildren all suggest families in conflict. Given the prevalence of stepfamilies, the continuing prejudice against this form remains a puzzle. And even though first-marriage families no longer constitute the majority of families in this country, they remain the standard, the ideal against which stepfamilies are measured—and nearly always found wanting.

On the Methodology Used in This Book

Examining the cultural and lived experiences of stepfamilies in the past required an examination of a variety of print and manuscript sources. I consulted legal treatises, legal digests and commentaries, court records, case law, statute law, probate material, church records, family correspondence, and diaries. For some manuscript sources, I literally combed through every collection with a genealogically trained eye. Some finding aids were useful, but most guides to manuscript collections do not mention stepfamilies; they can, however, include clues that demonstrate the occurrence of a remarriage. I accessed these resources through a combination of patience, time, and the help of archivists.

A large number of print sources are now available in keyword-searchable formats. I worked with Early American Imprints, Series I, Evans (1639–1800); Early American Imprints, Series II, Shaw-Shoemaker (1800–1819); American Periodical Series; and America's Historical Newspapers. I also used Literature Online and Early English Books Online to access English sources. Although Early English Books Online is not keyword searchable, it has a useful index.

I used certain keywords to query the different databases. I began my search for stepfamilies with some familiar terms: "stepmother" (and "stepdame"), "stepfather" (and "stepsire"), "stepdaughter," "stepson," "stepsister," "stepbrother," and "stepchild/children." Using alternative labels that I often found in legal sources, I searched for "mother-in-law," "father-in-law," "daughter-in-law," and "son-in-law." I excluded "brother-in-law" and "sister-in-law" because the *Oxford English Dictionary* and my review of the sources indicated that these terms were not used as alternatives to "stepbrother" and "stepsister." I then broadened my search to include other possible alternative terms gleaned from my research, among them "second marriage," "second husband," "second wife," "now-wife," "natural mother," "natural father," "unnatural mother," "unnatural father," "real mother," and "real father."

Some of these labels were more useful than others. For example, I chose "now-wife" because this term is the focus of one of the few historical studies of these families in colonial North America.[1] In the print sources studied here, however, "now-wife" was almost exclusively used in advertisements and legal notices as a short for "now the wife of," whether or not the remarriage included children. Likewise, "natural mother" and "natural father" as well as "real mother" and "real father" could refer to biological mothers and biological fathers; however, "unnatural mothers" and "unnatural fathers" usually referred not to stepmothers or stepfathers but to murderous or sexually abusive parents.

Finally, family correspondence of the period demonstrated that stepfamily members could be referred to simply as "mother," "father," "son," "daughter," "sister," and "brother." I first searched for these terms in newspapers with the intention of reading each reference for content, but the searches generated too many results. I turned, therefore, to a subset, examining just two newspapers, the *Boston Newsletter* (1704–69) and *Connecticut Courant* (1764–1837). I chose these publications because they had the longest runs and minimal overlap. Because a search of these publications for these terms still found too many articles, I searched only for the term "mother" and sampled 20 percent of the 3,659 items found. In none of those instances did "mother" refer to a stepmother. Based on this research, I concluded that newspapers did not use "mother" as an alternative to "stepmother," although people commonly did so in private letters. However, the press frequently substituted "sister" and "brother" for "stepsister" and "stepbrother," paralleling the practice in family letters and diaries. Searches for "stepsister" or "stepbrother" returned no results, although I did find examples of stepfamily stories referring to such relationships using the terms "sister" and "brother."

These methods enabled me to find stepfamilies that did not appear in indexes and finding aids. Thus, the evidence for this study was obtained using a combination of traditional methods and a digital humanities' approach.

NOTES

PREFACE

1. Charles Perrault, *Histories, ou Contes du Temps Passé, avec des Moralités: Contes de ma Mère l'Oye* (Paris: Barbin, 1697). The first English translation was by Robert Sampler or Guy Miège, *Histories, or Tales of Past Times, Told by Mother Goose* (London: Pote, 1729). In New England, the first edition was likely by Oliver Goldsmith (under the pen name William Shakespeare), *Mother Goose's Melody; or, Sonnets for the Cradle* (Worcester, Mass.: Thomas, 1785). For the pre-Perrault origin of this tale, see Ruth B. Bottigheimer, *Fairy Tales: A New History* (Albany: Excelsior/State University of New York Press, 2009). The Cinderella story to this day remains a favorite in the United States and around the world: scholars have now identified as many as 345 variations (Marian Rolfe Cox, *Cinderella* [London: Nutt, 1893]).

2. Jacob and Wilhelm Grimm, *Kinder- und Hausmärchen* [Children's and Household Tales] (Berlin: Realschulbuch, 1812).

3. For an outline of the Grimms' revisions of these tales, see Jack Zipes, *The Brothers Grimm: From Enchanted Forests to the Modern World* (New York: Routledge, 1988), 10–15; Jacob and Wilhelm Grimm, "Snow-White," http://www.pitt.edu/~dash/type0709.html#snowwhite (1 January 2006); Jacob and Wilhelm Grimm, "Little Snow-White," http://www.pitt.edu/~dash/grimm053a.html (1 January 2006). For various interpretations of the reasons for these revisions, see Jack Zipes, *Happily Ever After: Fairy Tales, Children, and the Culture Industry* (New York: Routledge, 1997), 49–55; Maria Tatar, *The Hard Facts of the Grimms' Fairy Tales* (Princeton: Princeton University Press, 1987), chapter 6.

4. Jacob and Wilhelm Grimm, "Hansel and Gretel," http://www.pitt.edu/~dash/grim015a.htm 1 (1 January 2006).

5. Some scholars suggest that pleasure reading for children became a new publishing niche in this period. Others also connect this development to a new focus on childhood as a stage of life. Both contentions have been highly debated. For an overview of the literature and varying scholarly perspectives, see John Morgenstern, "The Rise of Children's Literature Reconsidered," *Children's Literature Association Quarterly* 26 (Summer 2001): 64–73. Bruno Bettelheim is among those who argue that fairy tales reveal a fundamental truth about the human condition. See Bruno Bettelheim, *The Uses of Enchantment: The Meaning and Importance of Fairy Tales* (New York: Vintage, 1977). Jack Zipes takes a historical approach, arguing that folktales simply replicated themselves as cultures interacted, thus accounting for their apparently ever-present nature. See Jack Zipes, *Breaking the Magic Spell: Radical Theories of Folk and Fairy*

Tales (1979; New York: Routledge, 1992), 11. For a similar approach, see Eugene Weber, "Fairies and Hard Facts: The Reality of Folktales," *Journal of the History of Ideas* 42 (January–March 1981): 93–113. Some feminist scholars argue that these stories did not reflect an emerging middle-class mentality, as Zipes would have it, or a long-ago peasant tradition, as Weber suggests, but rather embodied an ancient matriarchal tradition. For a summary of feminist work on fairy tales, see Donald Haase, "Feminist Fairy-Tale Scholarship," in *Fairy Tales and Feminism: New Approaches*, ed. Donald Haase (Detroit: Wayne State University Press, 2004), 10–14.

INTRODUCTION

1. Joseph J. Ellis, *His Excellency: George Washington* (New York: Vintage, 2004), 42–43, 135–37, 255–56; Patricia Brady, *Martha Washington: An American Life* (New York: Viking, 2005), 145–46.

2. Mantle Fielding, "Edward Savage's Portraits of Washington," *Pennsylvania Magazine of History and Biography* 48 (July 1924): 193–200; http://www.nga.gov (13 September 2013); http://www.mountvernon.org (13 September 2013).

3. H. W. Brands, *The First American: The Life and Times of Benjamin Franklin* (New York: Anchor, 2002), 20–34. This and other recent biographies fail to note that James Franklin was Benjamin Franklin's half brother. See Edmund S. Morgan, *Benjamin Franklin* (New Haven: Yale University Press, 2003); Gordon S. Wood, *The Americanization of Benjamin Franklin* (New York: Penguin, 2005).

4. Catherine Allgor, *A Perfect Union: Dolley Madison and the Creation of an American Nation* (New York: Holt, 2007), 181, 351–99.

5. David Hackett Fischer, *Paul Revere's Ride* (New York: Oxford University Press, 1995), 15; www.paulreverehouse.org (13 September 2013).

6. For the United States, see Marylynn Salmon, *Women and the Law of Property in Early America* (Chapel Hill: University of North Carolina Press, 1986), chapter 5. For England, see Lawrence Stone, *Road to Divorce: England, 1530–1987* (Oxford: Oxford University Press, 1990).

7. Isaac, "The Good Step-Mother," *Congregational Visitor*, June 1848, 139–43; reprinted as Cong. Visitor, "The Good Step-Mother," *Father's and Mother's Manual*, October 1848, 106–10.

8. "Step-, comb. form," "Stepbairn, n.," "Stepchild, n.," *Oxford English Dictionary Online*, 2nd ed. (8 June 2011).

9. In early modern England, for example, the figure was 25–30 percent. See Roger Schofield and Edward A. Wrigley, "Remarriage Intervals and the Effect of Marriage Order on Fertility," in *Marriage and Remarriage in Populations of the Past*, ed. J. Pupâquier, E. Hèlin, P. Laslett, M. Livi-Bacci, and S. Sogner (London: Academic, 1981), 212. In sixteenth- and seventeenth-century France, 20–33 percent of marriages were remarriages, despite Catholic authorities' traditional discouragement of remarriage. See Guy Carbourdin, "Remarriage in France during the Sixteenth and Seventeenth Centuries," in *Marriage and Remarriage*, ed. Pupâquier et al., 284. In eighteenth-century New England, the number is thought to be slightly higher, at 40 percent. See Gloria L. Main, *Peoples of a Spacious Land* (Cambridge: Harvard University Press,

2001), 85, 264 (n. 69); Toby L. Ditz, *Property and Kinship: Inheritance in Early Connecticut, 1750–1820* (Princeton: Princeton University Press, 1986), 180 (n. 5); William F. Ricketson, "To Be Young, Poor, and Alone: The Experience of Widowhood in the Massachusetts Bay Colony, 1675–1676," *New England Quarterly* 64 (March 1991): 113–27; Susan Grigg, "Toward a Theory of Remarriage: A Case Study of Newburyport at the Beginning of the Nineteenth Century," *Journal of Interdisciplinary History* 8 (Autumn 1977): 83–120. Remarriage rates varied by location, but in general, healthier seventeenth-century New England likely had fewer stepfamilies. See Alexander Keyssar, "Widowhood in Eighteenth-Century Massachusetts: A Problem in the History of the Family," *Perspectives in American History* (1974): 83–119; Philip J. Greven Jr., *Four Generations: Population, Land, and Family in Colonial Andover, Massachusetts* (Ithaca: Cornell University Press, 1970), 110–11; John Demos, *A Little Commonwealth: Family Life in Plymouth Colony* (New York: Oxford University Press, 1970), 67; Richard Archer, "New England Mosaic: A Demographic Analysis for the Seventeenth Century," *William and Mary Quarterly*, 3rd ser. 47 (October 1990): 495–96. In some seaports, stepfamilies may have remained more common. See Maris A. Vinovskis, "Mortality Rates and Trends in Massachusetts before 1860," *Journal of Economic History* 32 (March 1972): 184–213.

10. Laurel Thatcher Ulrich suggests that deaths in childbirth were lower in rural New England than comparable areas in England and much lower than in the cities of Dublin and London. In the diary of the early Maine midwife that she studied, five or six maternal deaths occurred per one thousand births, numbers comparable to early twentieth-century rates in the United States. See Laurel Thatcher Ulrich, *A Midwife's Tale: The Life of Martha Ballard, Based on Her Diary, 1785–1812* (New York: Knopf, 1990), 172–73. Roger Schofield suggests that maternal mortality rates have been exaggerated for early modern England and that women were just as likely to die from other causes. See Roger Schofield, "Did the Mothers Really Die?: Three Centuries of Maternal Mortality in 'The World We Have Lost,'" in *The World We Have Gained: Histories of Population and Social Structure*, ed. Lloyd Bonfield, Richard M. Smith, and Keith Wrightson (Oxford: Blackwell, 1986), 231–60. In addition, colonial North America was in a constant state of war prior to the revolution, increasing the death rate for young men. For the implications of King Philip's War for family life, see Ricketson, "To Be Young, Poor, and Alone."

11. For eighteenth-century New England, Main has found that widows married less often than widowers and did so in age-specific patterns (*Peoples of a Spacious Land*, 264 [n. 69]). Ditz has found similar patterns in eighteenth-century Connecticut (*Property and Kinship*, 180 [n. 5]). Looking at the 1774 census in Connecticut, Robert V. Wells concludes that widows remarried less often than widowers (*The Population of the British Colonies in America before 1776: A Survey of Census Data* [Princeton: Princeton University Press, 1975], 94–96). Keyssar has found a similar pattern for Woburn, Massachusetts ("Widowhood in Eighteenth-Century Massachusetts"). Grigg finds that this pattern continued into the nineteenth century ("Toward a Theory of Remarriage"). In seventeenth- and eighteenth-century France, 50 percent of widowers remarried, while only 20 percent of widows did so. See André Burguière, "Remarriage in France under the *Ancien Régime* during the Seventeenth and Eighteenth Centuries:

Differences between Theory and Practice," in *Marriage and Remarriage*, ed. Pupâquier et al., 48. Margaret Pelling found very few spouseless men in Norwich, England, before 1700, which she interprets as evidence of virtually universal remarriage for men ("Finding Widowers: Men without Women in English Towns before 1700," in *Widowhood in Medieval and Early Modern Europe*, ed. Sandra Cavallo and Lyndan Warner [Harlow: Longman, 1991], 50–51). Barbara J. Todd, looking at Abington, traces widows through their deaths or remarriages and concludes that between 14.6 percent and 50 percent remarried between 1540 and 1710 ("Demographic Determinism and Female Agency: The Remarrying Widow Reconsidered . . . Again," *Continuity and Change* 9 [December 1994]: 433). Demos has said that for both men and women, marriage within a year and often within six months of the death of a spouse was common in seventeenth-century Plymouth, Massachusetts; however, such was not the case in the more settled communities of the eighteenth and nineteenth centuries (*Little Commonwealth*, 66). A study of eighteenth-century widows in Woburn, Massachusetts, finds that women remarried an average of 2.5 years after the death of their husbands (Keyssar, "Widowhood in Eighteenth-Century Massachusetts," 93). In early nineteenth-century Newburyport, Massachusetts, men remarried more quickly than women—on average, 5.6 years for widows and 1.9 years for widowers (Grigg, "Toward a Theory of Remarriage"). In eighteenth-century New France, New England's northern neighbor, Molly G. Richter has found that men remarried more quickly than women ("Widowhood in New France: Consequences and Coping Strategies," *French Colonial History* 4, no. 1 [2003]: 49–62). In general, remarriage intervals in northwestern Europe between the seventeenth and eighteenth centuries were 15.5 months for men and 39.2 months for women (Antoinette Fauve-Chamoux, "Marriage, Widowhood, and Divorce," in *The History of the European Family*, vol. 1, *Family Life in Early Modern Times, 1500–1789*, ed. David I. Kertzer and Marzio Barbagli [New Haven: Yale University Press, 2001], 225). For England, the gendered patterns of remarriage intervals were similar but less pronounced than for northwestern Europe as a whole: widowers waited 12.6 months, while widows waited 19.4 months (Schofield and Wrigley, "Remarriage Intervals," 214). According to one group of scholars studying early modern England, "Very rapid remarriage was never common: in late Elizabethan and early Stuart England about 6 per cent of male remarriages took place within two months of the death of the wife, but by the end of the eighteenth century the figure was down to about 1 per cent." The speed of remarriage was also linked to the number of dependent children in a household, the age of a widow or widower, and the rural or urban nature of the community studied (E. A. Wrigley, R. S. Davies, J. E. Oeppen, and R. S. Schofield, *English Population History from Family Reconstitution, 1580–1837* [Cambridge: Cambridge University Press, 1997], 176–82). Vivien Brodsky argues that for Londoners, and particularly for widows of craftsmen and tradesmen, remarriage could be swift ("Widows in Late Elizabethan London: Remarriage, Economic Opportunity, and Family Orientations," in *World We Have Gained*, ed. Bonfield, Smith, and Wrightson, 122–54).

12. Peter Laslett first proposed the idea of the nuclear family in northwestern Europe in "Characteristics of the Western Family Considered over Time," *Journal of Family History* 2 (June 1977): 89–115. He elaborates on this view in Peter Laslett, *The*

World We Have Lost: England before the Industrial Age, 3rd ed. (New York: Scribner's, 1984); Peter Laslett, "Family and Household as Work Group and Kin Group: Areas of Traditional Europe Compared," in *Family Forms in Historic Europe*, ed. Richard Wall, Jean Robin, and Peter Laslett (Cambridge: Cambridge University Press, 1983), 513–64. David Herlihy has argued that the nuclear family was a common pattern back to at least the medieval period (*Medieval Households* [Cambridge: Harvard University Press, 1985]). In fact, the extended family became more rather than less common as time progressed. See Michael Anderson, *Family Structure in Nineteenth Century Lancashire* (Cambridge: Cambridge University Press, 1971); Steven Ruggles, *Prolonged Connections: The Rise of the Extended Family in Nineteenth-Century England* (Madison: University of Wisconsin Press, 1987); Steven Ruggles, "Multigenerational Families in Nineteenth-Century America," *Continuity and Change* 18 (May 2003): 139–65. Glen Elder proposed a life-course analysis to take into consideration the evolving family structure among primarily nuclear households ("History and the Family: The Discovery of Complexity," *Journal of Marriage and the Family* 43 [August 1981]: 489–519). See also Tamara K. Hareven, "Cycles, Courses, and Cohorts: Reflections on the Theoretical and Methodological Approaches to the Historical Study of Family Development," *Journal of Social History* 12 (Autumn 1978): 97–109. Households if not families included unrelated servants, although Naomi Tadmor argues that people used "household" and "family" interchangeably in early modern England (*Family and Friends in Eighteenth-Century England: Household, Kinship, and Patronage* [Cambridge: Cambridge University Press, 2001]). Greven finds that the "modified extended family" was common in colonial Andover, Massachusetts (*Four Generations*, chapters 7, 8). For an overview of the history of the idea of nuclear families, see Daniel Scott Smith, "The Curious History of Theorizing about the History of the Western Nuclear Family," *Social Science History* 17 (Autumn 1993): 325–53.

13. André Burguière, "The Formation of the Couple," *Journal of Family History* 12 (March 1987): 39–53.

14. For an example of a colony that returned to English patterns after early demographic disruption, see Lois Green Carr and Lorena S. Walsh, "The Planter's Wife: The Experience of White Women in Seventeenth-Century Maryland," *William and Mary Quarterly*, 3rd ser., 34 (October 1977): 542–71.

15. Recent work in European family history has suggested that kin networks were not replaced by the nuclear family but rather remained important even after 1750. The focus of the clan shifted from lineage and inheritance to "alliance and affinity." See David Warren Sabean, Simon Teuscher, and Jon Mathieu, eds., *Kinship in Europe: Approaches to Long-Term Development (1300–1900)* (New York: Berghahn, 2007), 3.

16. For example, prejudice against stepmothers has been traced to ancient Greece and Rome. See Patricia A. Watson, *Ancient Stepmothers: Myth, Misogyny, and Reality* (Leiden: Brill, 1995); David Noy, "Wicked Stepmothers in Roman Society and Imagination," *Journal of Family History* 16 (October 1991): 345–61.

17. This transformation has been studied and debated, but most scholars conclude that a new ideology emerged about family life in Enlightenment Europe and in North America in the eighteenth century. For the idea of a real transition to "modern" families based on marital affection and enlightened child rearing in Europe, see Philippe Ariès,

Centuries of Childhood (New York: Vintage, 1965); Lawrence Stone, *The Family, Sex, and Marriage in England, 1500–1800* (London: Weidenfeld and Nicolson, 1977); Edward Shorter, *The Making of the Modern Family* (New York: Basic Books, 1975). All three of these authors argue that a change in middle-class family ideology occurred by the end of the eighteenth century (though they disagree about precisely when that change took place); Shorter contends that the change affected the lower sort as well. For a summary of recent works participating in the ongoing discussion about the timing of this ideological change and its translation into reality in Europe, see Mary S. Hartman, *The Household and the Making of History: A Subversive View of the Western Past* (New York: Cambridge University Press, 2004). For colonial North America, see Carl N. Degler, *At Odds: Women and the Family in America from the Revolution to the Present* (New York: Oxford University Press, 1980); Steven Mintz and Susan Kellogg, *Domestic Revolutions: A Social History of American Family Life* (New York: Free Press, 1988); Karin Calvert, *Children in the House: The Material Culture of Early Childhood, 1600–1900* (Boston: Northeastern University Press, 1992). For more specific regional studies, see Daniel Blake Smith, *Inside the Great House: Planter Family Life in Eighteenth-Century Chesapeake Society* (Ithaca: Cornell University Press, 1980); Jan Lewis, *The Pursuit of Happiness: Family and Values in Jefferson's Virginia* (New York: Cambridge University Press, 1983); Barry Levy, *Quakers and the American Family: British Settlement in the Delaware Valley* (New York: Oxford University Press, 1988); Anya Jabour, *Marriage in the Early Republic: Elizabeth and William Wirt and the Companionate Ideal* (Baltimore: Johns Hopkins University Press, 1998). For the role of the American Revolution in this transformation, see Jay Fliegelman, *Prodigals and Pilgrims: The American Revolution against Patriarchal Authority, 1750–1800* (Cambridge: Cambridge University Press, 1982); Melvin Yazawa, *From Colonies to Commonwealth: Familial Ideology and the Beginnings of the American Republic* (Baltimore: Johns Hopkins University Press, 1985). From the legal point of view, Carole Shammas argues that the revolution had little impact on family relationships (*A History of Household Government in America* [Charlottesville: University of Virginia Press, 2002]). Others argue that affective families were not new and can even be found as early as the fourteenth century in Europe. See Alan Macfarlane, *Marriage and Love in England: Modes of Reproduction, 1300–1840* (Oxford: Blackwell, 1986). In *Forgotten Children: Parent-Child Relations from 1500 to 1900* (Cambridge: Cambridge University Press, 1983), Linda Pollock argues for a remarkable continuity in child rearing. Mary Abbott likewise argues that family patterns tend to resist change (*Family Ties: The English Family, 1540–1920* [London: Routledge, 1993]). Others have written persuasively that ideology changed but that the relationship between ideology and reality was not direct. For example, according to Sarah M. S. Pearsall, a change in expressions of "family feeling" acted as a kind of glue to keep transatlantic families connected rather than simply reflecting a new development in family interaction (*Atlantic Families: Lives and Letters in the Later Eighteenth Century* [Oxford: Oxford University Press, 2008]). Kenneth Lockridge contends that affective language had little impact on family life but rather was a new way to reinforce patriarchy ("Colonial Self-Fashioning: Paradoxes and Pathologies in the Construction of Genteel Identity in Eighteenth-Century America," in *Through a*

Glass Darkly: Reflections on Personal Identity in Early America, ed. Ronald Hoffman, Mechal Sobel, and Frederika J. Teute [Chapel Hill: University of North Carolina Press, 1997], 274–339). In Holly Brewer's view, change was reflected in the legal discussion about the age of reason for children in the eighteenth century (*By Birth or Consent: Children, Law, and the Anglo-American Revolution in Authority* [Chapel Hill: University of North Carolina Press, 2005], 350–51).

18. Ann Marie Plane, *Colonial Intimacies: Indian Marriage in Early New England* (Ithaca: Cornell University Press, 2002); Richard Godbeer, *Sexual Revolution in Early America* (Baltimore: Johns Hopkins University Press, 2002), 156–57.

19. For New England, see Daniel R. Mandell, *Behind the Frontier: Indians in Eighteenth Century Eastern Massachusetts* (Lincoln: University of Nebraska Press, 1996); Jean M. O'Brien, *Dispossession by Degrees: Indian Land and Identity in Massachusetts, 1650–1790* (Cambridge: Cambridge University Press, 1997).

20. For a general overview, see "The History of the Family in Africa," a special issue of the *Journal of African History* 24 (1983). On extended family patterns, see Raymond T. Smith, "The Nuclear Family in Afro-American Kinship," *Journal of Comparative History* 1 (Autumn 1970): 55–70.

21. Stephanie Smallwood, *Saltwater Slavery: A Middle Passage from Africa to American Diaspora* (Cambridge: Harvard University Press, 2008).

22. Herbert G. Gutman, *The Black Family in Slavery and Freedom, 1750–1925* (New York: Vintage, 1977); Ira Berlin, *Many Thousands Gone: The First Two Centuries of Slavery in North America* (Cambridge: Belknap Press of Harvard University Press, 2000).

23. On polygyny, see Godbeer, *Sexual Revolution*, 151–52. For sixteenth- and early seventeenth-century African communities dealing with the slave trade, see Linda M. Heywood and John K. Thornton, *Central Africans, Atlantic Creoles, and the Foundation of the Americas, 1585–1660* (Cambridge: Cambridge University Press, 2007), 66, 305; Berlin, *Many Thousands Gone*, 189.

24. For the difficulty of comparing African and European family traditions in the past, see David Warren Sabean, "The History of the Family in Africa and Europe: Some Comparative Perspectives," *Journal of African History* 24 (1983): 163–71.

25. For the link between family patterns and class formation, see Burton J. Bledstein and Robert D. Johnson, eds., *The Middling Sorts: Explorations in the History of the American Middle Class* (New York: Routledge, 2001). Most scholars of early modern England would agree that by the eighteenth century, some sort of middling group existed between the gentry and the "lower sort." Did this group between the poor and the elite, the "middling sort" of the eighteenth century, have a Marxist sense of class consciousness, an awareness that they were unique? If class categories existed, who belonged to the middle class? An economic approach, for example, might insist on defining the boundaries of this group by income or profession. In contrast, those taking a social or cultural history approach might focus on *mentalité*—cultural markers of status. Finally, did a middle class "rise" in the eighteenth century, or had it existed all along? For a summary of some of these arguments for England, see John Seed, "From 'Middling Sort' to Middle Class in Late Eighteenth- and Early Nineteenth-Century England," in *Social Orders and Social Class in Europe since 1500: Studies*

in Social Stratification, ed. M. L. Bush (London: Longman, 1992), 114–35; Margaret Hunt, *The Middling Sort: Commerce, Gender, and the Family in England, 1680–1780* (Berkeley: University of California Press, 1996); Leonore Davidoff and Catherine Hall, *Family Fortunes: Men and Women of the English Middle Class, 1780–1850* (Chicago: University of Chicago Press, 1987), 225–343. The cultural seeds of the British North American middle class were planted in the eighteenth century. See Mary P. Ryan, *Cradle of the Middle-Class: The Family in Oneida County, New York, 1790–1865* (New York: Cambridge University Press, 1981); Paul Johnson, *Shopkeeper's Millennium: Society and Revivals in Rochester, New York, 1815–1837* (New York: Hill and Wang, 1978); Stuart Blumin, *The Emergence of the Middle Class: Social Experience and the American City, 1700–1900* (New York: Cambridge University Press, 1989); Konstantin Dierks, "Middle-Class Formation in Eighteenth-Century North America," in *Class Matters: Early North America and the Atlantic World*, ed. Simon Middleton and Billy G. Smith (Philadelphia: University of Pennsylvania Press, 2008), 99–108. I use "middle class" and "middling sort/s" interchangeably, given that this study ends in antebellum America, a place and time that most scholars would agree included an identifiable middle class.

26. Historian Ruth Wallis Herndon uses the term "mates" to designate individuals in the extralegal unions that were common among the early American poor (*Unwelcome Americans: Living on the Margins in Early America* [Philadelphia: University of Pennsylvania Press, 2001]). On informal marriage, see Clare A. Lyons, *Sex among the Rabble: An Intimate History of Gender and Power in the Age of Revolution, Philadelphia, 1730–1830* (Chapel Hill: University of North Carolina Press, 2006).

27. See, for example, Stephanie Coontz, *The Way We Never Were: American Families and the Nostalgia Trap* (New York: Basic Books, 2000).

28. Peter Laslett, *The World We Have Lost: England before the Industrial Age*, 3rd ed. (New York: Scribner's, 1984), 115.

29. Helena M. Wall, *Fierce Communion: Family and Community in Early America* (Cambridge: Harvard University Press, 1990), 89.

30. Work on stepfamilies as a separate group has appeared in both article form and in conference settings. For the singular work for early North America, see Darrett B. Rutman and Anita H. Rutman, " 'Now-Wives and Sons-in-Law': Parental Death in a Seventeenth-Century Virginia County," in *The Chesapeake in the Seventeenth Century: Essays on Anglo-American Society*, ed. Thad W. Tate and David L. Ammerman (Chapel Hill: University of North Carolina Press, 1979), 153–75. For a later period in Canadian history, see Peter Gossage, "*La Marâtre*: Marie-Anne Houde and the Myth of the Wicked Stepmother in Quebec," *Canadian Historical Review* 76 (December 1995): 563–95; Peter Gossage, "Tangled Webs: Remarriage and Family Conflict in Nineteenth-Century Quebec," in *Family Matters; Papers in Post-Confederation Canadian Family History*, ed. Edgar-André Montigny and Anne Lorene Chambers (Toronto: Canadian Scholars' Press, 1998), 355–76; Peter Gossage, "Remarried with Children: Stepfamilies in Quebec, 1866–1920," paper presented at the annual meeting of the American Historical Association, Boston, January 2001; Peter Gossage, "Living in Step: Narratives of Remarriage and Stepfamily Life in Quebec, 1870–1940," paper

presented at the annual meeting of the American Historical Association, San Francisco, January 2002. For Europe, see Stephen Collins, "British Stepfamily Relationships, 1500–1800," *Journal of Family History* 16 (October 1991): 331–45; Stephen Collins, "'Reason, Nature, and Order': The Stepfamily in English Renaissance Thought," *Renaissance Studies* 13 (September 1999): 312–23; Sylvie Perrier, "The Blended Family in *Ancien Régime* France: A Dynamic Family Forum," *History of the Family* 3, no. 4 (1998): 459–71; Sylvie Perrier, "Coresidence of Siblings, Halfsiblings, and Step-Siblings in *Ancien Régime* France," *History of the Family* 5 (June 2000): 299–314; Janice Leidl, "Honour Thy Stepmother: Complicating Family Dynamics in Early Modern England," paper presented at the Berkshire Conference on the History of Women, Amherst, Mass., June 2011.

31. Ruth H. Bloch, "Changing Conceptions of Sexuality and Romance in Eighteenth-Century America," *William and Mary Quarterly*, 3rd ser., 60 (January 2003): 18.

32. On the historical importance of genealogical material, see Karin Wulf, "Bible, King, and Common Law: Genealogical Literacies and Family History Practices in British America," *Early American Studies* 10 (Fall 2012): 467–502.

33. Rutman and Rutman, "'Now-Wives and Sons-in-Law'"; Carr and Walsh, "Planter's Wife."

34. For an overview of the scholarship on literacy, see Ross W. Beales Jr., "Studying Literacy at the Community Level: A Research Note," *Journal of Interdisciplinary History* 8 (Spring 1978): 93–102. The literate in New England included women and some people of color. See E. Jennifer Monaghan, "'She Loved to Read in Good Books': Literacy and the Indians of Martha's Vineyard, 1643–1725," *History of Education Quarterly* 30 (Winter 1990): 492–521; E. Jennifer Monaghan, "Literacy Instruction and Gender in Colonial New England," *American Quarterly* 40 (March 1988): 18–41. For the underrepresentation of non-property-holding New Englanders in this literature, see Ruth Wallis Herndon, "Research Note: Literacy among New England's Transient Poor, 1750–1800," *Journal of Social History* 29 (Summer 1996): 963–65. For details on the early publishing industry, see David D. Hall, "The Uses of Literacy in New England, 1600–1850," in *Printing and Society in Early America*, ed. William L. Joyce, David D. Hall, Richard D. Brown, and John Hench (Worcester, Mass.: American Antiquarian Society, 1983), 1–47; Richard D. Brown, *Knowledge Is Power: The Diffusion of Information in Early America, 1700–1865* (New York: Oxford University Press, 1989); William J. Gilmore, *Reading Becomes a Necessity of Life: Material and Cultural Life in Rural New England, 1780–1835* (Knoxville: University of Tennessee Press, 1989).

CHAPTER ONE

1. James Sullivan to Rufus King, 29 January 1786, James Sullivan Transcripts, 1770–1867, Massachusetts Historical Society, Boston.

2. James Sullivan to Rufus King, 23 April 1786, in ibid.

3. Thomas C. Amory, *Life of James Sullivan* (Boston: Phillips, Sampson, 1859), 1:178–80, 273.

4. See, for example, Lawrence Stone, *The Family, Sex, and Marriage in England, 1500-1800* (London: Weidenfeld and Nicolson, 1977); Carl N. Degler, *At Odds: Women and the Family in America from the Revolution to the Present* (New York: Oxford University Press, 1980); Steven Mintz and Susan Kellogg, *Domestic Revolutions: A Social History of American Family Life* (New York: Free Press, 1988). Ruth H. Bloch argues that both love and money were important ("Changing Conceptions of Sexuality and Romance in Eighteenth-Century America," *William and Mary Quarterly*, 3rd ser., 60 [January 2003]: 14). Lorri Glover makes the case that in South Carolina, property always trumped affection, at least among elites (*All Our Relations: Blood Ties and Emotional Bonds among Early South Carolina Gentry* [Baltimore: Johns Hopkins University Press, 2000], 8).

5. Not until women's rights expanded in the mid-nineteenth century were married women allowed to own property. See Susan Staves, *Married Women's Separate Property in England, 1660-1833* (Cambridge: Harvard University Press, 1990); Marylynn Salmon, *Women and the Law of Property in Early America* (Chapel Hill: University of North Carolina Press, 1986). For ways of circumventing these laws, see Amy Louise Erickson, *Women and Property in Early Modern England* (New York: Routledge, 1995); Linda L. Sturtz, *Within Her Power: Propertied Women in Colonial Virginia* (New York: Routledge, 2002); Lisa Wilson, *Life after Death: Widows in Pennsylvania, 1750-1850* (Philadelphia: Temple University Press, 1992).

6. See, for example, Barbara J. Todd, "The Remarrying Widow: A Stereotype Reconsidered," in *Women in English Society, 1500-1800*, ed. Mary Prior (London: Methuen, 1985), 54–92; Barbara J. Todd, "Demographic Determinism and Female Agency: The Remarrying Widow Reconsidered . . . Again," *Continuity and Change* (December 1994): 421–50; Susan Grigg, "Toward a Theory of Remarriage: A Case Study of Newburyport at the Beginning of the Nineteenth Century," *Journal of Interdisciplinary History* (Autumn 1977): 183–220.

7. Richard L. Bushman, *The Refinement of America: Persons, Houses, Cities* (New York: Vintage, 1993), 90–92. For the power of family letters and their style, see Sarah M. S. Pearsall, *Atlantic Families: Lives and Letters in the Later Eighteenth Century* (Oxford: Oxford University Press, 2008).

8. John Langdon Sibley, *Biographical Sketches of Graduates of Harvard University, in Cambridge, Massachusetts* (New York: Johnson Reprint, 1967), 7:27–50.

9. Thomas Clap, "Memoirs of Some Remarkable Occurances of Divine Providence," 9 November 1736, Thomas Clap, President of Yale College, Records (RU 130), Manuscripts and Archives, Yale University Library, New Haven, Conn.

10. Ibid.

11. Ibid.

12. Thomas Clap, "Rev. Thomas Clap's Thoughts on a Second Marriage," 9 April 1737, Baldwin Family Papers (MS-55), Manuscripts and Archives, Yale University Library.

13. Ibid; see also Daniel Vickers, "Competency and Competition: Economic Culture in Early America," *William and Mary Quarterly*, 3rd ser., 47 (January 1990): 3–29.

14. Clap, "Thoughts on a Second Marriage."

15. Clap, "Memoirs."

16. Ibid.

17. Joy Day Buel and Richard Buel Jr., *A Way of Duty: A Woman and Her Family in Revolutionary America* (New York: Norton, 1984), 61–66.

18. Ibid.

19. Mary (Fish) Noyes, "Essay on the Characteristics of a Good Husband," 3 August 1773, Silliman Family Papers (MS 450), Manuscripts and Archives, Yale University Library. Steven Mintz, *Huck's Raft: A History of American Childhood* (Cambridge: Belknap Press of Harvard University Press, 2004), 58–59, chapter 4.

20. Noyes, "Essay on the Characteristics of a Good Husband."

21. As quoted in Buel and Buel, *Way of Duty*, 82.

22. Gold Selleck Silliman to Mary (Fish) Noyes, 14 March 1775, Silliman Family Papers.

23. Mary (Fish) Noyes to Gold Selleck Silliman, 26 March 1775, and Gold Selleck Silliman to Mary (Fish) Noyes, 31 March 1775; both in ibid.

24. Mary (Fish) Noyes to Gold Selleck Silliman, 20 April 1775, in ibid.

25. See Charles Carlton, "The Widow's Tale: Male Myths and Female Reality in 16th and 17th Century England," *Albion* 10 (Summer 1978): 118–29. See also Jennifer Panek, *Widows and Suitors in Early Modern English Comedy* (Cambridge: Cambridge University Press, 2004); Elizabeth Foyster, "Marrying the Experienced Widow in Early Modern England: The Male Perspective," in *Widowhood in Medieval and Early Modern Europe*, ed. Sandra Cavallo and Lyndan Warner (Harlow: Longman, 1999), 108–24.

26. For a discussion of the *Spectator*'s general influence and significance among the eighteenth-century English middle class, see Erin Mackie, ed., *The Commerce of Everyday Life: Selections from "The Tatler" and "The Spectator"* (Boston: Bedford/St. Martin's, 1998), introduction.

27. Joseph Addison and Richard Steele, *The Spectator, Volumes 1, 2, and 3: With Translations and Index for the Series*, ed. Henry Morley (London: Routledge, 1891), No. 561, 30 June 1714, http://www.gutenberg.net (13 September 2013).

28. James Littlejohn, Esq. [Timothy Dwight], "The Friend, No. IX, by James Littlejohn, Esq.," *New-Haven Gazette, and the Connecticut Magazine*, 8 June 1786, 130.

29. Ibid.

30. James Littlejohn, Esq. [Timothy Dwight], "The Friend, No. IX, by James Littlejohn, Esq.," *New-Haven Gazette, and the Connecticut Magazine*, 15 June 1786, 137.

31. Ibid.

32. Ibid.

33. Ibid.

34. Mather Byles [Jr.] to Catherine Byles, 15 March 1787, Mather Byles [Jr.] to Catherine and Mary Byles, 12 October 1787, both in Byles Family Papers, 1757–1915, Massachusetts Historical Society.

35. [W. W. Woolsey] to George Woolsey, 1 May 1816, W. W. Woolsey to Theodore D. Woolsey, 23 November 1820, both in Woolsey Family Papers (MS 562), Manuscripts and Archives, Yale University Library.

36. Sarah C. Woolsey to Theodore D. Woolsey, 12 December 1820, 26 November 1821, both in ibid.

37. Ebenezer Turell, *The Life and Character of the Reverend Benjamin Colman, D.D.* (1749; Delmar, N.Y.: Scholars, 1972), 208.

38. Mrs. Cutts to Eliphalet Pearson, 27 July 1784, Park Family Papers (MS 384), Manuscripts and Archives, Yale University Library.

39. Mary Hubbard to Gardner Greene, 3 August 1799, 28 February 1801, both in Hubbard-Greene Papers, 1784–1851, Massachusetts Historical Society.

40. Harrison Gray Otis to Sally (Foster) Otis, 16 April 1820, Harrison Gray Otis Papers, 1691–1870, Massachusetts Historical Society.

41. Elizabeth Ellery Dana, "Extracts from the Diary of William Watson," *New England Historical and Genealogical Register* 80 (January 1926): 60.

42. C. Dallett Hemphill notes this possibility in *Siblings: Brothers and Sisters in American History* (New York: Oxford University Press, 2011), 44. Leonore Davidoff makes a similar observation about the English debate in *Thicker Than Water: Siblings and Their Relations, 1780–1920* (Oxford: Oxford University Press, 2012), 92.

43. Julia Cowles, *The Diaries of Julia Cowles: A Connecticut Record, 1797–1803*, ed. Anna Roosevelt Cowles (New Haven: Yale University Press, 1931), 59.

44. Although marrying a wife's sister was prohibited in the colonies as in England, such marriages nonetheless occurred. In New England, Increase Mather acknowledged but lamented this fact in a 1695 sermon: "It is a burning Shame, that ever it should be heard of in such a Land of Uprightness as *New England*" (*The Answer of Several Ministers in and near Boston, to That Case of Conscience, Whether It Is Lawful for a Man to Marry His Wives Own Sister?* [Boston: Green, 1695], 8).

45. Brian Connolly, "'Every Family Become a School of Abominable Impurity': Incest and Theology in the Early Republic," *Journal of the Early Republic* 30 (Fall 2010): 413–42.

46. Walter King, *A Farewell Discourse, Delivered to the Congregational Church and Society of Chelsea, in Norwich, Connecticut, August 18, 1811, Together with an Appendix, Giving Some Account of the Ground of Difficulty between the Pastor and Society Together with the Result of Council by Walter King* (New York: Seymour, 1811), 28.

47. James Finley, *A Brief Attempt to Set the Prohibitions in the XVIIIth and XXth Chapters of the Book of Leviticus in a Proper Light, Wherein an Answer to the Two Following Questions Is More Especially Attended to, viz. I. Whether It Be Right for a Man, after the Death of His Wife, to Marry Her Sister? II. Supposing the Marriage to Be Wrong, Whether They, Continuing to Cohabit, May Be Admitted to Church Privileges?* (Wilmington, Del.: Adams, 1783), 4.

48. Jonathan Edwards, *The Marriage of a Wife's Sister Considered in a Sermon Delivered in the Chapel of Yale-College, on the Evening after the Commencement, September 12, a.d. 1792; Being the Anniversary Concio ad Clerum* (New Haven, Conn.: Green, 1792), 22–23.

49. Domesticus, *The Doctrine of Incest Stated, with an Examination of the Question Whether a Man of the Presbyterian Church . . .* , 2nd ed. (New York: Carvill, 1827), 30–33. This author also noted a dark side to the legal change: as a potential future mate, a spinster might be suspect by her sister and a temptation to her brother-in-law.

50. Citizen, *The Marriage of a Deceased Wife's Sister Vindicated, in a Letter from a Citizen to a Friend* (New York: Swords, 1797), 24–25.

CHAPTER TWO

1. Tapping Reeve, *Law of Baron and Feme* (New York: Sourcebook, 1970), 225.

2. *Phillips v. Medbury*, 7 Conn. 568; 1829 Conn. LEXIS 33.

3. In the 1840s, married women gained more power as married women's property acts allowed them to own their own property. This change permitted widows to care for their children's immediate and future needs with less dependence on the good behavior of a second husband. See Carole Shammas, "Re-Assessing the Married Women's Property Acts," *Journal of Women's History* 6 (Spring 1994): 10–30; Kathleen S. Sullivan, *Constitutional Context: Women and Rights Discourse in Nineteenth-Century America* (Baltimore: Johns Hopkins University Press, 2007).

4. E. Anthony Rotundo, "American Fatherhood: A Historical Perspective," *American Behavioral Scientist* 29 (September–October 1985): 7–23; Robert L. Griswold, *Fatherhood in America: A History* (New York: Basic Books, 1993); Stephen M. Frank, *Life with Father: Parenthood and Masculinity in the Nineteenth-Century American North* (Baltimore: Johns Hopkins University Press, 1998); Robert Griswold, "Introduction to the Social Issue on Fatherhood," *Journal of Family History* 24 (July 1999): 251–54; Lisa Wilson, "Ye Heart of a Father: Male Parenting in Colonial New England," *Journal of Family History* 24 (July 1999): 255–74; Shawn Johansen, *Family Men: Middle-Class Fatherhood in Early Industrializing America* (New York: Routledge, 2001).

5. For an overview of the property rights of married women, see Marylynn Salmon, *Women and the Law of Property in Early America* (Chapel Hill: University of North Carolina Press, 1986).

6. If a man with children died intestate (without a will), his widow got one-third of his personal estate outright and one-third of his real estate. Men could write wills stipulating that their widows would receive more or less than the standard widow's share, but widows could often go to court to get at least that amount. Creditors were paid after the widow's third was extracted from the estate (this was true in most of the colonies; one notable exception was Pennsylvania where creditors were paid first). When women remarried, they could lose their life interests in their third of their husbands' real estate, a provision that had the potential to keep a stepfather from accessing at least some of his stepchildren's future property. Connecticut law governing those who died intestate suggests this kind of link between death and remarriage. In other words, when a woman died or remarried her share of the real estate went to her children. See Toby L. Ditz, *Property and Kinship: Inheritance in Early Connecticut, 1750–1820* (Princeton: Princeton University Press, 1986), 130 (n. 28). However, wills suggest a more complicated understanding. Some testators seem to connect life estates and remarriage, while other men simply left their wives life estates, with no language addressing what would happen if the women wed again. The need to make this link explicit in a will suggests that a life estate and remarriage were not automatically linked in practice. Such a linkage was not automatic elsewhere in the eighteenth century; for

Virginia and New York, see Joan R. Gundersen and Gwen Victor Gampel, "Married Women's Legal Status in Eighteenth-Century New York and Virginia," *William and Mary Quarterly*, 3rd ser., 39 (January 1982): 122–23; for Jamaica, see Trevor Burnard, "Inheritance and Independence: Women's Status in Early Colonial Jamaica," *William and Mary Quarterly*, 3rd ser., 48 (January 1991): 113. In addition, a stepfather could get access to another man's real estate if he was named as administrator of an unsettled estate when he married a widow or alternatively became the guardian of his stepchildren.

7. In the Chesapeake, thanks to a high death rate and weak kin networks, an Orphans' Court system developed to focus on the protection of widows and orphans from among others, unscrupulous stepfathers. See Lois Green Carr, "The Development of the Maryland Orphans' Court, 1654–1715," in *Law, Society, and Politics in Early Maryland*, ed. Aubrey C. Land, Lois Green Carr, and Edward C. Papenfuse (Baltimore: Johns Hopkins University Press, 1977), 41. Even in the early Chesapeake, stepfathers generally resisted the temptation to exploit orphans. See Darrett B. Rutman and Anita H. Rutman, *A Place in Time: Middlesex County, Virginia, 1650–1750* (New York: Norton, 1984), 117. No such court developed in the healthier environment of New England.

8. For a summary of Deane's life, see Kalman Goldstein, "Silas Deane: Preparation for Rascality," *Historian* 43 (November 1980): 75–97. Goldstein looks to Deane's less documented early life for explanations of his later behavior, an approach I replicate in using Deane's role as a stepfather to understand the blended family of which he was a part. By twenty-first-century standards, marrying a widowed client may seem like unseemly behavior for a lawyer, but Deane's actions were hardly unique in the eighteenth century. Samuel Sewall, a well-known Boston diarist and merchant/lawyer, also used settling estates as courting opportunities. See Samuel Sewall, *The Diary of Samuel Sewall, 1674–1729*, ed. M. Halsey Thomas (New York: Farrar, Straus and Giroux, 1973), 2:889–92.

9. Zephaniah Swift, *A Digest of the Laws of the State of Connecticut* (New Haven: Converse, 1822–23), 30. Henry Dutton, another Connecticut legal commentator, went even further, saying that a new husband had no choice but to join with her in this responsibility. In his view, a husband *must* take on the role of executor of his predecessor's estate: "Where the wife is executrix or administratrix, they must join, and they must be named as executors or administrators." He added, "In 1 Sw. Dig. p. 38, it is said, probably by mistake, that in such cases they *may* join" (*The Connecticut Digest* [New Haven: Howe, 1833], 13).

10. Indenture, Silas Deane and Mehitable Webb, 2 November 1763, Samuel Blachley Webb Papers (MS 539), Manuscripts and Archives, Yale University Library, New Haven, Conn. All further references to the prenuptial agreement between Mehitable Webb and Silas Deane are to this document.

11. For more on prenuptial agreements in England, see Susan Staves, *Married Women's Separate Property in England, 1660–1833* (Cambridge: Harvard University Press, 1990). For the Anglo-American case in Virginia, see Linda L. Sturtz, *Within Her Power: Propertied Women in Colonial Virginia* (New York: Routledge, 2002). See also Marylynn Salmon, "Women and Property in South Carolina: The Evidence

from Marriage Settlements, 1730 to 1830," *William and Mary Quarterly*, 3rd ser., 39 (October 1982): 680–83; Suzanne Lebsock, *The Free Women of Petersburg: Status and Culture in a Southern Town, 1784–1860* (New York: Norton, 1984), 76; Lisa Wilson, *Life after Death: Widows in Pennsylvania, 1750–1850* (Philadelphia: Temple University Press, 1992), 34–37.

12. Salmon argues that prenuptial agreements were not effective in Connecticut because the colony had no official court to deal with equity issues (*Women and the Law of Property*, chapter 6). In Connecticut, women got more support in the courts if they created jointure agreements (which stipulated what the women would receive if their husbands died) rather than separate estates (which gave them the power to control their own inheritances while married). See Cornelia Hughes Dayton, *Women before the Bar: Gender, Law, and Society in Connecticut, 1639–1789* (Chapel Hill: University of North Carolina Press, 1995), 41. The signed agreement between Silas Deane and Mehitable Webb was a hybrid of the two.

13. For England, see Mary Louise Erickson, *Women and Property in Early Modern England* (New York: Routledge, 1995), 31–32.

14. For New England, see Gloria L. Main, *Peoples of a Spacious Land* (Cambridge: Harvard University Press, 2001), 265 (n. 76).

15. Gary Boyd Roberts, ed., *Genealogies of Connecticut Families: From the New England Historical and Genealogical Register* (Baltimore: Genealogical Publishing, 1983), 3:623–24.

16. Sir William Blackstone, *Commentaries on the Laws of England* (Oxford: Clarendon, 1765–69), book 3, chapter 14, p. 223.

17. Ibid., book 2, chapter 18, pp. 281–82.

18. James Kent, *Commentaries on American Law* (New York: Halsted, 1826–30), 4:73–76.

19. *The Public Records of the State of Connecticut* (Hartford: Case, Lockwood, and Brainard, 1894–2007), 9:147–50.

20. Ibid.

21. Ibid.

22. Connecticut Archives, Private Controversies, 2d ser., vol. 29, 145a, Connecticut State Library, Hartford.

23. Silas Deane to Samuel Blachley Webb, 31 October 1783, Webb Papers.

24. *Public Records*, 9:148.

25. Joseph Webb, Wethersfield, 1761, Hartford Probate District, CSL.

26. Silas Deane to Samuel Blachley Webb, 14 May 1775, Webb Papers.

27. Silas Deane, *The Deane Papers: Collections of the New-York Historical Society* (New York: New-York Historical Society, 1886–91), 1:369.

28. Ibid., 2:177–78.

29. Ibid., 4:131.

30. Ibid., 163.

31. Ibid., 177.

32. Ibid., 5:220.

33. Ibid., 323.

34. Ibid., 490.

35. [Silas Deane to Samuel Blachley Webb], 31 October 1783, Webb Papers.

36. Deane, *Deane Papers*, 4:130–31.

37. Ibid., 4:162–64.

38. Ibid.

39. [Silas Deane to Samuel Blachley Webb], 31 October 1783, Webb Papers. Some evidence supports Deane's claims about Joseph's mismanagement of money. He and his wife were such lavish hosts that their home was dubbed Hospitality Hall. In addition, he purchased supplies for the war effort and accepted badly devalued Continental currency, an act of patriotic generosity that landed him in debtor's prison in 1781. See Sherman W. Adams, *The History of Ancient Wethersfield*, ed. Henry R. Stiles (New York: Grafton, 1904), 1:480–81; Wendell Garrett, "Antiques in Wethersfield," *Antiques*, March 1976, 534; www.webb-deane-stevens.org (13 September 2013).

40. [Silas Deane to Samuel Blachley Webb], 31 October 1783, Webb Papers.

41. Deane, *Deane Papers*, 5:220.

42. *Cooper v. Martin*, 4 East. 82 (1803).

43. Swift, *Digest*, 1:415.

44. Reeve, *Law of Baron and Femme*, 285. Reeve strongly opposed this custom on the grounds that it had no legal basis.

45. *Mulhern v. McDavitt*, 82 Mass. 404; 1860 Mass. LEXIS 330; 16 Gray 404.

46. Kent, *Commentaries*, 2:192.

47. Nathan Dane, *General Abridgment and Digest of American Law: With Occasional Notes and Comments* (Boston: Cummings, Hillard, 1823–29), 353.

48. *Stone v. Carr* (1799), 3 Espinasse, 1–3.

49. According to Adele Stuart Meriam, the idea of in loco parentis was codified in the American court system with two cases: *Williams v. Williams*, 3 N.Y. (3 Comstock) 512 (1850) and *Lantz v. Frey and Wife*, 14 Pa. 201 (1850) (*The Stepfather in the Family* [Chicago: University of Chicago Press, 1940], 23–27).

50. *James Freto v. John Brown*, 4 Mass. 6751; 1808 Mass. LEXIS 184; 4 Tyng 675.

51. *Cooper v. Martin*, 76–84.

52. Connecticut Archives, Private Controversies, 2nd ser., vol. 29, 145f, 1463, 145g.

53. Ibid. Ultimately, however, the Webb children had no evidence other than Sally's testimony that Deane had taken the deeds, and the court ruled that no "proof was produced" (*Public Records*, 9:149).

54. Silas Deane, Wetherfield, 1792, Hartford Probate District, CSL.

CHAPTER THREE

1. Rev. Thomas Cooke, *The New Universal Letter Writer: Containing Letters on Duty, Amusement, Love, Courtship, Marriage, Friendship, Trade, Religion, and Other Useful Subjects* (Boston: Hastings, Etheridge, and Bliss, 1809), 73–81. Versions of this manual continued to circulate in England and Scotland through 1841. See Eve Tavor Bannet, *Empire of Letters: Letter Manuals and Transatlantic Correspondence, 1688–1820* (Cambridge: Cambridge University Press, 2005), 194–97. More than 40 percent of books exported from England in the eighteenth century went to British North America or the West Indies. American publishers in the eighteenth century could not

compete with cheaper English imports. See James Raven, "'The Atlantic World,' Part 3, 'The Importation of Books in the Eighteenth Century,'" in *A History of the Book in America*, vol. 1, *The Colonial Book in the Atlantic World*, ed. Hugh Amory and David D. Hall (Cambridge: Cambridge University Press, 2000), 183–98.

2. Patricia A. Watson argues that wicked stepmothers emerged in Greece in the fifth century B.C. (*Ancient Stepmothers: Myth, Misogyny, and Reality* [Leiden: Brill, 1995], 84, 91). David Noy suggests this tradition began with the spread of Christianity ("Wicked Stepmothers in Roman Society and Imagination," *Journal of Family History* 16 [October 1991]: 345–61).

3. The idea of the "natural" mother received new attention in eighteenth-century Europe, and she was depicted as an enlightened mother who saw children as innately good or at the worst as blank slates ready for instruction. See Jean-Jacques Rousseau, *Émile*, trans. Barbara Foxley, intro. P. D. Jimack (1762; London: Dent, 1993); John Locke, *Some Thoughts Concerning Education; and Of the Conduct of the Understanding*, ed. and intro. Ruth W. Grant and Nathan Tarcov (Indianapolis: Hackett, 1996).

4. This metaphor was also used by the Irish during the Rebellion of 1798. See *Extract from the Press a Newspaper Published in the Capital of Ireland, during the Part of the Years 1797 and 1798, Including Numbers Sixty-Eight and Sixty-Nine, Which Were Suppressed by Order of the Irish Government, before the Usual Time of Publication* (Philadelphia: Duane, 1802).

5. For the link between the American Revolution and motherhood, see Linda K. Kerber, *Women of the Republic: Intellect and Ideology in Revolutionary America* (Chapel Hill: University of North Carolina Press, 1980); Mary Beth Norton, *Liberty's Daughters: The Revolutionary Experience of American Women, 1750–1800* (Boston: Little, Brown, 1980); Ruth H. Bloch, "American Feminine Ideals in Transition: The Rise of the Moral Mother, 1785–1815," *Feminist Studies* 4 (June 1978): 101–26; Rosemarie Zagarri, "Morals, Manners, and the Republican Mother," *American Quarterly* 44 (June 1992): 192–215. On the issue of sensibility see, G. J. Barker-Benfield, *The Culture of Sensibility: Sex and Society in Eighteenth-Century Britain* (Chicago: University of Chicago Press, 1992); Sarah Knott, *Sensibility and the American Revolution* (Chapel Hill: University of North Carolina Press, 2009).

6. For the link between revolutionary rhetoric and familial metaphors focusing on the character of America as an overgrown child fighting for independence from a cruel father, the king, see Edwin G. Burrows and Michael Wallace, "The American Revolution: The Ideology and Psychology of National Liberation," *Perspectives in American History* 6 (1972): 167–306; Winthrop D. Jordan, "Familial Politics: Thomas Paine and the Killing of the King, 1776," *Journal of American History* 60 (September 1973): 294–308; Jay Fliegelman, *Prodigals and Pilgrims: The American Revolution against Patriarchal Authority, 1750–1800* (Cambridge: Cambridge University Press, 1982). In the case of the French Revolution, the child literally killed the father (and mother), with the bond of *fraternité* replacing the bond of parent and child. See Lynn Hunt, *The Family Romance of the French Revolution* (Berkeley: University of California Press, 1992).

7. Clifford K. Shipton, ed., *Biographical Sketches of Those Who Attended Harvard College* (Cambridge: Harvard University Press, 1933–75), 13:163–74.

8. John Adams to Abigail Adams, 15 July 1776, in *Adams Family Correspondence*, ed. L. H. Butterfield (Cambridge: Belknap Press of Harvard University Press, 1963–93), 2:49.

9. "From the New-York Gazette, Oct. 17," *Newport Mercury*, 28 October 1765, 2.

10. *Boston Gazette, and Country Journal*, 21 March 1774, 1.

11. "Watertown, June 10," *Boston Gazette, and Country Journal*, 10 June 1776, 3.

12. The Watchman, "Mr. Humphreys, If the Enclosed Be Deserving a Place in Your Paper, Your Inserting It Will Oblige a Customer," *Pennsylvania Ledger*, 20 April 1776, 1.

13. "Philadelphia, Feb. 5," *New-Hampshire Gazette, and General Advertiser*, 18 February 1789, 3; "Philadelphia, February 7," *Connecticut Journal*, 18 February 1789, 2.

14. "New-Hampshire," *Salem (Massachusetts) Mercury*, 28 August 1787, 3.

15. "From the Providence Advertiser: British Monopoly," *Middlesex (Massachusetts) Gazette*, 17 February 1820, 2.

16. "Boston, August 11," *Falmouth (New Hampshire) Gazette and Weekly Advertiser*, 20 August 1785, 3.

17. "An Oration," *Boston Gazette, and Weekly Republican Journal*, 19 September 1796, 1.

18. Isaac Gardner Reed, *An Oration Delivered in Warren, on the Fourth of July, a.d. 1809 in Commemoration of the Declaration of American Independence, at the Request of the Library Society in Warren, by Isaac G. Reed* (Portland, Conn.: Shirley, 1809).

19. *Middlesex (Massachusetts) Gazette*, 27 September 1826, 3.

20. "Extract of a Letter from a Gentleman in _____ to His Friend in Alexandria, Dated October 5, 1791," *New-Hampshire Gazette, and General Advertiser*, 3 November 1791, 2.

21. Katherine Henderson and Barbara F. McManus, *Half Humankind: Contexts and Texts about the Controversy about Women, 1540–1640* (Champaign: University of Illinois Press, 1985). Female writers began a counterattack after the mid-seventeenth century. See Joan Kelly, "Early Feminist Theory and the '*Querelle des Femmes*,'" *Signs* 8 (Autumn 1982): 4–28.

22. D. E. Underdown, "The Taming of the Scold: The Enforcement of Patriarchal Authority in Early Modern England," in *Order and Disorder in Early Modern England*, ed. Anthony Fletcher and John Stevenson (New York: Cambridge University Press, 1985), 116–36.

23. See, for example, James Sharpe, *Instruments of Darkness: Witchcraft in Early Modern England* (Philadelphia: University of Pennsylvania Press, 1997); Carol F. Karlsen, *The Devil in the Shape of a Woman: Witchcraft in Colonial New England* (New York: Norton, 1987).

24. Stephen Collins, "'Reason, Nature, and Order': The Stepfamily in English Renaissance Thought," *Renaissance Studies* 13 (September 1999): 323.

25. In England and in Anglo-America, a stepmother could be called a stepmother, but she could also be labeled a mother-in-law or simply a mother. A mother-in-law referred to both a mother-in-law in the modern sense and a mother "by law"—in this case, by marriage. The term "mother-in-law" was the most neutral way to refer to a stepmother and was often used in legal documents. "Mother," conversely, was the term

most commonly used in family letters. The use of "mother" could suggest something about the quality of a woman's relationship with her stepchildren. Just as often, however, it was simply a title that reflected her position in the family. In Jamaica and in parts of southwestern England, "mother-in-law" can still mean stepmother. See "Mother-in-law, n. and adj.," *Oxford English Dictionary Online*, draft rev., December 2008 (7 August 2009); "in-law," *Oxford English Dictionary Online*, 2nd ed., 1989 (7 August 2009).

26. Henry Goodcole, *Natures Cruell Step-Dames; or, Matchlesse Monsters of the Female Sex; Elizabeth Barnes, and Anne Willis Who Were Executed the 26. day of April, 1637. at Tyburne, for the Unnaturall Murthering of Their Own Children* (London: Coules, 1637).

27. John Newnham, *Newnams Nightcrowe: A Bird That Breedeth Braules in Many Families and Housholdes* (London: Wolfe, 1590). A nightcrowe is "a bird supposed to croak or cry at night and to be of evil omen" or an "evil or malicious person; a nocturnal thief or criminal." This word is now obsolete but was still used as late as 1658. See "Night-crowe, n.," *Oxford English Dictionary Online*, 3rd ed., September 2003 (7 July 2011).

28. Ibid.

29. William Shakespeare, *Cymbeline* (First Folio, 1623).

30. Robert Stapylton, *The Step-Mother: A Tragi-Comedy* (London: Streater, 1664).

31. For more on "cheap print" and motherhood, see Mary E. Fissel, *Vernacular Bodies: The Politics of Reproduction in Early Modern England* (Oxford: Oxford University Press, 2006).

32. *Newes from Perin in Cornwall: A Most Bloody and Un-Exampled Murther Very Lately Committed by a Father on His Sonne (Who Was Lately Returned from the Indyes) at the Instigation of a Merciless Step-Mother* (London: [Allde], 1618).

33. Nicholas Rowe, *The Ambitious Stepmother* (London: J. and R. Townson, 1746). Rowe produced his play in London in 1700, but it enjoyed a following in the colonies as well. *The Ambitious Stepmother* appeared in library and book catalogs in New England into the early nineteenth century.

34. See the entry for "step" in Samuel Johnson, *A Dictionary of the English Language, on CD-ROM*, ed. Anne McDermott (Cambridge: Cambridge University Press in association with the University of Birmingham, 1996). Both Johnson's first edition, published in 1755, and the fourth edition, published in 1773, are the same in this regard.

35. Noah Webster, *A Compendious Dictionary of the English Language* (New Haven; Sidney's, 1806). As late as the 1828 edition, Webster included both "stepmother" and "stepdame" (Noah Webster, *An American Dictionary of the English Language* [New York: Converse, 1828]). The word "stepdame" appeared in Johnson's work as well but only in the quotations he used to illustrate the use of the prefix "step" (Samuel Johnson, *Dictionary*).

36. *The Cruel Step-Mother; or, The Unhappy Son* (London, 1760). This popular story was reissued multiple times between 1760 and 1810. At least one Boston author had read this tale before penning a similar story, *The Damsel's Tragedy; or, The Cruel Step-Mother* (Boston, between 1790 and 1806).

37. Geoffrey of Monmouth, *The Historia Regnum Britanniae of Geoffrey of Monmouth*, trans. R. Ellis Jones, ed. A. Griscom (1136; London: Longman Green, 1929), 6:11–15.

38. William Henry Ireland, *Vortigern, an Historical Tragedy, in Five Acts* (London: Barker, 1799), act 1, scene 2, act 5, scene 1.

39. Thomas Worcester, *The Solemnity of Marriage Illustrated: A Discourse, Occasioned by the Re-Marriage of the Rev. Noah Worcester* (Concord, N.H.: Hough, 1798), 22–23.

40. "The Step Mother," *Providence Gazette*, 22 January 1825, 1.

41. "The Daughters-in-Law: For the Ladies' Port Folio Amelia; Belina," *Ladies Port Folio*, 1820, 173; "The Mother-in-Law: For the Ladies' Port Folio Elizabeth," *Ladies Port Folio*, 1820, 188.

42. *The Lady Isabella's Tragedy* (Newcastle upon Tyne: White, [1730?]). This song was reissued multiple times between 1670 and 1730 in England. Songs were one of the most accessible and widely distributed popular culture forms, not even requiring literacy. See Frances E. Dolan, *Dangerous Familiars: Representations of Domestic Crime in England, 1550–1700* (Ithaca: Cornell University Press, 1994), 7.

43. *(By Authority.) At the Theater in Baltimore, on Tuesday, the 27th of May, 1783, Will Be Presented, a Tragedy. (Never Acted Here) called Isabella; or The Fatal Marriage* (Baltimore: Goddard, 1783).

44. "The Admonisher—No. II: Dedicated to Stepmothers," *Connecticut Courant*, 10 December 1792, 2.

45. "The Step Mother," *Providence Gazette*, 22 January 1825, 1.

46. "From the Emporium: The Tomb Stone," *Farmer's Cabinet*, 7 June 1823, 1.

CHAPTER FOUR

1. Elizabeth (Murray) Campbell Smith to James Murray, 17 February 1762, James Murray Papers, 1732–1781, Massachusetts Historical Society, Boston.

2. James Murray to Dolly Murray, 14 December 1753, in ibid.

3. Elizabeth (Murray) Campbell Smith to Dolly Murray, 17 February 1762, in ibid.

4. J. Benet to Dolly Murray, 16 March 1762, in ibid.

5. Margaret (MacKay) Thompson Murray to Dolly Murray, 30 April 1767, in ibid.

6. On the rarity of such sources and the implications of this scarcity for the study of children's historical agency, see Mary Jo Maynes, "Age as a Category of Historical Analysis: History, Agency, and Narratives of Childhood," *Journal of the History of Childhood and Youth* 1 (Winter 2008): 114–24. Modern studies tend to ignore stepchildren's views of their families. See Aino Ritala-Koskinen, "Stepfamilies from the Child's Perspective: From Stepfamily to Close Relationships," in *Stepfamilies: History, Research, and Policy*, ed. Irene Levin and Marvin B. Sussman (New York: Haworth, 1997), 135–51.

7. Ernest Hawkins, *Missions of the Church of England in the North American Colonies* (London: Fellowes, 1845), 249–50; John Langdon Sibley, *Biographical Sketches of Graduates of Harvard University, in Cambridge, Massachusetts* (New York: Johnson Reprint, 1967), 13:6–26, 7:206–14.

8. [Elizabeth Cuming] to Catherine Byles, 28 April 1778, Byles Family Papers, 1757–1915, Massachusetts Historical Society.

9. Elizabeth Byles to Mary and Catherine Byles, 29 September 1778, in ibid.

10. Eliza[beth] Byles to Mary Byles, 9 May 1782, in ibid.

11. Mather Byles [III] to Catherine and Mary Byles, 10 April 1784, and Mather Byles [Jr.] to Mather Byles [Sr.], 21 June 1784, both in ibid.

12. Rebecca Byles to Catherine Byles, 2 June 1784, and Mather Byles [III] to Catherine and Mary Byles, 10 April 1784, both in ibid.

13. Mather Byles [III] to Catherine Byles, 22 October 1784, in ibid.

14. Mather Byles [III] to Catherine Byles, 10 November 1784, in ibid.

15. Rebecca Byles to Catherine and Mary Byles, 7 December [1784], in ibid.

16. Rebecca Byles to Catherine and Mary Byles, 26 March 1785, in ibid.

17. Rebecca (Byles) Allmon to Catherine and Mary Byles, 1786, in ibid.; Lois K. Kernaghan, "Almon (Allmon), William James," *Dictionary of Canadian Biography*, http://www.biographi.ca/en/bio/almon_william_james_5E.html (10 March 2014).

18. Mather Byles [Jr.] to Catherine Byles, 15 March 1787, and Rebecca (Byles) Allmon to Catherine and Mary Byles, 29 March, 3 May 1787, all in Byles Family Papers; Kernaghan, "Almon (Allmon), William James"; Wallace Brown, "Byles, Mather," *Dictionary of Canadian Biography*, http://www.biographi.ca/en/bio/byles_mather_5E.html (10 March 2014).

19. Eliza[beth] Byles to Catherine and Mary Byles, 14 May 1787, in ibid.

20. Eliza[beth] Byles to Catherine and Mary Byles, 18 August 1788, and Mather Byles [III] to Catherine and Mary Byles, 26 August 1788, 12 January 1789, all in ibid.

21. Anna Byles to Catherine and Mary Byles, [8?] November 1788, in ibid.

22. Mather Byles [Jr.] to Catherine and Mary Byles, [February or March 1789], and Elizabeth Byles to Catherine and Mary Byles, 28 October 1789, both in ibid.

23. Jacob Norton Diaries, 1787–1818, 24, 25, 28 January 1811, Massachusetts Historical Society.

24. Ibid., 16 March–22 April 1811. Although the girls' move was not discussed directly, it is clear from the correspondence subsequent to the Cranches' deaths that they were living with the Greenleafs.

25. A[bby] A. Shaw to Mary Cranch, 1 March 1811, Jacob Norton Papers, 1774–1840, Massachusetts Historical Society.

26. Jacob Norton Diaries, 24 April, 7 May, 30 May–2 June 1813.

27. Ibid., 2, 18 August 1813, 1 January 1814.

28. Elizabeth Norton to Mary Norton, 18 September 1824, 26 December 1827, Norton Papers.

29. Mary Norton to Hannah (Bowers) Norton, 3 August 1829, in ibid.

30. Elizabeth Norton to Mary Norton, 15 April 1829, Jacob Norton Papers, Massachusetts Historical Society. Guide to the Collection, First Church (Weymouth, Mass.) Records, 1724–1839, Massachusetts Historical Society.

31. Mary Norton to Lucy Ann Norton, 10 May 1829, in ibid.

32. Richard Norton to Jacob Norton, 27 March, 14 July 1813, Norton Papers; Richard Cranch Norton Journals and Letterbooks, 1811–1821, 11 June 1813, Massachusetts Historical Society.

33. Richard Norton to Hannah (Bowers) Norton, 14 July, 21 August 1813, Norton Papers; Richard Cranch Norton Journals and Letterbooks, 13 July 1813.

34. Richard Norton to Jacob Norton, 1 March 1817, in ibid.

35. Catharine Maria Sedgwick Journal, 2 January 1849–28 December 1854, Catharine Maria Sedgwick Papers I, Massachusetts Historical Society.

36. In light of Theodore Sedgwick's constant absence and Pamela Sedgwick's incapacity, Freeman likely did much of the day-to-day child care. She is the only non-Sedgwick buried in the family plot, and her epitaph, written by the youngest Sedgwick, Charles, ends "Good Mother, farewell." See *African American and the End of Slavery in Massachusetts*, http://www.masshist.org/endofslavery/index.php?id=54 (19 March 2014).

37. Theodore Sedgwick [Sr.] to Henry Sedgwick, 12 November 1808, Sedgwick Family Papers, 1717–1946, Massachusetts Historical Society; Theodore Sedgwick [Sr.] to Catharine Maria Sedgwick, 26 November 1808, Catharine Maria Sedgwick Papers III.

38. Theodore Sedgwick [Jr.] to Henry Sedgwick, 12 June 1808, and Theodore Sedgwick [Jr.] to Theodore Sedgwick [Sr.], 18 October 1808, both in Sedgwick Family Papers.

39. Henry Sedgwick to Catharine Maria Sedgwick, 1 January 1809, Catharine Maria Sedgwick Papers III.

40. Eliza (Sedgwick) Pomeroy to Henry Sedgwick, 1 January 1812, and Charles Sedgwick to Catharine Maria Sedgwick, 27 March 1812, both in Sedgwick Family Papers; Catharine Maria Sedgwick to Henry Sedgwick, 18 June 1812, Catharine Maria Sedgwick Papers III.

41. Theodore Sedgwick [Jr.] to Theodore Sedgwick [Sr.], 10 February 1809, Sedgwick Family Papers.

42. Henry Sedgwick to Theodore Sedgwick, 24 February 1810, and Theodore Sedgwick [Sr.] to Henry Sedgwick, 16 July 1811, both in ibid.

43. Catharine Maria Sedgwick to Robert Sedgwick, 4 October 1811, and Robert Sedgwick to Catharine Maria Sedgwick, 16 October 1811, both in ibid.

44. Henry Sedgwick to Theodore Sedgwick [Jr.], 25 January 1813, and Robert Sedgwick to Catharine Maria Sedgwick, 28 February 1813, both in ibid.

45. Ebenezer Watson and Robert Sedgwick to Henry Sedgwick, 9 March 1813, Thaddeus Pomeroy to Henry Sedgwick, 26 March 1813, and Eliza (Sedgwick) Pomeroy to Henry Sedgwick, 2 January 1814, all in ibid.

46. Henry Sedgwick to Catharine Maria Sedgwick, 26 March 1812, and Catherine Maria Sedgwick to Henry Sedgwick, 5 April 1813, both in Catharine Maria Sedgwick Papers III; Robert Sedgwick to Henry Sedgwick with addition by Frances (Sedgwick) Watson, 4 April 1813, Sedgwick Family Papers.

CHAPTER FIVE

1. "Holyoke, Edward, 1689–1769. Papers of Edward Holyoke: An Inventory," http://oasis.lib.harvard.edu/oasis/deliver/~hua02005 (11 March 2014); Finding Aid, "Epes Family Papers, 1659–1793" http://www.pem.org/library/finding_aids/

MSS429_EpesFamilyPapers.pdf (22 March 2014); Copy of Will of Elizabeth Epes, 5 February 1759, Holyoke Family Papers, 1607–1905, Phillips Library, Peabody Essex Museum, Peabody, Mass.

2. Copy of Will of Elizabeth Epes, 5 February 1759, Holyoke Family Papers.

3. Copy of Will of Sam[ue]l Epes, Esq., 4 April 1760, Holyoke Family Papers; Clifford K. Shipton, *Sibley's Harvard Graduates: Biographical Sketches of Those Who Attended Harvard College* (Boston: Massachusetts Historical Society, 1937–75), 5:265–78, 13:41–42, 94, 18:385–87.

4. Family historians have taken up the topic of sibling relationships in England and Anglo-America but have yet to fully address the issue of stepfamily siblings. See Amy Harris, *Siblinghood and Social Relations in Georgian England: Share and Share Alike* (Manchester: Manchester University Press, 2012); Leonore Davidoff, *Thicker Than Water: Siblings and Their Relations, 1780–1920* (Oxford: Oxford University Press, 2012); Christopher H. Johnson and David Warren Sabean, *Sibling Relations and the Transformations of European Kinship, 1300–1900* (New York: Berghahn, 2011). For Anglo-America, see Wayne Bodle, "The Littlest Commonwealth?: The Neglected Importance of Sibling Relations in American Family History," *Reviews in American History* 30 (March 2002): 22; Lorri Glover, *All Our Relations: Blood Ties and Emotional Bonds among the Early South Carolina Gentry* (Baltimore: Johns Hopkins University Press, 2000); Lee Chambers, "Married to Each Other, Married to the Cause: Singlehood and Sibship in Antebellum Massachusetts," *Women's History Review* 17 (July 2008): 341–57; C. Dallett Hemphill, *Siblings: Brothers and Sisters in American History* (New York: Oxford University Press, 2011). Only Sylvie Perrier has addressed the topic of stepfamily siblings specifically for early modern Europe; see "Coresidence of Siblings, Halfsiblings, and Step-Siblings in Ancien Regime France," *History of the Family* 5 (June 2000): 299–314.

5. Hemphill has found a similar pattern (*Siblings*, 18). Harris notes this lack of distinction in naming for eighteenth-century England (*Siblinghood*, 14).

6. The legal term "half-blood" appeared in these papers, but I found it only fifty-eight times. I chose to focus on the *Boston Newsletter* (1704–76, 3,500 issues) and *Connecticut Courant* (1764–1850, 4,582 issues) because they were the New England papers with the longest runs and minimal overlap. I used the keyword search capability of NewsBank: America's Newspapers.

7. Samuel Johnson, *A Dictionary of the English Language, on CD-ROM*, ed. Anne McDermott (Cambridge: Cambridge University Press in association with the University of Birmingham, 1996).

8. Noah Webster, *A Compendious Dictionary of the English Language* (New Haven: Sidney's, 1806). "Stepsister" and "stepbrother" did appear in Webster's 1828 edition (*An American Dictionary of the English Language* [New York: Converse, 1828]).

9. Will of John Lay, 16 January 1675, New London Probate Records, 1675–1725, Connecticut State Library, Hartford.

10. Will of Peter Lay, 7 June 1682, in ibid.

11. William Blackstone, *Commentaries on the Laws of England* (Oxford: Clarendon, 1765–69), 2:227. "Half-blood, n. and adj.," *Oxford English Dictionary Online*, 2nd ed. (accessed 7 December 2009). It was not until the nineteenth century that the idea

of "half-blood" meant a mixed-raced person, usually of Native American and Euro-American ancestry, with a clear preference for the latter.

12. Blackstone, *Commentaries*, 2:234. In English law, half-blood inheritance was allowed if a child died under age, in which case the child's estate was absorbed by his or her parents and therefore indirectly diverted to a half sibling. Also, adults could bequeath land that they had acquired on their own to half siblings. For the history of British law in this regard, see *Sheffield v. Lovering*, 12 Mass. 490, 1815 WL 986 (Mass.).

13. Blackstone, *Commentaries*, 2:231–32.

14. William Blackstone, *A Treatise on the Law of Descents in Fee-Simple* (Oxford: Clarendon, 1759), 36. William Pollock and Frederic William Maitland argue that this law did not have an ancient origin, as Blackstone would suggest (*History of the English Law before the Time of Edward I* [Cambridge: Cambridge University Press, 1895], 2:302–5).

15. Blackstone, *Treatise*, 45, 47; Blackstone, *Commentaries*, 2:237.

16. Blackstone, *Treatise*, 53, 56; Blackstone, *Commentaries*, 2:231, 232–33; 3 & 4 Wm. IV, c. 106; David A. Thomas, "Anglo-American Land Law: Diverging Developments for a Shared History, Part III: British and American Real Property Law and Practice—A Contemporary Comparison," *Real Property, Probate, and Trust Journal* 34 (Fall 1999): 443–516. Edward Christian acknowledged in his edition of Blackstone's *Commentaries* that the legal analyst was "apologizing for the exclusion of the half-blood." According to Christian, "Surely nothing can be more cruel or contrary to our notions of propriety and consistency, than to give the estate to a distant relation or to the lord, in preference to a half brother, either when it has descended from the common parent or when the half brother has himself acquired it." See William Blackstone, *Commentaries on the Law of England*, ed. Edward Christian (Portland, Maine: Wait, 1807), 2:233n.

17. Mass. General Statutes. c. 91, §5 (1835): "The degrees of kindred shall be computed according to the rules of the civil law; and the kindred of the half blood shall inherit equally with those of the whole blood in the same degree." In practice, both primogeniture and entail were rarely used in Massachusetts. The southern colonies held on to an inheritance structure that privileged an indigenous, landed elite until Thomas Jefferson and others pushed for change as a result of the rhetoric of equality that fueled the revolution. See Stanley N. Katz, "Republicanism and the Law of Inheritance in the American Revolutionary Era," *Michigan Law Review* 76 (November 1977): 1–29.

18. John Adams, *The Legal Papers of John Adams*, ed. L. Kinvin Wroth and Hiller B. Zobel (New York: Athenaeum, 1968), 1:14.

19. Ibid., 6–7, 4. This entry was written while Adams was a law student, sometime between 1758 and 1759. According to Henry Campbell Black, maxims "are but attempted general statements of rules of law and are law only to extent of application in adjudicated cases." See *Black's Law Dictionary*, 4th ed. (St. Paul, Minn.: West, 1968), 1130.

20. Sir William Blackstone, *An Essay on Collateral Consanguinity, Its Limits, Extent, and Duration: More Particularly as It Is Regarded by the Statutes of All Souls College in the University of Oxford* (London: Owen and Clements, 1750), 12.

21. Blackstone, *Treatise*, appendix.

22. John Holyoke, Genealogy of the Family of the Holyokes, October 1746, Holyoke Family Papers.

23. These numbers are not an accurate record of the number of stepfamilies in the community. The records listed only one woman as remarrying during this eighty-year period, and only men who married, remarried, recorded their marriages, and died in Connecticut can be traced. Such men usually had property. Thus, the families I found are but are a subset of a subset, but they are verifiably stepfamilies. In Connecticut, the housing of many of the state's records in the same location, the existence of a unique name index, and the marriage records of a few towns that recorded remarriages by men allow for this kind of close examination. See Thomas R. Harlow, ed., *Vital Records of Saybrook, 1647-1834* (Hartford: Connecticut Historical Society and the Order of the Founders and Patriots of America, 1952); Probate Estate Papers Index, Connecticut State Library.

24. Peabody Grinell, Guilford, 1768, Guilford Probate District, Connecticut State Library.

25. Nathaniel Kirtland, Guilford, 1751, and Philip Kirtland, Guilford, 1779, both in ibid.; James Kent, *Commentaries on American Law* (New York: Halsted, 1826-30), vol. 2, part 4, lecture 29.

26. Thomas Merrill, Saybrook, 1711, New London Probate District, Connecticut State Library.

27. Thomas Silliman, Chester, 1839, Saybrook Probate District, Connecticut State Library.

28. Hemphill, *Siblings*, proposes that brothers did kin-keeping activities as surely as did sisters. These interactions have been found today among modern sibling groups. See Victor G. Cicirelli, *Sibling Relationships across the Life Span* (New York: Plenum, 1995), 42-44, 111-14; E. Mavis Hetherington, "Family Functioning in NonStepfamilies and Different Kinds of Stepfamilies: An Integration," *Monographs of the Society for Research in Child Development* 64 (December 1999): 184-91; Edward R. Anderson, "Sibling, Half Sibling, and Stepsibling Relationships in Remarried Families," *Monographs of the Society for Research in Child Development* 64 (December 1999): 101-26.

29. Barbara Hofland, *The Sisters, a Domestic Tale* (Hartford: Sheldon and Goodwin, 1815), 39-48.

30. James Hogg, "Duncan Campbell," in *Winter Evening Tales: Collected among the Cottagers in the South of Scotland* (New York: Kirk and Mercein, Wiley and Kalsted, Gilley and Haly, and Thomas, 1820), 1:84-102. This story was excerpted as "From 'Winter Evening Tales,' by James Hogg, Duncan Campbell," *Farmers' Cabinet*, 29 July 1820, 12 August 1820, 19 August 1820, 26 August 1820, 4. All quotations are from this New England version.

31. "A Cinderella Story: From the Philadelphia Chronicle," *Farmers' Cabinet*, 10 December 1831, 1.

32. Catherine Parr Strickland Traill, *The Step-Brothers: A Tale* (London: Harvey and Darton, 1828), 52-110.

33. Benjamin Franklin, *The Autobiography of Benjamin Franklin*, ed. John Bigelow (Philadelphia: Lippincott, 1869), 102-7. For more on "kin-keeping" among the male,

full-blood siblings of the Franklin family, see C. Dallett Hemphill, "Siblings for Keeps in Early America," *Early American Studies* 9 (Winter 2011): 30–58.

34. Carrie Rebora, Paul Staiti, Erica E. Hirshler, Theodore E. Stebbins Jr., and Carol Troyen, *John Singleton Copley in America* (New York: Metropolitan Museum of Art, 1995).

35. John Singleton Copley to Susanna Copley, 22 July 1775, as quoted in Martha Babcock Amory, *The Domestic and Artistic Life of John Singleton Copley* (Boston: Houghton, Mifflin, 1882), 63; Peter Pelham [Jr.] to John Singleton Copley, 10 September 1765, in *Letters and Papers of John Singleton Copley and Henry Pelham, 1739–1776*, Massachusetts Historical Society Collections, vol. 71 (Boston: Massachusetts Historical Society, 1914), 40; John Singleton Copley to Susannah Copley, 28 January 1775, John Singleton Copley Family Papers, microfilm (Washington, D.C.: Library of Congress, 1949).

36. Mather Byles [Jr.] to Catherine Byles, 18 August 1783, Mather Byles [Jr.] to Catherine and Mary Byles, 15 June 1776, 31 May, 12 October 1787, 2 August, 4 September 1788, 28 October 1789, and Catherine and Mary Byles to Mather Byles [Jr.], 18 September 1780, 8 April 1784, all in Byles Family Papers, 1757–1915, Massachusetts Historical Society, Boston.

37. Amelia Russell to Susan Burbeck, 26 February 1818, Amelia E. Russell Letters (typescript), 1817–1818, Jonathan Russell Family Papers, 1792–1863, Massachusetts Historical Society, Boston; Amelia Russell to Polly Foster, 31 May 1818, Jonathan Russell Family Papers, 1792–1863, Massachusetts Historical Society; Amelia E. Russell, *Home Life of the Brook Farm Association* (Boston: Little, Brown, 1900); J. Russell, 9 November 1818, Lydia Smith Russell Diary, 1818, Massachusetts Historical Society. These "step-sisters and brother" were in reality Amelia's half siblings.

38. Henry Pearson to Ephraim Abbott, 18 February 1818, Bromfield Family Papers (MS 599), Manuscripts and Archives, Yale University Library, New Haven, Conn.

39. Margaret [Pearson] Blanchard to Mary [Pearson] Abbott, 25 March 1829, and Bond of Ephraim Abbott, 8 February 1822, both in ibid.

CHAPTER SIX

1. Catharine M. Sedgwick, *Life and Letters of Catharine M. Sedgwick*, ed. Mary E. Dewey (New York: Harper, 1871), 67; Arnaud Berquin, *L'Ami des Enfans* (Paris: Javier and Fervier, 1782–83); translated into English as Arnaud Berquin, *The Children's Friend* (London: Cadwell and Elmsley, 1783–86). This collection had a large readership on both sides of the Atlantic. The original was published in French in twenty-four monthly installments between 1782 and 1783. It appeared first in the United States in 1789. All quotations are from Arnaud Berquin, *The Children's Friend* (Newburyport, Mass.: Mycall, 1793).

2. [Oliver Goldsmith], *Goody Two-Shoes: A Facsimile Reproduction of the Edition of 1766*, intro. Charles Welsh (London: Griffith and Farran, 1881), 131.

3. Lydia Smith Russell to Mrs. Barney Smith, 16 August 1818, Jonathan Russell Family Papers, 1792–1863, Massachusetts Historical Society, Boston; *The History of Little Goody Two Shoes* (Philadelphia: Johnson and Warner, 1811).

4. Fiction and short stories of the time did not take on this topic. Of the 875 works listed in the database Early American Fiction 1789–1875, only 30 mention stepmothers. These references are overwhelmingly negative, and none of these authors deal with the idea of reforming stepmothers.

5. "The Step-Mother," *Social Monitor and Orphans' Advocate* 3 (October 1844): 77.

6. S. A. Whelpley, "The Christian Step-Mother," *Christian Family Magazine and Annual* 4 (September 1844): 30–34.

7. On the rise of the moral mother and the cult of domesticity, see Barbara Welter, "The Cult of True Womanhood, 1820–1860," *American Quarterly* 18 (Summer 1966): 151–74; Nancy F. Cott, *The Bonds of Womanhood: "Woman's Sphere" in New England, 1780–1835* (New Haven: Yale University Press, 1977); Ruth H. Bloch, "American Feminine Ideals in Transition: The Rise of the Moral Mother, 1785–1815," *Feminist Studies* 4 (June 1978): 100–126; Mary P. Ryan, *The Empire of the Mother: American Writing about Domesticity, 1830–1860* (New York: Institute for Research in History and Haworth, 1982).

8. For the history of moral reform, Christianity, and womanhood, see Mary P. Ryan, *Cradle of the Middle-Class: The Family in Oneida County, New York, 1790–1865* (New York: Cambridge University Press, 1981); Nathan O. Hatch, *The Democratization of American Christianity* (New Haven: Yale University Press, 1989); Lori D. Ginzberg, *Women and the Work of Benevolence: Morality, Politics, and Class in the Nineteenth-Century United States* (New Haven: Yale University Press, 1990); Robert H. Abzug, *Cosmos Crumbling: American Reform and the Religious Imagination* (New York: Oxford University Press, 1994); Steven Mintz, *Moralists and Modernizers: America's Pre–Civil War Reformers* (Baltimore: Johns Hopkins University Press, 1995); Anne M. Boylan, *The Origins of Women's Activism: New York and Boston, 1797–1840* (Chapel Hill: University of North Carolina Press, 2002).

9. Some demographic changes may have influenced the timing of this reform effort. Maternal mortality declined between 1750 and the early nineteenth century, so stepmothers might have become less common. See Gloria Main, "Maternal Mortality and Sex Ratios," H-OIEAHC, 22 October 2004; Laurel Thatcher Ulrich, *The Midwife's Tale: The Life of Martha Ballard, Based on Her Diary, 1785–1812* (New York: Vintage, 1991), 173; for England, see E. A. Wrigley, R. S. Davies, J. E. Oeppen, and R. S. Schofield, *English Population History from Family Reconstitution, 1580–1837* (Cambridge: Cambridge University Press, 1997), 313. As maternal death from childbirth declined, so did men's need to remarry, a phenomenon that might have made stepmothers less threatening and thus resulted in the effort to bring them into the maternal fold. The start of a rise in divorce rates at the end of the period may suggest the failure of this effort. See Andrew J. Cherlin, *Marriage, Divorce, Remarriage*, rev. and enl. ed. (Cambridge: Harvard University Press, 1992), 21. With animosity at the root of divorce-based stepfamily formation, the open-armed efforts of reformers may have quickly become anachronistic.

10. Maria Jane Agard, "Step-Mother's Reward," *Ladies' Repository*, December 1847, 359–60.

11. "The Stepmother," *Youth's Companion*, November 1838, 102–3.

12. "Step-Mothers," *Ladies Garland*, September 1842, 83–88.

13. "The Stepmother," *Ladies' Monthly Museum*, July 1815, 12–19.

14. A Mother, "The Step-Mother," *Mothers' Journal and Family Visitant*, October 1849, 293–98.

15. "The Stepmother," *Ladies' Monthly Museum*, July 1815, 12–19.

16. "The Step-Mother," *Mothers' Journal and Family Visitant*, September 1849, 290–91.

17. "Step-Mothers," *Ladies Garland*, September 1842, 83–88.

18. Isaac, "The Good Step-Mother," *Congregational Visiter*, June 1848, 139–43; reprinted as Cong. Visitor, "The Good Step-Mother," *Father's and Mother's Manual*, October 1848, 106–10.

19. "Step-Mothers," *Mothers' Journal and Family Visitant*, April 1852, 103–6.

20. For a general history of the rise of children's books, see Gillian Avery, *Behold the Child: American Children and Their Books, 1621–1922* (Baltimore: Johns Hopkins University Press, 1994); Anne Scott MacLeod, *American Childhood: Essays on Children's Literature of the Nineteenth and Twentieth Centuries* (Athens: University of Georgia Press, 1994).

21. *Cheap Repository: The Good Step-Mother* (London: Marshall, 1797?). The Cheap Repository Tracts were written for early readers and sought to counter the inexpensive and unsavory material that peddlers and traders hawked to the lower classes. These stories had alluring titles and a similar cost but were in fact designed to provide religious uplift to the lower sorts while encouraging them to remain in their proper place. As many as three a month were published, and Hannah More wrote more than fifty. They also included woodcuts to provide visual appeal. The printer of the series, John Marshall of London, had a falling out with More but continued to print volumes written by other authors in 1798 and 1799. See G. H. Spinney, "Cheap Repository Tracts: Hazard and Marshall Editions," *The Library* 20 (1939–40): 295–340.

22. *Cheap Repository: The Good Step-Mother*.

23. Charles Lamb and Mary Lamb, "Father's Wedding Day," in *Mrs. Leicester's School; or, The History of Several Young Ladies, Related by Themselves* (London: Godwin, 1809; first U.S. publication, George Town, D.C.: Milligan, 1811). All quotations are from Charles Lamb and Mary Lamb, *Mrs. Leicester's School* (London: Dent, 1912).

24. Mary Pilkington, "The Amiable Mother-in-Law; or, Prejudice Subdued," in *Mentorial Tales, for the Instruction of Young Ladies Just Leaving School and Entering upon the Theatre of Life* (London: Harris, 1802). All quotations are from Mary Pilkington, "The Amiable Mother-in-Law; or, Prejudice Subdued," in *Mentorial Tales, for the Instruction of Young Ladies Just Leaving School and Entering upon the Theatre of Life* (Philadelphia: Johnson and Warner, 1811), 135–72.

25. "My Good Step-Mother," *Youth's Friend*, October 1843, 153. The story was essentially reprinted as "My Good Step-Mother," *Youth's Companion*, December 1843, 123.

26. "The Good Step-Mother," *Children's Magazine*, November 1848, 250–53.

27. "The Stepmother; or, Prejudice Vanquished," *Youth's Literary Messenger*, September 1838, 145–46.

28. Sophia S. Harrington, "The Stepdaughter," *Mother's Assistant and Young Lady's Friend*, May 1847, 125–35; Sophia S. Harrington, "The Stepdaughter," *Mother's Assistant and Young Lady's Friend*, June 1847, 146–54.

29. "The Stepmother," *Youth's Companion*, November 1838, 102–3.

30. Helen C. Knight, "The Step-Mother.—Fear and Love," *Mother's Assistant and Young Lady's Friend*, June 1846, 121–32.

31. "The Good Step-Mother," *Children's Magazine*, November 1848, 250–53.

32. "My Good Step-Mother," *Youth's Friend*, October 1843, 152–55; "My Good Step-Mother," *Youth's Companion*, December 1843, 123.

33. Of the 485 U.S. periodicals published between 1820 and 1852, 49 percent focused on reform. See Candy Gunther Brown, *The Word in the World: Evangelical Writing, Publishing, and Reading in America, 1789–1880* (Chapel Hill: University of North Carolina Press, 2004), 154–55.

34. Ibid., 183; Jennifer Phelgy, *Educating the Proper Woman Reader: Victorian Family Literary Magazines and the Cultural Health of the Nation* (Columbus: Ohio State University Press, 2004), 6–8; Patricia Okker, *Our Sister Editors: Sarah J. Hale and the Tradition of Nineteenth Century American Women Editors* (Athens: University of Georgia Press, 1995). In addition, women readers were invited to submit letters or contributions to these periodicals.

35. According to the 1850 census, about 90 percent of white Americans were literate (Candy Gunther Brown, *Word in the World*, 10), and by 1860, literacy rates for men and women were roughly equal (Okker, *Our Sister Editors*, 110–11).

36. See, for example, Phelgy, *Educating the Proper Woman Reader*, 16–17; Okker, *Our Sister Editors*, 112–13, 131–32.

37. A search for keywords such as "stepmother," "stepfather," "stepson," "stepdaughter" in the database American Periodical Series Online, 1741–1900, between 1691 and 1852 found eighty-one articles about stepfamilies in forty-seven different publications. Of these articles, 89 percent were focused on stepmothers and stepchildren. Thirty percent of the articles on stepfamilies were published in Boston, 22 percent in Philadelphia, and 22 percent in New York City. Other magazines with this kind of content were published in Springfield, Massachusetts; Burlington, Vermont; Frederick, Maryland; Utica and Albany, New York; Shiremanstown, Pennsylvania; and Harpers Ferry, West Virginia.

38. Ryan, *Empire of the Mother*, 19–20, 116. Members of contemporary maternal associations read these journals and thus were aware of such positive stepmother images. See Richard A. Meckel, "Education a Ministry of Mothers: Evangelical Maternal Associations, 1815–1860," *Journal of the Early Republic* 2 (Winter 1982): 403–23. These organizations focused on raising children, thereby opening the door for stepmother awareness and perhaps participation.

39. Catharine E. Beecher, *A Treatise on Domestic Economy: For the Use of Young Ladies at Home and at School* (Boston: Marsh, Capen, Lyon, and Webb, 1841); Lydia Maria Child, *The Mother's Book* (Boston: Carter, Hendee, 1831).

40. "Step-Mothers," *Mothers' Journal and Family Visitant*, April 1852, 103–6.

41. B., "Trials of Step Mothers," *Mother's Magazine*, August 1837, 189–91.

42. L. B. M., "Step-Mothers," *Mother's Monthly Journal*, August 1841, 117–19; L. B. M., "Step-Mothers," *Mother's Monthly Journal*, September 1841, 131–34.

43. Ibid.

44. A Mother, "The Step-Mother," *Mothers' Journal and Family Visitant*, October 1849, 293–98.

45. S. D. M., "The Stepmother," *Mrs. Whittelsey's Magazine for Mothers*, January 1850, 290–92.

46. "Step-Mothers," *Ladies Garland*, September 1842, 83–88.

47. L. B. M., "Step-Mothers," *Mother's Monthly Journal*, August 1841, 117–19; L. B. M., "Step-Mothers," *Mother's Monthly Journal*, September 1841, 131–34.

48. Ibid.

49. B., "Trials of Step Mothers," *Mother's Magazine*, August 1837, 189–91.

50. M. R. C., "Prejudice against Stepmothers," *Mother's Monthly Journal*, June 1842, 86–89.

51. Isaac, "The Good Step-Mother," *Congregational Visiter*, June 1848, 142.

52. "Step-Mothers," *Mothers' Journal and Family Visitant*, April 1852, 103–6.

53. M.R.C., "Prejudice against Stepmothers," *Mother's Monthly Journal*, June 1842, 86–89.

54. "The Stepmother," *Ladies' Monthly Museum*, July 1815, 12–19.

55. Isaac, "The Good Step-Mother," *Congregational Visiter*, June 1848, 142.

56. M. B. A., "The Step-Daughter," *Christian Parlor Magazine*, March 1847, 331–37.

57. Harriet N. Hathaway, "The Step-Mother," *Spirit Messenger and Harmonial Guide*, August 1851, 33–35.

58. "Letter to a Step-Mother.—No. 1," *Mother's Monthly Journal*, June 1837, 87–88.

59. Helen C. Knight, "The Step-Mother.—Fear and Love," *Mother's Assistant and Young Lady's Friend*, June 1846, 121–32.

60. "Letter to a Step-Mother.—No. 1," *Mother's Monthly Journal*, June 1837, 87–88.

61. Maria Jane Agard, "Step-Mother's Reward," *Ladies' Repository*, December 1847, 359–60.

62. Isaac, "The Good Step-Mother," *Congregational Visiter*, June 1848, 142.

63. Ibid.

64. "The Step-Mother," *Mother's Magazine*, July 1848, 210–12.

65. Maria Jane Agard, "Step-Mother's Reward," *Ladies' Repository*, December 1847, 359–60.

66. B., "Trials of Step Mothers," *Mother's Magazine*, August 1837, 189–91.

67. "Step-Mothers," *Ladies Garland*, September 1842, 83–88.

68. "Step-Mothers," *Mothers' Journal and Family Visitant*, April 1852, 103–6.

69. Isaac, "The Good Step-Mother," *Congregational Visiter*, June 1848, 142.

70. "Step-Mothers," *Mothers' Journal and Family Visitant*, April 1852, 103–6.

71. S. D. M., "The Stepmother," *Mrs. Whittelsey's Magazine for Mothers*, January 1850, 290–92.

72. "Letter to a Step-Mother.—No. 1," *Mother's Monthly Journal*, June 1837, 87–88.

73. L. B. M., "Step-Mothers," *Mother's Monthly Journal*, August 1841, 117–19; L. B. M., "Step-Mothers," *Mother's Monthly Journal*, September 1841, 131–34.

74. Grace Greenwood, "The Step-Mother," *Godey's Lady's Book*, December 1849, 448–54.

75. A Mother, "The Step-Mother," *Mothers' Journal and Family Visitant*, October 1849, 293–98.

76. "The Stepmother's Dream," *Advocate of Moral Reform and Family Guardian*, September 1852, 138.

77. S. D. M., "The Stepmother," *Mrs. Whittelsey's Magazine for Mothers*, 1850, 290–92.

78. L. B. M., "Step-Mothers," *Mother's Monthly Journal*, August 1841, 117–19; L. B. M., "Step-Mothers," *Mother's Monthly Journal*, September 1841, 131–34.

79. Z. X., "My Step-Mother," *Ladies Repository*, April 1846, 99–100.

EPILOGUE

1. For a discussion of the link between divorce and nineteenth-century family values, see Robert L. Griswold, *Family and Divorce in California, 1850–1880: Victorian Illusions and Everyday Realities* (Albany: State University of New York Press, 1982).

2. According to Glenda Riley, the legal permission to remarry following a divorce facilitated the increase in divorce rates (*Divorce: An American Tradition* [New York: Oxford University Press, 1991]).

3. Frank F. Furstenberg, "Divorce and the American Family," *Annual Review of Sociology* 16 (1990): 379–82; Riley, *Divorce*, 171.

4. In 1980, 44 percent of marriages in the United States were remarriages. See Laura V. Salwen, "The Myth of the Wicked Stepmother," *Women and Therapy* 10, nos. 1–2 (1990): 117.

5. Riley, *Divorce*, 52.

6. www.census.gov (2 August 2006).

7. If families formed without legal marriage are included, then 30 percent of children live in stepfamilies. See http://www.stepfamilies.info (28 November 2007).

8. Eighteen percent had living stepparents, 13 percent had stepchildren, and 30 percent had step- or half siblings. See www.pewsocialtrends.org (13 September 2013).

9. Marilyn Coleman and Lawrence H. Ganong, "Cultural Stereotyping of Stepfamilies," in *Remarriage and Stepparenting: Current Research and Theory*, ed. Kay Palsley and Marilyn Ihinger-Tallman (New York: Guilford, 1987), 21.

10. One alternative used by stepfamilies is calling stepparents by their first names. See www.pewsocialtrends.org (14 September 2013).

11. Carole Shammas, "Re-Assessing the Married Women's Property Acts," *Journal of Women's History* 6 (Spring 1994): 10–30; Kathleen S. Sullivan, *Constitutional Context: Women and Rights Discourse in Nineteenth-Century America* (Baltimore: Johns Hopkins University Press, 2007).

12. Bernard J. Berkowitz, "Legal Incidents of Today's 'Step' Relationships: Cinderella Revisited," *Family Law Quarterly* 209 (1970): 209–29.

13. Stephen Claxton-Oldfield, "Deconstructing the Myth of the Wicked Stepparent," *Marriage and Family Review* 30, nos. 1–2 (2000): 51–57.

14. On 2 January 2013, I searched all newspapers in EBSCOhost for the word "stepfather" in the title of articles published between 1985 and 2008: 85 percent of the stories I found were negative, with most focused on abuse.

15. "Maximum Term for Stepfather in Death of Girl," *New York Times*, 4 April 2008, 1; "Police Charge Stepfather in Murder of Battered Girl," *New York Times*, 23 November 2001, 8; "Stepfather Is Sentenced to Prison in Abuse of Girl Who Later Died," *New York Times*, 30 October 1996, 3; "Stepfather Gets 57 Years for Raping Two Children,"

New York Amsterdam News, 14 January 1995, 3; "Stepfather Sentenced in Rape and Sodomy," *New York Times*, 7 January 1995, 29.

16. All three movies are loosely based on an actual case in which a stepfather is a serial killer. On the negative images of both stepfathers and stepmothers in the movies, see Stephen Claxton-Oldfield and Bonnie Butler, "Portrayal of Stepparents in Movie Plot Summaries," *Psychology Reports* 82 (1998): 879–82.

17. The sociological literature remains inconclusive about whether stepfathers are more likely than biological fathers to be sexual abusers or even whether rates of abuse are higher in stepfamilies than in non-stepfamilies. See Lawrence H. Ganong and Marilyn Coleman, *Remarried Family Relationships* (Thousand Oaks, Calif.: Sage, 1994), 86–90; Francesca Alder-Baeder, "What Do We Know about the Physical Abuse of Stepchildren?: A Review of the Literature," *Journal of Divorce and Remarriage* 44, nos. 3–4 (2006): 67–81.

18. Lawrence H. Ganong and Marilyn Coleman, *Stepfamily Relationships: Development, Dynamics, and Interventions* (New York: Kluwer Academic/Plenum, 2004), 125.

19. Marianne Dainton, "The Myths and Misconceptions of the Stepmother Identity: Descriptions and Prescriptions for Identity Management," *Family Relations* 42 (January 1993): 93–98; Salwen, "Myth of the Wicked Stepmother," 117–25.

20. For a discussion of the impact of Walt Disney, see Jack Zipes, *Happily Ever After: Fairy Tales, Children, and the Culture Industry* (New York: Routledge, 1997), 34–38, chapter 3.

21. Anne W. Simon, *Stepchild in the Family: A View of Children in Remarriage* (New York: Odyssey, 1964), 138. For the historical and cultural assumption that stepmothers are and were "wicked," see M. Radomisli, "Stereotypes, Stepmothers, and Splitting," *American Journal of Psychoanalysis* 41 (Summer 1981): 121–27; Maria Tatar, "From Nags to Witches: Stepmothers in the Grimms' Fairy Tales," in *Opening Texts: Psychoanalysis and the Culture of the Child*, ed. Joseph H. Smith and William Kerrigan (Baltimore: Johns Hopkins University Press, 1985), 28–41; Coleman and Ganong, "Cultural Stereotyping," 19–41; Richard L. Dukes, "The Cinderella Myth: Negative Evaluations of Stepparents," *Social Science Research* 73 (January 1989): 67–69; Ann C. Bernstein, "Gender and Stepfamily Life: A Review," *Journal of Feminist Family Therapy* 1, no. 4 (1989): 1–27; Dainton, "Myths and Misconceptions," 93–98; Stephen Collins, "British Stepfamily Relationships, 1500–1800," *Journal of Family History* 16 (October 1991): 331–45; Stephen Collins, "'Reason, Nature, and Order': The Stepfamily in English Renaissance Thought," *Renaissance Studies* 13 (September 1999): 312–24. Modern sociologists have remarked that women in the present either overcompensate to fend off this stereotype or morph into the wicked stepmother they fear becoming. See Christina Hughes, *Stepparents: Wicked or Wonderful?: An Indepth Study of Stepparenthood* (Brookfield, Vt.: Gower, 1991), chapter 3; E. B. Visher and J. S. Visher, *Stepfamilies: Myths and Realities* (Secaucus, N.J.: Citadel, 1979), 56–57; Salwen, "Myth of the Wicked Stepmother," 119–21.

22. Some researchers have argued that traditional gender roles mean that women interact with their stepchildren more than men do, a phenomenon that might account

for additional conflict between stepmothers and children. See Lucile Duberman, "Step-Kin Relationships," *Journal of Marriage and Family* 35 (May 1973): 290.

23. Molly Ladd-Taylor and Lauri Umansky, eds. *"Bad Mothers": The Politics of Blame in Twentieth-Century America* (New York: New York University Press, 1998), introduction.

24. Susan J. Douglas and Meredith W. Michaels, *The Mommy Myth: The Idealization of Motherhood and How It Has Undermined All Women* (New York: Free Press, 2004).

25. For example, Ladd-Taylor and Umansky conflate the two in *"Bad Mothers,"* 6.

26. Dainton, "Myths and Misconceptions," 95.

27. Judith Wallerstein and Sandra Blakeslee, *Second Chances* (London: Bantam, 1989); E. Mavis Hetherington and Josephine D. Arasteh, eds., *The Impact of Divorce, Single Parenting, and Stepparenting on Children* (Hillsdale, N.J.: Erlbaum, 1988). More recent work has argued that not all stepchildren do poorly in stepfamilies; for the English case, see Gill Gorell Barnes, Paul Thompson, Gwyn Daniel, and Natasha Burchardt, *Growing Up in Stepfamilies* (Oxford: Clarendon, 1998).

28. For an overview of some of these studies, see Paul R. Amato, "The Implications of Research Findings on Children in Stepfamilies," in *Stepfamilies: Who Benefits? Who Does Not?*, ed. Judith Dunn and Alan Booth (Hillsdale, N.J.: Erlbaum, 1994), 81–88. One recent study found that educational outcomes for stepchildren are similar to those for other children if variables other than family structure are taken into account. See Donna K. Ginther and Robert A. Pollack, "Family Structure and Children's Educational Outcomes: Blended Families, Stylized Facts, and Descriptive Regressions," *Demography* 41 (November 2004): 671–96.

29. S. Hugh Bryan, Lawrence H. Ganong, Marilyn Coleman, and Linda R. Bryan, "Counselors' Perceptions of Stepparents and Stepchildren," *Journal of Counseling Psychology* 32 (April 1985): 279–82.

30. Linda R. Bryan, Marilyn Coleman, Lawrence H. Ganong, and S. Hugh Bryan, "Person Perception: Family Structure as a Cue for Stereotyping," *Journal of Marriage and Family* 48 (February 1986): 169–74.

31. Aino Ritala-Koskinen, "Stepfamilies from the Child's Perspective: From Stepfamily to Close Relationships," *Marriage and Family Review* 26, nos. 1–2 (1997): 135–51.

APPENDIX

1. Darrett B. Rutman and Anita H. Rutman, "'Now-Wives and Sons-in-Law': Parental Death in a Seventeenth-Century Virginia County," in *The Chesapeake in the Seventeenth Century: Essays on Anglo-American Society*, ed. Thad W. Tate and David L. Ammerman (Chapel Hill: University of North Carolina Press, 1979), 153–75.

INDEX

Murray, Dolly, 58

Murray, Margaret (Mackay) Thompson, 55

Native American family, 4

New England, reason for focus on, 5–6

Norton, Edward, 66

Norton, Elizabeth, 66, 67

Norton, Elizabeth (Cranch): death of, 65–66

Norton, Hannah (Bowers), 66; as loving stepmother, 67–68

Norton, Jacob (father): mourning of, 65–66. *See also* Widowers: and remarriage

Norton, Jacob (son), 66

Norton, Lucy, 66

Norton, Mary, 66, 67

Norton, Richard: stepmother cannot replace mother for, 68; and prejudice against stepmother, 68–70; stepmother as second mother of, 69; stepmother compared to mother, 69–70; mother name as sacred for, 70

Noyes, John, 14

Noyes, Mary (Fish), 10, 14–17; and marriage proposal from Naphtali Daggett, 14–15

Nuclear family, 120–21 (n. 12); as brittle, 3, 66; mended through remarriage, 67, 94

Otis, Harrison Gray, 23

Pearson, Edward Augustus, 89; inheritance from half sister, 90

Pearson, Eliphalet, 22, 89

Pearson, Henry, 89–90

Pearson, Margaret, 89–90

Pearson, Maria, 22, 89–90

Pearson, Sarah, 89

Pearson, Sarah (Bromfield), 22, 89

Pelham, Henry, 87–88

Pelham, Mary (Singleton) Copley, 86

Pelham, Peter (father), 86–87

Pelham, Peter (son), 88

Polygyny and spouse loss, 4

Poor families and spouse loss, 4

Prenuptial contract of Mehitable Webb and Silas Deane, 30–32

Primogeniture, 80

Probate marriage settlements, 30

Querelle des Femmes, 49

Reading: and stories of good stepmothers, 91–92; literacy and, 125 (n. 34). *See also* Russell, Amelia: reading good stepmother story with stepmother; Sedgwick, Catherine Maria: and reading

Reed, Isaac Gardner, 48

Reid, Susanna (Lawlor), 59

Remarriage: divorce and, 2; death and, 2–3; rates of, 3, 118 (n. 9); speed of, 17, 70; and wife's sister, 23–25; and unsettled estate, 29. *See also* Widower: and remarriage; Widows: and remarriage

Revere, Paul, 1–2

Revere, Rachel (Walker), 1–2

Russell, Amelia: affectionate to half sister, 89; as surrogate parent to half sister, 89; reading good stepmother story with stepmother, 91–92

Russell, Jonathan, 89

Russell, Lydia (Smith), 89, 91–92

Russell, Penelope, 70–76

Saltonstall, Mary (Haynes) Lord, 10

Saybrook, Conn., 82–83

Second Great Awakening and stepmother reform, 93

Sedgwick, Catherine Maria, 70; compares stepmother to mother, 74; and Sedgwick family reputation, 75; and reading, 91–92

Sedgwick, Charles, 70, 74

Sedgwick, Eliza, 70, 72–73

Sedgwick, Frances, 70, 76

Sedgwick, Henry, 70, 71, 73; and stepmother as father's new lover, 72; idealize dead mother, 74

Watson, William, 23
Webb, Joseph (father), 27; real
 estate of, 34–35; personal property
 of, 35
Webb, Joseph (son), 32; Silas Deane
 blames, for unsettled Webb estate,
 39–40
Webb, Mehitable (Nott), 27–28
Webb, Sarah, 43
Whiting, Mary, 10

Widowers: and remarriage, 9–10, 59,
 64–65, 66–67, 119 (n. 11); marry inex-
 perienced mother, 19–21
Widows: and remarriage, 9–10, 119
 (n. 11); and sex, 17–18; and inheritance
 law, 27, 129–30 (n. 6)
Williams, William, 46
Woolsey, Sarah (Chauncey), 21–22
Woolsey, Theodore, 21–22
Woolsey, William, 21–22

CPSIA information can be obtained
at www.ICGtesting.com
Printed in the USA
LVOW11s0013100518

576576LV00003B/205/P